# JESUS IS THE CHRIST

THE MESSIANIC TESTIMONY
OF THE GOSPELS

# JESUS IS
# THE CHRIST

MICHAEL F. BIRD

**IVP** Academic

An imprint of InterVarsity Press
Downers Grove, Illinois

*InterVarsity Press*
*P.O. Box 1400, Downers Grove, IL 60515-1426*
*Internet: www.ivpress.com*
*Email: email@ivpress.com*

*InterVarsity Press® is the book-publishing division of InterVarsity Christian Fellowship/
USA®, a movement of students and faculty active on campus at hundreds of universities,
colleges and schools of nursing in the United States of America, and a member movement of
the International Fellowship of Evangelical Students. For information about local and
regional activities, write Public Relations Dept., InterVarsity Christian Fellowship/USA,
6400 Schroeder Rd., P.O. Box 7895, Madison, WI 53707-7895, or visit the IVCF website at
<www.intervarsity.org>.*

*All Scripture quotations, unless otherwise indicated, are taken from the Holy Bible, Today's New
International Version™. Copyright © 2001 by International Bible Society. All rights reserved.*

*Cover design: Cindy Kiple*

*ISBN 978-0-8308-2823-4*

*Printed in the United States of America ∞*

 *InterVarsity Press is committed to protecting the environment and to the
responsible use of natural resources. As a member of Green Press Initiative we use
recycled paper whenever possible. To learn more about the Green Press Initiative,
visit <www.greenpressinitiative.org>.*

**Library of Congress Cataloging-in-Publication Data**
*A catalog record for this book is available from the Library of Congress.*

| P | 17 | 16 | 15 | 14 | 13 | 12 | 11 | 10 | 9 | 8 | 7 | 6 | 5 | 4 | 3 | 2 | 1 |
|---|----|----|----|----|----|----|----|----|---|---|---|---|---|---|---|---|---|
| Y | 27 | 26 | 25 | 24 | 23 | 22 | 21 | 20 | 19 | 18 | 17 | 16 | 15 | 14 | 13 | | |

# CONTENTS

| | | |
|---|---|---|
| Preface | | vii |
| Abbreviations | | ix |
| Introduction: When Did Jesus Become the Messiah? | | 1 |
| 1 | The Gospel of Mark: The Crucified Messiah | 32 |
| 2 | The Gospel of Matthew: The Davidic Messiah | 57 |
| 3 | The Gospel of Luke (and Acts): The Prophetic Messiah | 79 |
| 4 | The Gospel of John: The Elusive Messiah | 97 |
| | Conclusion: Believing in the Messiah | 141 |
| | Bibliography | 148 |
| | Endnotes | 166 |
| | General Index | 206 |

# Preface

This book is a follow-up to my earlier volume *Are You the One Who Is to Come? The Historical Jesus and the Messianic Question* (Grand Rapids, MI: Baker, 2009). There I argued, contrary to much modern scholarship, that Jesus did in fact claim to be the anointed deliverer referred to in Israel's sacred traditions and hoped for in diverse ways among some Second Temple Jewish groups. The shape of all four Gospels was determined by the messianism of Jesus and its impact upon his first followers. Whereas in my former volume I focused on the claims of the historical Jesus in his Jewish context, here I am concerned with the function of Jesus' messiahship in the narrative and theological horizons of the evangelists.

Accordingly, this volume examines the various ways in which Jesus as 'the Messiah' is construed as part of the story, Christology, and purpose of the four canonical Gospels. It is the significance of the title and role of 'Messiah' that is explicated in the Gospels, and this tells us something of the evangelists themselves and the audiences for which they wrote. In the end, I conclude that Jesus' messiahship is the 'mother of all Christology' and that this facet of the evangelists' Christology needs to be better appreciated in discussion of their narrative, rhetorical, social, and historical aims.

Chapters 1 and 3 have appeared previously in *Reformed Theological Review*. I am grateful to the editor of *RTR*, Dr Allan Harman, for allowing me to reuse the material here. These two chapters have been significantly revised and expanded since their initial publication. The other chapters in this book were written specifically for this volume and appear in print for the first time.

The making of any book requires a great amount of energy, patience, and dedication – and that is just from the people around the author. As ever, I am only able to find the time and motivation to write thanks to so many people around me. First, my longsuffering wife, Naomi, remains my constant anchor with her support and care. My growing children are a wonderful distraction from the loneliness of academic life. My colleagues at Crossway Col-lege provide ongoing encouragement for my research. My poor students continue to suffer under my teaching and humour (often intermixed). I've also had the chance to preach through the Gospels among my good friends at Acacia Ridge Presbyterian Church. My Paternoster editors Robin Parry and then Michael Parsons helped direct this project from proposal to submission and gave me the extra time I needed to complete it. Also thanks go to David Byrd for doing a really good proofread of the manuscript.

In terms of family, it appears that our quiver is now full with the birth of our fourth child, Theodore Titus Bird (and even if our quiver is not full our house certainly is). He is to us, as his name suggests, a gift from God, and to him this book is dedicated in celebration of his entrance into the world. When he is old enough perhaps he too shall read it and from here learn the story of Jesus and make the good confession that 'Jesus is the Christ'.

*Michael F. Bird*
*Brisbane, Australia*
*May 2011*

# Abbreviations

Abbreviations of writings from Philo, Josephus, the apostolic fathers, Dead Sea Scrolls, Apocrypha, Pseudepigrapha, rabbinic writings, patristic literature, Nag Hammadi Codices, and Greco-Roman literature are taken from C.A. Evans and S.E. Porter, *Dictionary of New Testament Background* (Downers Grove, IL: IVP, 2000).

| | |
|---|---|
| AB | Anchor Bible |
| *ABD* | *Anchor Bible Dictionary* |
| ABRL | Anchor Bible Reference Library |
| *BBR* | *Bulletin for Biblical Research* |
| BDAG | Walter Bauer, et al., *A Greek-English Lexicon of the New Testament and Other Early Christian Literature* (Chicago: University of Chicago Press, 3rd edn, 2000) |
| *Bib* | *Biblica* |
| BS | Biblical Seminar |
| *BTB* | *Biblical Theology Bulletin* |
| BTNT | Biblical Theology of the New Testament |
| BZNW | *Biblische Zeitschrift für die neutestamentliche Wissenschaft* Supplement |
| CBET | Contributions to Biblical Exegesis and Theology |
| *CBQ* | *Catholic Biblical Quarterly* |
| *CBR* | *Currents in Biblical Research* |
| CEB | Common English Bible |
| CITM | Christianity in the Making |
| CNTUOT | Commentary on the New Testament Use of the Old Testament |
| COQG | Christian Origins and the Question of God |

| | |
|---|---|
| CTR | *Criswell Theological Review* |
| EBC | Expositor's Bible Commentary |
| ed. | editor/edited by |
| edn | edition |
| ESV | English Standard Version |
| FS | festschrift |
| *DNTB* | *Dictionary of New Testament Background* |
| *DJG* | *Dictionary of Jesus and the Gospels* |
| *EJT* | *European Journal of Theology* |
| *ExpT* | *Expository Times* |
| HNT | Handbuch zum Neuen Testament |
| HNTC | Herder's New Testament Commentary |
| *HTR* | *Harvard Theological Review* |
| *HTS* | *Harvard Theological Studies* |
| ICC | International Critical Commentary |
| *Int* | *Interpretation* |
| *JBL* | *Journal of Biblical Literature* |
| *JETS* | *Journal of the Evangelical Theological Society* |
| *JGRChJ* | *Journal of Greco-Roman Christianity and Judaism* |
| *JSHJ* | *Journal for the Study of the Historical Jesus* |
| *JSNT* | *Journal for the Study of the New Testament* |
| JSNTSup | Journal for the Study of the New Testament: Supplement Series |
| *JTS* | *Journal of Theological Studies* |
| KJV | King James Version |
| LHJS | Library of Historical Jesus Studies |
| LNTS | Library of New Testament Studies |
| NASB | New American Standard Bible |
| NCBC | New Century Bible Commentary |
| NCCS | New Covenant Commentary Series |
| NET | New English Translation |
| NICNT | New International Commentary on the New Testament |
| NIGTC | New International Greek Textual Commentary |
| NIV | New International Version (1984, 2010) |
| NJB | New Jerusalem Bible |
| NLT | New Living Translation |
| *NovT* | *Novum Testamentum* |
| NovTSup | Novum Testamentum Supplement |

| | |
|---|---|
| NRSV | New Revised Standard Version |
| NSBT | New Studies in Biblical Theology |
| NTL | New Testament Library |
| *NTS* | *New Testament Studies* |
| PNTC | Pillar New Testament Commentary |
| *RTR* | *Reformed Theological Review* |
| SBLDS | Society of Biblical Literature Dissertation Series |
| SBLGNT | Society of Biblical Literature Greek New Testament |
| SBT | Studies in Biblical Theology |
| SNTSMS | Society of New Testament Studies Monograph Series |
| SP | Sacra pagina |
| *TDNT* | *Theological Dictionary of the New Testament* |
| TNIV | Today's New International Version |
| trans. | translation/translated by |
| *TrinJ* | *Trinity Journal* |
| *TynBul* | *Tyndale Bulletin* |
| vols | volumes |
| WBC | Word Biblical Commentary |
| WUNT | Wissenschaftliche Untersuchungen zum Neuen Testament |
| *ZNW* | *Zeitschrift für die neutestamentliche Wissenschaft* |

# Introduction

# When Did Jesus Become
# the Messiah?

What was arguably the most basic and universal christological belief in the early church was the claim that Jesus is Israel's Messiah. Or as we are accustomed to saying, Jesus is the Christ. This belief is reflected above all in the canonical Gospels. The incipit of the Gospel of Mark includes the words, 'The beginning of the Gospel of Jesus the Messiah' (Mark 1:1), and the story ends with the crucifixion of 'the Messiah, the King of Israel' (Mark 15:32).[1] Whatever genre Mark thought he was writing, his Jesus-story is explicitly identified as a Messiah-story. Mark redefines the meaning of 'Christ' (*Christos*, Χριστός) in terms of the life, ministry, and death of Jesus of Nazareth. As we will see later, Mark writes a Greco-Roman biography about a Palestinian religious teacher, set in the context of Judean history, and explained in light of his apocalyptic worldview. Mark's Gospel is an apology for the concept of a messianic death in light of a particular reading of Israel's sacred traditions.

Mark was not alone in this task. For all the diversity within the Gospels about Jesus, each of the other three evangelists, in his own way, shares Mark's contention that the Jesus-story is a messianic narrative. The opening line of Matthew immediately situates Jesus in the context of a Davidic genealogy with the words, 'This is the scroll of the beginning of Jesus the Messiah, the Son of David' (Matt. 1:1, my trans.). In fact the genealogy functions as a compressed summary of Israel's story, one wracked by tragedy, failure, and hope. The history of Israel is retold with the birth of Jesus the Messiah reckoned as the most climactic event since the exile (Matt. 1:16–18). Matthew invests a great amount of effort in establishing the Jewish credentials and Davidic pedigree of this Messiah. Such a task is undertaken with a view to demonstrating that the faith of Jesus-believers is not a departure from Judaism; rather, it is the very fulfilment of it. The Matthean Jesus holds together the new and the old revelation (Matt. 9:17; 13:52). He is the deliverer of the Jewish people from their sins and a light to the Gentiles (Matt. 1:21; 4:15–16; 28:19–20).

In the case of Luke, Jesus emerges as the messianic herald of salvation. In the birth narratives, Jesus is identified as 'Messiah, the Lord' (Luke 2:11) and the salvific agent 'the Lord's Messiah' (Luke 2:26). Here the ascription to Jesus of the titles 'Messiah' (Χριστός) and 'Lord' (Κύριος) is not haphazard or accidental (see Acts 2:36). Luke identifies the redeeming action of Israel's God as operating through this messianic agent who effects salvation for his people. In the developing narrative, Jesus is uniquely commissioned, anointed, and empowered to be the Messiah-from-Israel for the sake of the entire Roman world. Jesus fearlessly follows the Isaianic script for salvation that entails his death and resurrection. Luke regards this not as an adulteration of the Jewish messianic story, but instead Jesus' death-resurrection-exaltation constitutes the proper resolution of the entire sway of scriptural hopes. In the end, Luke's two-volume work is a community-defining narrative about salvation, the saved, and the saviour. For Luke these are all tunes played in a messianic key.

The Gospel of John, different in texture and type from the Synoptic Gospels, is remarkably similar to the Synoptics in its construction of a messianic narrative. The messiahship of Jesus and the type of divine agent that he represents constitute the primary cause of the tension between Jesus and the Judean authorities. The messianic question constantly hangs in the air and serves to perplex crowds and ingrain opposition against Jesus (John 7:26–52; 9:22; 10:24–39; 12:34–43). It is quite probable that the Fourth Gospel was written at a time when the messianic identity of Jesus was arguably *the* singularly dividing issue between non-Jesus-believing-Jews and Jesus-believing-Jews (John 9:22; 12:42; 16:2; cf. 1 John 2:22; 5:1).[2] Accordingly, for John the messiahship of Jesus is the fulcrum of the entire narrative. It is not only the claim of Andrew, but also of the entire network of Christians for whom John wrote that 'We have found the Messiah' (John 1:41). John can imagine no faith in Jesus other than that of faith in Jesus as the Messiah. The purpose of the evangelist, then, through a parade of signs and witnesses, is to lead his audience to believe that 'Jesus is the Messiah, the Son of God, and that by believing you may have life in his name' (John 20:31). Ultimately the testimony of the Beloved Disciple is that the Logos, the light of the world, the new grace – all anticipated in Judaism – are realities disclosed in the ministry of Jesus the Messiah of Israel.

The significance of Jewish messianism as the background for New Testament Christology is recognized widely enough, as is the claim that the Gospels announce that Jesus is the Messiah. Yet an underlying background question is: When did Jesus become the Messiah? A common script in scholarship, with variations of lines, has been something like this: Jesus never claimed to be the Messiah; in fact, he repudiated the title. Jesus only claimed to be a prophet of God's kingdom. The crucifixion of Jesus on trumped-up charges of being a messianic pretender was undertaken by the Judean leadership in order to have the troublesome Galilean permanently silenced. His earliest followers experienced visions of Jesus after his death and thereby considered to him to be raised and exalted as God's viceroy. On the basis of either Jesus' resurrection/exaltation or out of hope for his future return, Palestinian Christianity then labelled him the Messiah as a way of expressing his elevated status. The title 'Messiah' was then read back into the story of Jesus' death, creating the martyrological formula 'Χριστός died for . . .' as we find in short summaries in Paul's letters. The linking of Jesus' death with his messiahship was then imported into the passion stories underlying the Gospels. Soon after, Χριστός became a proper name for Jesus when Christianity spread into Gentile circles that did not know of a messianic deliverer referred to in the Jewish Scriptures. Viewed this way, the identification of Jesus as the Messiah is something of an ad hoc addition to the tradition, made in order to indicate that Jesus is a person of some importance in the divine plan.

Such paradigms, which propose the development of Christology from non-messianic to messianic, imply the relative insignificance of Jesus as Messiah in the New Testament in general and in the Gospels in particular. For instance, Rudolf Bultmann contended that 'the synoptic tradition leaves no doubt about it that *Jesus' life and work* measured by traditional messianic ideas was *not messianic.*'[3] More recently, Lidija Novakovic states that 'the confession of Jesus as Messiah is the presupposition of New Testament Christology, not its content'.[4] The effect is to move Jesus, the early church, and the Gospels away from the aegis of messianism.

In contrast, it is the contention of this study that the messianic identity of Jesus is the earliest and most basic claim of early Christology. What is more, it is precisely the testimony to Jesus as the Messiah that is arguably the most defining christological affirmation of the canonical Gospels. In my view, the designation of Jesus as Messiah is not a late, secondary, or dispensable category applied to Jesus. The messiahship of Jesus comprises the primary framework in which the sum of all christological affirmations in the Gospels are to be understood, that is, all Christology is a subset of Messianology. A Christian messianism explains the scriptural exegesis of the Old Testament in the Gospels, it accounts for the distinctive shape of the narratives in terms of their plot and characterization, and it provides explanations for the didactic, apologetic, and evangelistic purposes of the evangelists. It is time to bring the messiahship of Jesus back to the front and centre of Gospel studies and explore the background, content, and purpose of these messianic narratives and what they tell us about early Christianity.

Before delving into the Gospels with a view to describing the exact way in which the messiahship of Jesus functions in their narrative and theological horizons, we first have to situate the Gospels in the context of early Christianity. The Gospels were not the first written documents to announce Jesus as the Messiah. Therefore, a preliminary task is to answer the question: When did Jesus become the Messiah?

## When Did Jesus Become the Messiah?

According to Helmut Koester, 'Among the most difficult and as yet unsolved problems of the history of early Christian christology are why and when Jesus was given the title "Messiah".'[5] Good question. In answering it we have to say several things about Jewish messianism, whether Jesus claimed to be a messianic figure, and how belief in Jesus as the Messiah emerged in the early church.

## Messianic expectations

Not all Jews in the first century were anxiously waiting for a Messiah. Despite popular misconceptions that Judea was filled with every Tobias, David, and Herschel claiming to be the Messiah, the only two figures unambiguously spoken of as the Messiah between AD 30 and 132 are Jesus of Nazareth and Simon bar Kokhba (known also as Simeon ben Kosiba).[6] Yes, other figures emerged from time to time who excited hopes for future deliverance, set themselves up as royal claimants, and echoed biblical traditions in their actions, but few as far as we know were explicitly hailed as messianic leaders.

Among those Jewish authors and Jewish groups who did anticipate a Messiah, there were diverse opinions as to what type of figure he would be.[7] Some looked for a Messiah with militaristic qualities, who would lead the people in a successful purge of Gentiles and sinners (e.g. 1QM; *Pss. Sol.* 17 – 18). Others imagined a Messiah with transcendent qualities and supernatural powers (e.g. *1 Enoch* 37 – 71; *4 Ezra*). The Qumran community envisaged two 'anointed' leaders in the final days: a 'Messiah of Aaron' and a 'Messiah of Israel' (e.g. 1QS 9.11; CD 12.22–23; 1QSa 2.17–22). Philo held out a hope for a Hebrew king who would establish a Jewish kingdom and subjugate the nations (e.g. *Moses* 1.290–291; *Rewards* 95–96). There is also a variety of names and titles for such a deliverer other than 'Messiah', including: Son of David, Son of God, Son of Man, the Prophet, Elect One, Prince, Branch, Root, Sceptre, Star, Chosen One, Coming One.

Messianism grew out of reflection on Israel's sacred traditions in light of the mixed socio-political fortunes of the Jewish people in the Persian, Greek, and Roman periods. The shared thread of Jewish messianism in the various tapestries that hung around from time to time was a future hope for a royal and eschatological deliverer to liberate Israel and establish a renewed Jewish kingdom.[8] In the end we might define the Messiah as 'an agent of God in the end-time who is said somewhere in the literature to be anointed, but who is not necessarily called "messiah" in every passage'.[9]

### The historical Jesus as a messianic claimant

Did Jesus claim to be the Messiah? For many the answer is an obvious 'yes', and for others it is an equally obvious 'no'! Why the confusion?[10] Well, consider the fact that Jesus never once uses the title 'Messiah' to describe himself. At the very most, he is called Messiah, king, and Son of David by others. By itself such data might suggest that Jesus inspired messianic hopes but did not himself embrace the title as the best label for what his ministry was about. The other problem is that the places in the Gospels where Jesus supposedly accepts the messianic designation (Mark 8:29; 14:61–62; John 4:25–26; 18:33–34) are thought to bear an uncanny resemblance to early Christian confessions of Jesus' identity. In other words, some of the Gospel accounts look as if the evangelists or their sources have read their messianic faith back into stories of Jesus' pre-Easter life. So where does one go with this?

First, a denial that Jesus thought of himself as a messianic leader creates more problems than it solves. We still have the matter of why Jesus was crucified as a messianic pretender, how the messianic faith of the early church arose in the first place, and why the evangelists put the story of Jesus into a messianic matrix. One standard explanation is that the early church *inferred* Jesus' status as Messiah from his resurrection. If God had raised him, then surely he must be the Messiah – but it is not that simple. The problem is that there is no precedent for deducing messiahship from resurrection. How does 'resurrected' equal 'Messiah'? John the Baptist died a martyr; some even thought he had come back to life in Jesus (Mark 6:14–16; 8:28), but no-one thereafter considered the Baptist to be the Messiah. We could say the same about the two witnesses in Revelation 11 who are martyred, brought back to life, and ascend to heaven. The revivification of the two witnesses was not met with messianic acclaim. Or again, in the *Testament of Job* 39 – 40, the disappearance of the bodies of Job's children and their assumption into heaven effects no change in their status. Belief in Jesus' resurrection certainly accentuated messianic beliefs about him (e.g. Rom. 1:2–4), but it did not of itself create that messianic belief. As Johannes Weiss said nearly a century ago, 'Only because his death seemed to be a proof against messiahship could his resurrection be perceived as a proof in favour of it'.[11]

Another explanation appeals to the seeming 'messianic secret' found in the earliest Gospel, the Gospel of Mark. One notices in Mark that Jesus is constantly telling supplicants of healing and his disciples things like, 'Don't speak to anyone about this.' This is seen rather dramatically in Jesus' response to Peter's confession of Jesus as the Messiah, and some even contend that Jesus' rebuke to Peter is a rebuke for calling him 'Messiah' in the first place (Mark 8:29–31)! William Wrede picked up on this and argued that the messianic secret was not historical, but was theologically motivated. The purpose of the secret was to account for the fact that Christians had believed Jesus to be the Messiah since his resurrection, even though there was no extant memory of Jesus ever claiming to be such during his lifetime. In other words, the messianic secret is a literary device to show that the reason why no-one in the early Jerusalem church really knew about Jesus claiming to be the Messiah is that he kept it a deliberate secret from outsiders.[12] The thesis has been very influential in the course of scholarship, but it has not gone unchallenged. Probably the biggest problem with Wrede's thesis is that what is silenced in the Gospel of Mark is not necessarily messianic (such as healings and exorcisms [e.g. 1:44; 7:36]), and some material that is very messianic is not silenced at all (such as Bartimaeus calling Jesus 'Son of David' [10:47–49], Jesus' triumphal entry [11:1–10], and Jesus' enigmatic remarks about David and his Lord [12:35–37]). Moreover, the injunctions to secrecy fail, and word about Jesus continues to get out, resulting in crowds being drawn to Jesus. There is indeed a messianic secret in Mark and it operates differently at the historical and literary levels. In terms of history, it is probable that Jesus did ask people to be quiet about things he said and did because he did not want to draw the attention of the Herodian or Roman authorities, who would interpret his activities as subversive and express alarm at the crowds he was attracting. On the literary level, Mark uses the secrecy motif to accentuate the mystery and power surrounding Jesus himself, and that secret is gradually disclosed as the narrative presses towards its climactic conclusion in Jerusalem.

Second, there actually are some fairly good reasons for thinking that Jesus did in fact claim to be a messianic figure. Though much could be said, I enumerate the key evidence as follows:

(1) Isaiah 61, about a coming anointed figure, seems to have played a significant part in Jesus' own understanding of his role. There is an explicit appeal to a Spirit-anointed ministry in special Lucan material (Luke 4:18–21) and similarly Isaianic echoes in the material common to Luke and Matthew about John the Baptist's question as to whether Jesus really is the 'one to come' (Luke 7:18–23; Matt. 11:2–6). In fact, this later unit possesses a striking similarity with a text from the Dead Sea Scrolls that attributes a similar list of deeds to Israel's Messiah (4Q521 2.1–10).

(2) It is commonly recognized that Jesus' central message pertained to the kingdom of God. What role did Jesus think that he played in that kingdom, its announcement and consummation? Jesus' choice of twelve disciples was symbolic of the restoration of Israel that he believed he was effecting (Mark 3:13–16). There is also an eschatological saying that the twelve would sit on twelve thrones judging Israel and have a kingdom conferred on them the same way that the Father confers a kingdom on Jesus (Luke 22:28–30/Matt. 19:28–30). It seems that Jesus saw himself as the royal leader-to-be of the restored people of God – a king of a future kingdom.

(3) We also have to take into account the prominence of allusions to David and Solomon in Jesus' teaching activities (Matt. 12:42/Luke 11:31; Mark 2:23–28; 12:35–37). Solomon and David were both regarded as prophets and allegedly performed exorcisms, which aligns also with the pattern of Jesus' ministry. In any case, Jesus saw himself in a lineage associated with the greatest of royal figures from Israel's ancient past as ways of explicating his eschatological role.

(4) Several of the 'I have come' sayings appear to associate Jesus with activities that, in comparison with other Jewish literature, may be suitably classified as messianic (Mark 2:17; Luke 12:49–51/Matt. 10:34; Luke 19:10).

(5) Jesus' final week was thoroughly messianic. We have a messianic action in the triumphal entry that deliberately acts out

Zechariah 9 (Mark 11:1–10). There is a messianic act in the temple where he warns of the destruction of the temple unless Israel repents (Mark 11:11–18), and elsewhere we are told that he predicted the rebuilding of the temple, which is a messianic task (Mark 14:58; John 2:19; cf. 2 Sam. 7:11–14). Jesus engages the scribes on several topics, including the identity of the Messiah as David's Lord (Mark 12:35–37). In the passion scene, Jesus is depicted as a messianic shepherd who saves his people from the danger of tribulation by his vicarious death (Mark 14:27 = Zech. 13:7). At his trial before Caiaphas, Jesus is asked point blank a messianic question and responds with an oblique but affirmative answer that conflates Psalm 110:1 and Daniel 7:13 (Mark 14:62).[13]

(6) Finally, Jesus was executed on the charge of being a messianic pretender, hence the titulus that mocked him as 'the King of the Jews' (ὁ βασιλεὺς τῶν Ἰουδαίων) in derisive fashion (see Matt. 27:37; Mark 15:26; Luke 23:38; John 19:19). As Dale Allison says, the 'Romans probably crucified Jesus as "king of the Jews" because he did not distance himself from that derisive epithet'.[14]

I do not have the space to argue in detail why I think these units are historically authentic in content or at least outline. I and others have done the work on that elsewhere. Here it is sufficient to say that in looking over all of this, we are led to the conclusion that the root cause of the messianic faith of the early church has to go back to Jesus himself. Postulating a messianic movement arising from a non-messianic Jesus is a bit like trying to explain why people celebrate Martin Luther King Day if the story of Martin Luther King as a civil rights leader who spoke about a certain 'dream' was invented by later civil rights leaders who wanted to devise a lovely story to honour a nice pastor with a social conscience. The messianic faith of the early church did not combust into existence as people tried to figure out great titles to lavish upon their fallen leader. We all know that where there is smoke there is fire, and from nothing nothing comes. True, Jesus did not go around flying a banner saying, 'Look, I'm the Messiah.' But if you proclaim the kingdom of God, declare that the day of national restoration is dawning, compare yourself to David and

Solomon, perform what various people considered to be signs of messianic deliverance, enter Jerusalem on a donkey with people shouting 'Hosanna to the Son of David', and end up on trial on a messianic charge and mocked in death as a Jewish king, well, you don't need a PhD in rabbinic literature to see what was going on here. Jesus deliberately acted out a messianic role, and it was this motif to his ministry that explained why the church began and why it took the shape that it did. The resurrection certainly brought about a transformation for many of his followers. The resurrection turned the debris of a messianic failure into a messianic victory that inaugurated a messianic kingdom. Still, resurrection alone, some kind of cognitive dissonance, or supposed sociological models, cannot adequately account for the emergence of the church as a messianic movement or for the veneration of Jesus as 'Lord and Messiah' if Jesus never gave cause for thinking so. Oscar Cullmann put it wonderfully when he said: 'The early church believed in Christ's messiahship only because it believed that Jesus believed himself to be the Messiah.'[15]

### The early church as a messianic movement

The disciples of Jesus were not, after his death, all set, primed, and ready to believe in Jesus as the Messiah despite the fact he obviously wasn't. It was not a matter of sitting around waiting for a sign to confirm that Jesus was really a 'somebody' after all, despite the horrendous events that had just transpired, and latching onto 'Messiah' as a way of expressing his true status. Jesus had narrated in advance his forthcoming death and vindication. So in the view of his followers – who were probably hiding out in a place equivalent to where Salman Rushdie and Danish cartoonists take refuge – he was at best a martyr who might be vindicated as righteous at the resurrection of the dead at the end of history.

From all accounts it looks as if the disciples thought they had backed the wrong horse of the apocalypse. After narrating the events of Jesus' sudden death to the stranger, the travellers to Emmaus opine, 'but we had hoped that he was the one who was going to redeem Israel' (Luke 24:21). Obviously things had not gone according to script – their script, for as Luke continues, the risen Jesus was working off another script (Luke 24:25–27). Even when Jesus does appear to the disciples we are told that they asked him, 'Lord, are you at this time going to restore the kingdom to Israel?' (Acts 1:6). The question is just so inapt and irreverent that it has to be authentic. They are in effect asking, Now that Yahweh has granted you a second bite of the apple, will you at last succeed in what you failed to do the first time around and restore the Jewish nation to regional hegemony? The point of the story, at least in Luke's version, is that while the hope for national restoration remains valid, there is one important thing that is being missed out here. The point of course is that the restoration of Israel has already begun in their midst. It began with the ministry and suffering of the Messiah, and is continued in his vindication and exaltation, the soon-to-be effusion of the Holy Spirit, and the proclamation of the kingdom to all nations. The marks of restoration were already present. The restoration of the covenant people had begun with the followers of Jesus. There was now a new Davidic king, a new covenant, a new cultic symbol in the form of a communal meal, and a new spiritual breath blowing into God's people. This was the presupposition behind all future missionary endeavours, namely, that a transformed Israel would transform the world.[16] The resurrection of Jesus represented the vindication of the messianic ministry that he had begun.

It was remembrance of Jesus as an anointed prophet, testimony to his royal and eschatological role in a future kingdom, impressions he made upon his disciples by his teaching, fresh memories of his death on a messianic charge, knowledge of his Davidic family origins, belief in his resurrection, the experience of the Spirit – and reading Scripture in light of those convictions – that arguably led early Christians to reflect on the identity of Jesus in relation to Israel's God and to Israel's hope. The key designation that summarized their convictions about him, God, and Israel was that he was the Messiah. Belief in Jesus' resurrection and exaltation did not create messianic hopes as much as it served to define 'Messiah' in a new way.[17] Thereafter, mission became the 'mother of all theology' as the early church had to wrestle with 'who is this Jesus' whom they were to proclaim to their fellow Jews. As such, the messianic story and the story of Jesus were combined with traditions about the Suffering Servant and Son of Man and other motifs from Israel's sacred traditions, creating an amalgam of royal, priestly, and prophetic functions set within apocalyptic co-ordinates that explicated Jesus' person and work.

If the early speeches of Acts are anything to go by,[18] the early Jerusalem church used a number of christological terms to explicate what kind of eschatological redeemer Jesus was. God's raising Jesus from the dead and elevating him to the highest place in the heavenlies designated his key role as the 'Lord', 'Messiah', 'Righteous One', 'Prophet', 'Leader and Saviour' (2:33–36; 3:14–15,20–24; 5:31; my trans.) and the one in whom salvation comes (4:10–12). These stand in correlation with similar claims found in pre-Pauline materials where Jesus was declared to be the Son of God in power (Rom. 1:4) and installed by God the Father as Lord (Phil. 2:9–11). The royal-messianic emphases mediated via the title Χριστός are everywhere present (e.g. Acts 3:18–20; 5:31; 8:5), and his messianic function spans the period from his earthly life through to his *parousia*.

Primitive Christian proclamation had a messianic character. A shorthand rundown of early Christian preaching can be summed up with the words, 'Jesus is the Messiah' (Acts 5:42; 8:5; 9:22; 17:3; 18:5,28). That is probably derived from something in Aramaic like המשיחא ישוע ('Jesus [is] the Messiah'). The leading spokespersons for the early church saw themselves as witnesses to God's kingdom and its king. This king, Jesus, was the divinely appointed heir to David's throne through whom Israel could attain forgiveness, redemption, and renewal (Acts 2:36,39; 3:20–21; 4:18–21,26; 26:23). The reference to Jesus as the Messiah reflected the Jewish hope for the time of God's messianic mercy. For the early church, the salvation/blessing/mercy associated with the messianic age had dawned in the coming of Jesus and would be completed at his return.[19] It would be entirely unsurprising that a message directed at Israel would take on a messianic theme if the fulfilment of Israel's eschatological hopes were the main fabric of the preaching. So pervasive was Χριστός as a regular appellation for Jesus in Acts, pre-Pauline materials, and Paul's letters that it became a standard feature of Christian vocabulary by the 50s AD and even penetrated into Gentile-majority churches.

The name 'Jesus Christ' (*Iēsous Christos*, Ἰησοῦς Χριστός) represents an abbreviation of the title 'Jesus the Messiah', which itself was an expression of the confession 'Jesus *is* the Messiah'. It is from the title, whatever it was in Aramaic, that we get the Greek Ἰησοῦς Χριστός ('Jesus Christ') and Χριστός Ἰησοῦς ('Christ Jesus'). References to Ἰησοῦς Χριστός are ubiquitous in the New Testament. Received wisdom dictates that the appellation 'Messiah' was assigned to Jesus from the christological innovations fashioned by Jewish Christian Hellenists. Soon after, Χριστός evolved into a proper name for him as Ἰησοῦς Χριστός when Christianity spread into Gentile circles. On this view, we could glibly say that 'Christ' was his surname and 'Jesus' was his Christian name. Scholars are, of course, more clever than that, and put it into proper Roman terms of 'Jesus' as his praenomen (given name) and 'Christ' as his cognomen (family name). While Ἰησοῦς Χριστός certainly was used in a nominal sense, I am not so sure that we can leave it there.

First, even the nominal use of Ἰησοῦς Χριστός does not evacuate the designation of its titular and messianic significance.[20] Ἰησοῦς Χριστός might well function as a proper name for some audiences, particularly those who did not know the Jewish significance of Χριστός as 'anointed one' or 'Messiah'.[21] However, the name Ἰησοῦς Χριστός appears in documents that also use Χριστός as a title, as seen in the Gospel of Matthew (Matt. 1:1,18; cf. 1:16,17; 2:4; 11:2; 16:16,20; 22:42; 23:10; 24:5,23; 26:63,67; 27:17,22), Gospel of Mark (Mark 1:1; cf. 8:29; 9:41; 12:35; 14:61; 15:32), Gospel of John (John 1:17; 17:3; cf. 4:25–29; 7:26–42; 9:22; 10:24; 11:27; 12:34; 20:31), Acts (Acts 2:38; 3:6; 4:10; 8:12; 9:34; 10:36,48; 16:18; 24:24; cf. 2:31,36; 3:18–21; 5:42; 9:22; 17:3; 18:5; 18:28; 26:23), Paul's letters (e.g. Rom. 1:1,4,6–8; 2:16; 3:22,24; cf. 9:5; 15:6–7), Hebrews (Heb. 10:10; 13:8; cf. 3:14; 5:5; 6:1; 9:14,28; 11:26), 1 Peter (1 Pet. 1:1–3,7,13; 2:5; 3:21; 4:11,14; cf. 1:11,19; 2:21; 3:15–16,18; 4:1,13; 5:10,14), Johannine letters (1 John 1:3; 2:1; 3:16,23; 4:2; 5:6,20; 2 John 3,7; cf. 1 John 2:22; 5:1), and Revelation (Rev. 1:1–2,5; cf. 11:15; 12:10; 20:4–6).[22] Where the nominal use of Ἰησοῦς Χριστός appears as a proper name in the same document as the titular reference to Χριστός, we are right to think that Ἰησοῦς Χριστός has not lost its titular significance as designating a messianic agent. In such instances it is probable that the nominal usage is a contraction of the title, not a retraction of it.[23]

Second, even in places where reference is made to the 'name' Jesus Christ/Christ Jesus/Lord Jesus Christ (Acts 2:38; 4:10; 8:12; 10:48; 15:26; 16:18; 1 Cor. 1:2,10; 6:11; Eph. 5:20; 2 Thess. 1:12; 3:6; 1 John 3:23) there is presupposed a particular narrative about this Jesus who is saviour, healer, benefactor, mediator, sanctifier, dispenser of the Spirit, and divine agent. Appeal to the name Ἰησοῦς Χριστός implies a certain set of assumptions about the status and story of 'Jesus Christ' as a divine agent. This is the presupposition for the power that operates through his name and for attaining benefits from his name. Only because Χριστός means 'Messiah' does it makes sense for anyone to appeal to the name Ἰησοῦς Χριστός to receive some kind of benefit from him. For it is only as the Messiah that he has any benefits to confer on others. This explains why writers such as Luke can move so freely between titular and nominal usages of Χριστός (see Acts 2:36–38). The name of Jesus is efficacious only because of the messianic narrative associated with him. In which case, the nominal usage presupposes the titular meaning when the benefits of the name Ἰησοῦς Χριστός are declared.

Third, where we find Χριστός on its own, we are not to think of it as a further abbreviation of the name Ἰησοῦς Χριστός into Χριστός (like 'Julius Caesar' into 'Caesar'). Instead the unqualified usage of Χριστός marks a regression to the titular usage of Χριστός as 'Messiah'. That seems required in narratives that especially link Χριστός with the advent of God's kingdom such as those found in 1 Corinthians 15 and Revelation 11 – 12; 20. It is impossible to think of the Χριστός who inaugurates God's kingdom, executes the final judgement, and effects the restoration of creation as anyone other than the Messiah, if you know anything of the scriptural background.

We must also consider the messianic beliefs of the early church as proof that the messiahship of Jesus was early and pervasive. Within ten years of Jesus' death, segments of the early church became known as 'Christians' (*Christianoi*, Χριστιανοί). Up and until the late 30s the church went by a variety of names. The followers of Jesus were known as 'the Way', 'disciples', 'saints', 'believers', 'brothers', 'church', and 'Nazarenes'.[24] It is reported by Luke in Acts 11:26 (see also Acts 26:28; 1 Pet. 4:16; Tacitus, *Ann.* 15.44) that it was in the ethnically mixed congregation of Antioch that a group of Jesus-believers were first called Χριστιανοί. In my mind, Luke is not being anachronistic here by applying the name 'Christians' to believers at this juncture. The designation could be applied to Christians in Rome in the early 60s according to Tacitus, so why not in Antioch in the late 30s or early 40s according to Luke? The designation Χριστιανοί is similar to the names of other political groupings like the *Herodianoi, Caesarianoi,* or Latin equivalents like *Pompeiani, Galbiani,* and *Augustiani,* which indicate the loyalty and benefaction of adherents to a certain figure. I think it probable that the name 'Christian' first emerged in Antioch when a divide opened up between Jewish followers of Jesus with their Gentile companions and other Jews of Antioch. Sooner or later a name had to be given by local authorities in order to distinguish this peculiar Jewish group from other religious associations in Antioch. The significance of naming Jesus' followers as 'Christians' is that it identifies the church as a messianic faction from Judea who venerated a messianic figure named 'Jesus [the] Messiah'. Followers of Jesus were called, in effect, 'messianists' within ten years of his death. Thus, by the late 30s or early 40s, the early church was already known for and characterized by its messianic faith.[25]

Surely if anyone believed that Jesus was the Messiah it was Paul. Again there are dissenters who dispute the meaning and significance of Χριστός in Paul's letters.[26] Paul uses Χριστός more than any other New Testament writer, some 270 times, but whether his regular usage of Χριστός is actually messianic is an open question. Arguments based on the presence or the absence of the article are exceedingly weak, and it is contextual factors that are determinative for charting messianism in Paul.[27] In Paul's earliest letter, 1 Thessalonians, the basic building blocks for Paul's Christ-language are already in place. This is evident in the ascription of the honorific designation ὁ κύριος ἡμῶν Ἰησοῦς Χριστός ('our Lord Jesus Christ' [1 Thess. 1:1,3; 5:9,23,28), in terms nominating Christ as Paul's apostolic patron ὡς Χριστοῦ ἀπόστολοι ('as Christ's apostles' [1 Thess. 2:7]), the incorporative ἐν Χριστῷ ('in Christ' [1 Thess. 2:14; 4:16; 5:18),[28] and finally the summary of Paul's message as εὐαγγελίῳ τοῦ Χριστοῦ ('Gospel of Christ' [1 Thess. 3:2]).[29] The same types of Χριστός language occur throughout the rest of Paul's letters with only minor variation. In which case, Paul's usage of Χριστός remained remarkably consistent across his missionary career.[30] Why is this the case and why does Paul never explain the meaning of the peculiar noun Χριστός?

For the most part it seems that Χριστός functions as a proper name for Jesus in Paul's letters. But it also looks as if the titular background to the name was never far away from Paul's mind either.[31] On a careful reading it appears that it is not possible to absolutely separate the nominal and titular uses of Χριστός in Paul's letters.[32] A first hint towards that conclusion is the fact that Paul can easily reverse Ἰησοῦς Χριστός ('Jesus Christ') and Χριστός Ἰησοῦς ('Christ Jesus') as seen in their interchangeability in, for example, Rom. 1:1–8 and 15:5–6. Neither Jewish nor Roman names were reversed in sequence, and the reversibility of Ἰησοῦς Χριστός / Χριστός Ἰησοῦς is comprehensible only if Χριστός has some titular connotation.[33] In view of Paul's voluminous usage of Χριστός and its associations in Jewish messianism, several scholars have maintained the importance of Χριστός in Paul's letters as a messianic title.[34] Kramer took a minimalist approach when he proposed that only 1 Cor. 11:3 and Rom. 9:5 'might possibly mean "Messiah" in the literal sense'.[35] Dahl identified a string of references to Χριστός that were potentially laden with messianic content in Paul's letters (1 Cor. 10:4; 15:22; 2 Cor. 5:10; 11:2–3; Eph. 1:10,12,20; 5:14; Phil. 1:15,17; 3:7), James Dunn suggested some additions (Rom. 9:3,5; 15:3,7,19; 1 Cor. 1:23), Blomberg extends the list even further (1 Cor. 1:12; 11:1,3; 12:12; Eph. 5:2,23–25,29),[36] and I would add another (Gal. 3:16). Below I explore the significance of several of these texts along with aspects of Paul's thought which indicate a titular messianism attached to Jesus.

First, what exactly motivated Paul's pre-conversion persecution of the early church is a rather slippery issue (see Acts 8:3; 9:1; 1 Cor. 15:9; Gal. 1:23; Phil. 3:6; 1 Tim. 1:13). The reasons are probably multiple and complex. Veneration of Jesus, continued proclamation of Jesus, inter-sectarian Judean rivalry, Jewish Christian fraternization with Gentiles, and remarks about Jesus vis-à-vis the Torah and temple would have prompted zealous reprisals from those who believed that the holiness of Israel's faith was being compromised by this vocal new Galilean sect. A certain motivation for Saul's (i.e. Paul's) violent campaign against the church was the claim that the crucified Jesus was the Messiah. By the norms of Torah, the crucified Jesus could be neither a righteous man, nor a messianic figure. As Torah declared of such criminals, he was 'accursed' (Deut. 21:23, my trans.; cf. Gal. 3:13). If God was operating through Jesus, then the whole symbolic framework of Judaism was threatened.[37] Saul of Tarsus had a preformed messianism, and that messianism was transformed by the Damascus road experience (see 1 Cor. 15:7–8; Gal. 1:15–16; Phil. 3:2–21). The primary impact of the Damascus road event was to reverse Saul's verdict about Jesus. Jesus was not a pseudo-messiah; rather he had been vindicated as Israel's royal Messiah (see Rom. 1:4; 1 Cor. 1:20; 1 Tim. 3:16; cf. Acts 9:22; 26:20–24), and even more than that, he was the Lord of Glory (see 1 Cor. 2:8; 2 Cor. 3:18; 4:4–6; 8:19,23; 2 Thess. 2:14; Titus 2:13; cf. *1 Enoch* 22.14; 25.3,7; 27.3; 36.4; 63.2; 83.8). It was the identity of Jesus as the Messiah and the redefinition of messiahship that was the chief result of Paul's Damascus road experience. Understandably Paul's preaching after his Damascus road experience can be summarized as τὸ εὐαγγέλιον τοῦ Χριστοῦ ('the gospel of the Messiah') in Rom. 15:19 (cf. 16:25), 1 Cor. 9:12, 2 Cor. 2:12; 4:4; 9:13; 10:14, Gal. 1:7, Phil. 1:27, and 1 Thes. 3:2.[38] Thus, Saul's opposition to the Jesus movement presupposes its messianic character, and the content of Paul's gospel reflects the transformation of Paul's beliefs around a redefined messianism generated by his Damascus road christophany.

Second, Paul was fully aware that Χριστός means 'anointed one'. The apostle wrote: 'Now it is God who makes both us and you stand firm in Messiah (εἰς Χριστὸν). He anointed us (χρίσας ἡμᾶς), set his seal of ownership on us, and put his Spirit in our hearts as a deposit, guaranteeing what is to come' (2 Cor. 1:21–22).[39] In context, Paul is saying that the covenant faithfulness of Israel's God is revealed in Jesus. Jesus, the Son of God, is preached as the fulfiller of Israel's hopes by Paul, Silvanus, and Timothy. In him there is a divine 'yes' to Israel's promises with the concomitant result that the 'anointed one' (the bearer of the Spirit and the one raised by the Spirit) now anoints others with the same Spirit. In many ways, this is part and parcel of what we find in other Jewish literature, namely, the democratization of the messianic concept. In this the elect participate in the reign of the Messiah (see Dan. 7:27; Luke 22:30/Matt. 19:28; Eph. 2:6; 2 Tim. 2:12; Rev. 5:10; 20:4–6; 22:5).[40] In this case, the anointed one shares his anointing with others.

Third, in Romans 1:3–4 we read, 'regarding his Son, who as to his human life was from the seed of David, and who through the Spirit of holiness was appointed the Son of God in power by resurrection from the dead: Jesus Christ our Lord'. This text represents a piece of traditional material known to Paul. It does not regard the resurrection as the beginning of Jesus' messiahship because his Davidic lineage is presupposed. Here, divine sonship is transposed rather than triggered by the event of resurrection. Jesus' resurrection marks a transition into a higher rank of sonship, and his sonship exercises a new eschatological function that he did not previously discharge before Easter.[41]

Fourth, there is a clear and unambiguous use of Χριστός as a title in Romans 9:5: 'Theirs are the patriarchs, and from them is the Messiah (ὁ Χριστὸς) according to the flesh, who is God over all, forever praised! Amen.' In the foregoing sequence, Paul lists the privileges of God's covenant people, including adoption to sonship, glory, covenants, the law, temple, and the promises. The list is capped with reference to the Messiah. In which case, the Messiah is the climax and ultimate privilege that God has given to his people.[42]

Fifth, again drawing from Romans, the climax of the epistle is arguably found in the words of Romans 15:8–12:

> For I tell you that [Messiah] (Χριστὸν) has become a servant of the Jews on behalf of God's truth, so that the promises made to the patriarchs might be confirmed and, moreover, that the Gentiles might glorify God for his mercy. As it is written:

> 'Therefore I will praise you among the Gentiles;
>  I will sing the praises of your name' [Ps. 18:49].

Again, it says,

> 'Rejoice, you Gentiles, with his people' [Deut. 32:43].

And again,

> 'Praise the Lord, all you Gentiles;
>    let all the peoples extol him' [Ps. 117:1].

And again, Isaiah says,

> 'The Root of Jesse will spring up,
>    one who will arise to rule over the nations;
> in him the Gentiles will hope' [Isa. 11:10].

In the conclusion to his pastoral exhortation in Rom. 14:1–15:13, Paul sets forth the priority of Israel in the mission of the Messiah with the upshot that it is the basis for the inclusion of the Gentiles in God's mercy since this is precisely what Scripture foresaw. This is a well-thought-out counter-argument to any apparent smug anti-Jewish sentiment among Gentile Christians in Rome. It also complements the claim that the Roman Christians, irrespective of ethnicity or views of Torah, must accept one another just as the Messiah accepted them (Rom. 15:7). Richard Hays correctly sees Paul offering a christological reading of the Psalms with the psalms of lament understood as prayers of the Messiah himself (Ps. 69:9 in Rom. 15:3, and Ps. 18:49 in Rom. 15:9).[43] Such a reading only makes sense if the Messiah is the representative of God's people and acts for their deliverance. Also, I would add that the citation of Isaiah 11:10 is interesting for a couple of reasons. Whereas Rom. 13:1–7 might be understood as Paul propounding a social inactivism that accepts the political status quo, Paul writes to Christians in Nero's Rome (albeit during the good years) and mentions in passing the belief that Israel's Messiah will rule over the nations. I think it more likely that Rom. 13:1–7 is realistic and sage advice as to how Christians can stay underneath the radar of the imperial security apparatus despite their politically charged christological claims.[44] For Paul, it is the Son of David and not the Son of Augustus who will rule the world. In this sense, Paul's Christology is completely in line with other Jewish messianic expectations that utilized Isaiah 11 in a similar fashion.[45] Interestingly enough, Rom. 1:2–4 and 15:12 form a messianic *inclusio* that brackets the letter at front and back with the theme of Jesus as the Messiah.

Sixth, it is not merely the title 'Messiah', but it is the role that Jesus exercises that provides one of the primary reasons for regarding Paul's 'Christ' as a messianic figure.[46] Several instances could be cited. The repeated references to Jesus as judge (Rom. 2:16; 14:10; 2 Cor. 5:10; cf. John 5:27,30; Acts 10:42; 17:31; 2 Tim. 4:1) correspond to views in Jewish literature of the Messiah as judge (see *1 Enoch* 1.7–9; 25.4; 62.4–5; *Pss. Sol.* 17.4; *4 Ezra* 11 – 12; *2 Bar.* 72.1–5; *Sib. Or.* 3.652-54,741-60,772–82).[47] A better example is the function of Jesus as Messiah in the eschatological narrative of 1 Cor. 15:24–28 (see similarly Eph. 5:5; Col. 1:13; 2 Tim. 4:1,18):

> Then the end will come, when he hands over the kingdom to God the Father after he has destroyed all dominion, authority and power. For he must reign until he has put all his enemies under his feet. The last enemy to be destroyed is death. For he 'has put everything under his feet' [Pss 8:6; 110:1]. Now when it says that 'everything' has been put under him, it is clear that this does not include God himself, who put everything under Messiah (Χριστός). When he has done this, then the Son himself will be made subject to him who put everything under him, so that God may be all in all.

The royal and messianic emphasis is explicit with Jesus subjugating all enemies before handing the kingdom over to the Father. Paul envisages some kind of messianic interregnum as the penultimate stage of the kingdom's advent before it is handed over to the Father for consummation.[48] In the flow of thought, the resurrection of the Messiah is followed by the reign of the Messiah, and then the end with the resurrection of those 'in Messiah' (see 1 Cor. 15:18–19,21–22).

In view of this short survey it is clear that Jesus as Messiah is significant for Paul even if it was not his most extensive way of explicating Jesus' identity. The view of Jesus as Messiah was inherited from traditional Jewish Christian materials extant prior to Paul's missionary career and was arguably indebted to several messianic *testimonia* collections that Paul utilized in his letters (e.g.

2 Sam. 7:12–14; Ps. 2:7; Isa. 11:10). Attempts to flatten out the messianic character of Paul's Christology must be judged to be failures. The reason why Jesus' messiahship is never explicated at length in the Pauline letters is because Jesus' messianic identity was a settled and assumed matter that did not warrant further discussion. The reason why explicit messianic affirmations are mostly lacking from Paul's letters and yet abundant in the preaching of the Lucan Paul in Acts can be attributed to the fact that Paul expressed different concerns when addressing Gentile-majority Christians on the one hand and when engaging with unconverted Jews on the other hand.[49]

To recap, the early church became a messianic movement when it had every reason not to do so. Their leader was dead, crucified, and rejected, and Judaism had no established expectation for a dying and rising Messiah. Any messianic claims that Jesus had made to his followers or infused into the crowds should have died with him just as it was for Simeon ben Kosiba. Instead, the reports of his resurrection and exaltation reinforced his messianic claims and infused them with significant new content. Jesus was Lord as well as Messiah (Acts 2:36). He was not a nationalistic military Messiah, but a redeemer who mediates forgiveness and mercy (Acts 3:18–19). As his followers experienced the Spirit and reread their Scriptures, Jesus' death was regarded as part of the divine plan about the suffering and vindication of the Messiah that would lead to national renewal and a new creation. Leaders of 'the Way' preached openly to their Judean compatriots that Jesus was the Messiah promised in Israel's Scriptures. Their basic confession, 'Jesus is the Messiah', could be shortened in Greek to the designation Ἰησοῦς Χριστός. While Ἰησοῦς Χριστός evidently functioned as a proper name, it never lost connection with its titular origins. The fact that followers of Jesus were called 'Christians' (= 'messianists') in Antioch (Acts 11:26), Caesarea (Acts 26:28), and Rome (1 Pet. 4:16; Tacitus, *Ann.* 15.44) by the mid-first century further demonstrates that they were perceived to have been a messianic sect venerating a messianic figure. Paul is quite aware of the messianic narrative of a Messiah who establishes a kingdom (1 Cor. 15:24–28); he mentions traditional material that highlights Jesus' Davidic status (Rom. 1:2–3), and retains the titular usage of Χριστός (Rom. 9:5). The claim that

Jesus was 'the Messiah' became one of the central and defining characteristics of the new movement from its earliest phase.[50] Thus, the picture of the emerging Jerusalem church is that of a Judean renewal movement that attached a strong messianic interpretation to Jesus from the beginning.[51]

## Competing Histories of the Origin of Jesus as 'Messiah'

As I've already hinted at, the narrative I've described above is arduously contested. There are some scholars who hold to a history of Christianity in which messianism is either a late development or insignificant when it comes to the origins of Christology.

In the case of Rudolf Bultmann, he followed William Wrede in asserting that it was the resurrection that gave rise to the claims of Jesus' messianic status.[52] The real content of the Easter faith was that God had made the prophet and teacher Jesus of Nazareth the Messiah.[53] The title was added later in circles that wanted to dress Jesus in a messianic garment. Bultmann wrote that 'it was soon no longer conceivable that Jesus' life was unmessianic – at least in the circle of Hellenistic Christianity in which the Synoptics took form. That Jesus Christ, the Son of God, should have legitimated himself as such even in his earthly activity seemed self-evident, and so the gospel account of his ministry was cast in the light of messianic faith'.[54] In the early church the Son of Man and Messiah are just two sides of the same coin and signify Jesus as eschatological bringer of salvation.[55]

However, we are back again to the problem of Wrede's view, namely, that there is nothing about a resurrection that would automatically imply messiahship. According to Dale C. Allison: 'The resurrection alone cannot account for Christology, and Easter did not turn Jesus into someone or something altogether different than he was before. The resurrection, rather, sanctioned and so re-activated beliefs previously held about him. That is, post-Easter convictions confirmed pre-Easter expectations. The vindication of Jesus in the resurrection meant the vindication of hopes his followers had before the resurrection.'[56]

More specifically against Bultmann we have to note that the question remains as to why it was not 'conceivable' for Greek-speaking

Christians to imagine Jesus' life as unmessianic, while it supposedly was conceivable for Aramaic-speaking Christians? Beyond the artificial divide of Christianity into Jewish, Jewish Hellenistic, and Hellenistic tiers – a stratification that has collapsed under the sheer weight of evidence[57] – why would conceiving of Jesus as the Jewish Messiah become necessary in circles that were removed from the Jewish context in which messianism had its greatest influence? No sufficient answer can be found.

Ferdinand Hahn, in his study of the christological titles, advocated that Jesus deliberately distanced himself from messianism because it was caught up with Judean zealotry.[58] He does not think that the triumphal entry or the cleansing of the temple was in any sense messianic, and the charge of being a messianic pretender at the trial was entirely false.[59] He further believes that in the early church the concept of the Messiah was not used in reference to Jesus, as there was a 'one-sided interest in the Son of Man Christology'.[60] The notion of a kingly Messiah was applied to Jesus from the influence of apocalyptic thought. Jesus' messianic status was not inferred from his resurrection and exaltation but due to his authoritative action at his forthcoming *parousia* (i.e. his second coming).[61] It was then that the Son of Man was equated with the Messiah. That perspective is supposedly validated by the reference to messianism in the apocalyptic discourse of Mark 13, which refers to pseudo-messiahs in contrast to the coming Son of Man. Likewise, the Son of Man is correlated with the messianic office at the trial scene in Mark 14:61–62. Acts 3:20–21 also connects Jesus' messianic identity with his future return as saviour for Israel. In fact, when Jesus is called 'saviour' it is always in relation to Israel (Acts 5:31; 13:23).[62] Hahn finds a similar development behind the Christology of Matt. 25:31–46 and Revelation 11 – 12; 20 – 21.[63] Hahn asserts:

> It must be noted that the primitive Palestinian church at first completely avoided the concept of the kingly Messiah, then, however, though within the framework of an apocalyptic outlook, assimilated it and applied it to the ultimate work of Jesus. In this process there took place, in many ways, an absorption with the expectation of the coming Son of Man; at least there was a transference of specific characteristic traits of the other apocalyptic hope of salvation to Jesus as Messiah.[64]

As the *parousia* did not materialize in an immediate time frame as many Christians had hoped, the concept of messiahship was then extended to include his present work in heaven as God's viceroy. The connection is cogent on the grounds that in the Jewish framework real lordship was bound up with the messianic office. The messiahship of Jesus was then 'backdated' by persons within the Jewish Christian Hellenistic church from his *parousia* to his exaltation as Lord.[65] The importation of messianic ideas into the passion story was not the result of a further backdating of messianism, but arose instead on the basis of the placard on the cross, 'King of the Jews', which imbibed the idea that the Messiah must suffer and die. In Jewish Christian Hellenistic circles this impacted the Marcan passion story, basic formulations like 1 Cor. 15:3–4, and materials in 1 Peter 1.[66]

In Hahn's view, it was impossible to link Jesus' life to messiahship except insofar as his work was eschatological. Jesus' work as the new Moses and eschatological prophet made it possible then to smuggle messianic motifs into the Jesus tradition and to connect it with the miracle stories. As it turned out, much of this messianic role was subsumed under the title 'Son of God', and the loosening of contacts with Jewish origins in Hellenistic Christian circles meant that 'Jesus Christ' became in effect a proper name rather than a messianic title.[67] In sum, Hahn sees messiahship developing in several stages: (1) in association with the *parousia*; (2) backwards towards Jesus' exaltation; (3) imported into the passion story on the basis of the titulus on the cross; (4) through equating Jesus' eschatological deeds with messianic acts; and (5) leading to the creation of the name 'Jesus Christ'.[68]

There are problems here. If Jesus' first coming was not messianic, what should necessitate that his second advent should be? Jesus' identity as 'Son of Man' and 'Lord' created sufficient categories to designate his eschatological role at his *parousia*. What need is there to make him into a Messiah as well? One wonders if eschatology is being equated with messianism. That equation is problematic because an eschatological agent does not have to be a messianic one. On top of that, perhaps Jesus' messianic status at his *parousia* is an extension of the messianic role that he executed in his life and in his post-resurrection activity. It seems more likely to me that Acts 3:20 could be taken to mean 'that he may send the appointed Messiah *again* to you'.[69] The one already ordained as Messiah will return at the *parousia* for the benefit of the Jews, not to begin his messianic reign.[70] That is what Luke appears to be advocating, and his view does not seem to be peculiarly Lucan in any respect here. The New Testament authors constantly stress the unity between Jesus' life, exaltation, and *parousia* as part of his messianic vocation.[71] I also question whether identification of Jesus as Messiah could progress within Jewish Christianity in the pattern that Hahn suggests (*parousia* → exaltation → passion) in such a short time frame. The passion tradition that 'Χριστός died' (1 Cor. 15:3; 2 Cor. 5:15; 1 Thess. 4:14) is surely primitive.[72] In addition, why would a so-called Hellenistic stratum of the church, supposedly removed from the Jewish context of primitive Christology, revert to the Jewish category of Messiah to explicate Jesus' eschatological function? All the more surprising since we are often told that 'Messiah' had associations with zealotry and revolution that the Greek-speaking church wanted to avoid.

On a different track, Petr Pokorný contends that Jesus repudiated the title Messiah, and that the designation was applied to him as an explanation for the saving significance of his death.[73] Christians placed 'the concept of Messiah in a new context' and under 'the impact of the Easter experiences Christians dared to say that it was precisely the Jesus who had been crucified as a false political pretender who was the true messiah who brought salvation through his death'.[74] The suffering and dignity of the Messiah was inferred by linking together the Suffering Servant of Deutero-Isaiah (esp. Isaiah 53) with the anointed eschatological prophet of Trito-Isaiah (esp. Isaiah 61).[75]

Once more this view creates more questions than it answers. What inspired Christians to redefine the content of the messianic concept along these lines? If one replies, 'Easter experience', then one has only removed the problem back one step further. How did the Easter experience create messianism of this order? Once more, 'resurrection' *ergo* 'Messiah' is a non sequitur (i.e. it simply does not follow). Consequently the same can be said of crucified → resurrected → Messiah. The resurrection would make Jesus a divinely honoured martyr, but not necessarily a Messiah. In addition, the widespread appearance of Χριστός in relation to Jesus' suffering and death (e.g. Acts 3:18–19; 17:3; 26:23; Rom. 5:6,8; 8:34; 1 Cor. 8:11; 15:3; Gal. 2:21; 3:13; 1 Pet. 2:21; 3:18; 4:1; 5:10) suggests that interpretation of Jesus' death as a messianic death was primitive and pervasive (see also 'Messiah died and rose' etc. [Rom. 14:9; 2 Cor. 5:14–15; 1 Thess. 4:14]).[76] But from where did it come? Resurrection could not on its own create the messianic faith or a messianic atonement theology. A better point of origin for this formula would be Jesus himself, who enacted a messianic ministry in conjunction with references to his forthcoming rejection in Jerusalem.[77] In other words, it was Jesus' messianic claims combined with his intimations of his violent death that, in light of his resurrection, led Christians to find patterns in Scripture of a suffering/rejected figure who could be identified as the Messiah.

Maurice Casey has a slightly different view of the application of the Χριστός title to Jesus. He writes: 'The early Christians needed categories to express the centrality of Jesus, and this is the basic reason why some of them fastened on the expectation of a Davidic king.'[78] According to Casey, the roots for this lay in the mockery of Jesus at his death, but the real impetus arose from the subsequent creative exegesis of Hebrew texts by the early Christian community. This exegesis satisfied the need of Christian communities to venerate Jesus and it did so in categories focused on Davidic kingship. That the early church believed Jesus to be someone of divine importance and in a special relationship with God is beyond dispute. Equally indubitable is that they expressed Jesus' status in categories drawn from the Jewish Scriptures and their reception in Second Temple Judaism. However, to designate Jesus as Messiah after his suffering, without his having established a physical Israelite kingdom, would be somewhat of an anomaly unless we can find other ways of establishing why this redefinition of messiahship took place. Moreover, since the early church already had a repertoire of christological titles to apply to him, such as 'Lord', 'Son of Man', 'Leader', and 'Righteous One', can we really speak of a community 'need' to add another title like 'Messiah'? Although calling Jesus 'Messiah' was honorific to some extent, it was hardly the most honorific title that could be bestowed upon him. The titles 'Lord' and 'Son of God' are better significations of his transcendent qualities, divine authority, and proximity to God.

A more peculiar approach is undertaken by Merrill P. Miller and his collaborators in a volume on Christian origins.[79] Miller believes that Χριστός was added as a byname to Jesus, and the byname was then turned into a messianic title by the evangelists in order to turn Jesus into an ideal figure in his earthly life. On his reconstruction:

> [T]he term *christos* first took hold as a byname among Jewish followers of Jesus, perhaps in Damascus or Antioch, as a way of characterizing the founder of a community of mixed ethnic origin that was in the process of establishing itself as an independent association in interaction with but self-consciously distinguished from a network of Jewish synagogues. Since all the titles of Jesus in the Pauline corpus carry royal status, I assume that the connotations of the byname were royal, but I would also suggest that this was intended to say as much about the community as about the founder figure. It signified that followers constituted a royal realm that Jesus was divinely authorized to establish and over which he would come to be viewed as the one installed as ruler. The byname did not make Jesus an eschatological deliverer or expected king of Israel or a cosmic ruler but the anointed (and thus divinely approved) founder of a very self-conscious alternative community.[80]

I have several objections to this scenario. First, would it ever be possible for someone to apply the byname Χριστός to Jesus entirely independent of its messianic connotations? Χριστός appears in the Septuagint to designate an anointed king in David's line (Ps. 2:2)[81] and an eschatological Son of David (*Pss. Sol.* 17.32; 18.5). These were key ingredients of Jewish messianism. It is even harder to rip Χριστός away from messianic beliefs, especially when Χριστός is a translation of *mĕšîḥaʾ/māšîaḥ/messias* (Aram. מְשִׁיחָא; Heb. מָשִׁיחַ; Gk μεσσίας) in John 1:41 and 4:25. This was not a distinctively Christian equation and reports a fact well known to bilingual Greek-speaking Jews. In addition, the connotation of Χριστός as Messiah carried over into early Christian usage. Luke's references to the 'Lord's Messiah' (τὸν Χριστόν κυρίου) in Luke 2:26 and the 'Messiah of God' (Χριστὸν τοῦ θεοῦ) in Luke 9:20 are characteristic of Jewish

titles that always qualify 'Messiah' with some further description such as 'Messiah of Israel', 'his Messiah', 'Messiah of
Righteousness', or 'Messiah of Aaron'.[82] Consequently I cannot
imagine the label Χριστός being applied to Jesus by persons
seemingly unaware of its messianic connotations. Second, if
identifying Jesus and his followers as royal was the sole purpose
of giving him the byname Χριστός, would this not be better
served by attaching to him the byname 'king' (βασιλεύς) or
'prince' (ἀρχηγός) that is more properly 'royal'? No Greek lexi-
con in existence lists βασιλικός as a synonym for Χριστός. It is
impossible to (re)define Χριστός as royal unless one attaches it
to a Jewish narrative about a royal deliverer called the 'Anointed
One'. Yet to redefine Χριστός in such a way would constitute a
*de facto* messianic belief. Third, and similarly, even if Χριστός
connoted 'royal' for some persons, which I doubt, the label was
being applied to a person widely held to be an eschatological
deliverer. Jesus was an apocalyptic prophet and the early church
was an apocalyptic movement. As proof of that, the title 'Son of
Man' was frequently used to designate Jesus' role in the apocalyptic dénouement (Acts 7:56; Rev. 1:13; 14:14). If one applies an
apparently royal designation in the form of Χριστός to a person
venerated as an eschatological deliverer, then one has basically
created a messianic designation: 'anointed one' + royal status +
eschatological deliverer = messianism! Fourth, one should not
forget the cultic background of the word Χριστός ('Anointed
One') and its verbal form χρίω ('to anoint'). Anointing was associated with three primary offices in ancient Israel: king,[83] priest,[84]
and prophet,[85] but mostly with the first of these. In circles
outside of Jewish traditions, Χριστός would mean something
peculiar like 'smeared one', or else be mistaken for Χρηστός
meaning 'good, useful, beneficial'.[86] However, the anointed figures in Israel's sacred traditions all held roles that fundamentally involved mediation between Yahweh and the people. In
which case, to call Jesus Χριστός would suggest something of
his mediatory role, and it is not too far from considering his
mediatorship to include his being an agent of God's salvation.
Overall, to postulate a messianic descriptor like Χριστός being
applied non-messianically and then becoming messianic much
later is a rather odd reconstruction to entertain.[87]

In response to all of these alternatives I would also point out that, in effect, adding the title 'Messiah' to a crucified figure created more problems than it was worth given the divisions created in Jewish communities. It is hardly the kind of problem one would wish to create in the effort to venerate a departed leader, nor can messiahship be attached to a crucified Jesus on the back of some ad hoc scriptural proof-texting.[88] Let us remember that the 'Christ' element of Christianity proved to be a point of lasting division between Jews and Christians (e.g. John 9:22; 12:42; Justin, *1 Apol.* 31.5–6; *Dial. Tryph.* 10; 49; 90; 108).[89] That is because a crucified Messiah was far more than an 'insufferable paradox'.[90] A crucified Messiah was, to many, utter madness (Acts 26:23–25) or complete foolishness (1 Cor. 1:18). Yet this is precisely what Christians maintained under trying and difficult circumstances. As Joachim Jeremias put it, 'the scandal of the crucified Messiah is so enormous that it is hardly conceivable that the community should have presented itself with such a stumbling block.'[91] A messianic title that was secondary and late could be easily dispensed with if it became a catalyst for dangerous conflict. Capitulating on Jesus' messiahship in favour of something like an angelomorphized martyr sounds like a common-sense move if it promoted cordial relations with potentially hostile neighbours. Sensible unless, of course, messiahship was somehow indelibly connected to the primary structures of early faith in Jesus to the point that giving up Jesus' messianic identity was completely unthinkable. But, I must ask facetiously, I wonder what gave them that idea?

The creative lengths to which scholars go in their tradition-historical reconstructions of the origins of early Christology in order to explain how a non-messianic figure somehow evolved into the Messiah is truly staggering. In some cases they are grossly speculative about which part of Acts 2 – 3 contains the more primitive christological formula; resurrection faith becomes a magical messiah-making machine; the byname Χριστός, despite its linguistic connections to the Hebrew and Aramaic words for 'anointed one', never meant 'Messiah' until of course it evolved into a messianic title; and some group called 'Hellenistic Christianity' seems to do all the creative work in reading an honorific title back into Jesus' life without anyone objecting to the fiction.

What I find more compelling is that Jesus was a messianic claimant; the crucifixion should have meant the end of that story; but the resurrection vindicated that claim and gave impetus to a reinterpretation of the messianic concept in line with refocused Jewish eschatological hopes. Messiahship was redefined around the life and death of Jesus, while the more traditional role of the Messiah as a conquering figure was postponed until his *parousia*. This conception of messiahship led to a complete reconfiguration of beliefs about Jesus' relation to God, Israel, and salvation in the early church. The primitive church, under duress and persecution, continued to venerate Jesus as the long-awaited Davidic king and saviour who would usher in God's kingdom. Its confession of Jesus as Messiah remains embedded in the simple name 'Jesus Christ'. In sum, the story of Jesus as the Messiah remained basic to the church's faith from Jerusalem (Acts 2:36; 3:18–21; 5:42) to Cenchreae (Rom. 1:2–3; 9:5; 15:8–9) to Patmos (Rev. 20:1–6).[92]

## The Gospels of Jesus the Messiah

The relevance of the preceding discussion is that the Gospels were not the product of persons who were committed to reading Jesus' life as messianic when it was widely known that it was not. More likely, the Gospels where written between c. AD 70–100 when belief in Jesus as Israel's Messiah had been in currency for forty years or more. The Gospels were composed as conscious attempts to promote the gospel of Jesus, serve as an introduction to Israel's Messiah, and offer an explanation for the emergence of a messianic community that derived its praxis, symbols, and identity from Jesus called 'Messiah'. It is in the context of the church's pervasive faith in Jesus as a messianic deliverer that we come now to the Gospels.

The Gospels tell a story about the man Jesus of Nazareth who is identified with a number of titles such as Son of Man, Son of God, Son of David, Lord, and Messiah. The early church had maintained in preaching and through persecution that Jesus is the Messiah whom Israel has been waiting for. The Gospels are expressions of the church's deep-seated messianic faith, rather than narratives trying to legitimate a late messianic innovation. The Gospels are messianic stories about a messianic hope written for people wrestling with questions about the identity of Jesus in relation to the politics and pantheon of the Greco-Roman world.

Out of all the titles and roles ascribed to Jesus, it is the contention of this study that it is the messianic theme that is paramount. It is the testimony to Jesus as the Messiah that binds together the theological, literary, rhetorical, and social functions of the four canonical Gospels. Although we could rightly consider the Gospels as collectively teaching the same broad messianic story about Jesus, each of the Gospels articulates the messianic identity of Jesus in a different way, for a different end, in a different context, and with a different set of tools. It is the unique formulation of Jesus as the Messiah by the individual evangelists that is explored in what follows. In the end, Matthew, Mark, Luke, and John are like stained-glass windows offering different shapes and colours about a figure they all regard in their own unique way as the long-promised Messiah.

# 1.

# The Gospel of Mark:
# The Crucified Messiah

## Introduction

One of the major struggles of the early church was the attempt to convince other Jews that Jesus of Nazareth was and is Israel's Messiah. This proclamation of Jesus' messiahship had to over- come several persistent objections. First, Jesus was accused of blasphemy, being a false prophet, leading the nation astray, being demon-possessed, and practising magic.[1] Second, according to the titulus 'King of the Jews' (Mark 15:26; John 19:19), Jesus was crucified as a messianic pretender. Third, Jesus did not live up to the messianic expectation entertained by some Jewish groups. In the minds of some, the socio-political circumstances of Judea had not experienced the radical reversal that was often associated with the coming of the Messiah. After all, the Romans still ruled Palestine through the Herodian puppet kings, the current temple remained standing, the Diaspora had not returned to Palestine, the Jewish tribal league had not been reconstituted, and the Gentiles had not converged on Jerusalem with gifts and offerings. Thus whatever expectation there was for a Messiah, and the con- cept was diverse, some Jews evidently did not think that Jesus of Nazareth met the job description.[2]

In light of such unbelief it is understandable why a passage such as Psalm 118:22–23 was used polemically in early Christianity to show that Israel's rejection of her Messiah constituted another cycle of rebellion against God.[3] In 'Q' (traditions common to Matthew and Luke), one finds several contrasts between the unbelieving Israelites of Jesus' generation and believing Gentiles from Israel's antiquity.[4] In Romans 9 – 11, Paul concerns himself with the salvation–historical implications posed by Israel's current rejection of her Messiah. Consequently, Israel's failure to believe in Jesus as the Messiah constituted a serious theological problem for the early church.

It is certainly a testimony then to the robust nature of the Christology of the early church that it continued actively to proclaim Jesus as the Messiah in the face of unbelief, rejection, and even persecution by fellow Jews. Although I do not think that the messiahship of Jesus was the single factor that facilitated the 'parting of the ways' between Judaism and Christianity, the messiahship of Jesus still represented a point of division in the Jewish-Christian rift.[5] The question remains: How did early Christian authors attempt to tackle this division? I intend to argue that a significant purpose of the Gospels is to convince readers – Jewish readers in particular – that Jesus is the Messiah. The Gospels consciously set out to answer Jewish objections to the messiahship of Jesus, they perceive in Jesus the climax of the Jewish hope, and they proclaim Jesus as the saviour of Israel. My first port of call in this journey is to show how an apologetic messianism is at the heart of the narrative and theology of the Gospel of Mark.

## Mark's Messiah and the Cross

Martin Kähler was probably right when he said that the Gospels were passion narratives with an extended introduction.[6] That is especially true of the Gospel of Mark, so much so that Jack Kingsbury calls Mark 'the Gospel of the Cross'.[7] The whole direction of the narrative is propelled dramatically towards the dark and tragic moments of Gethsemane and Golgotha. Mark's literary and theological project is to reconcile the notion that 'Jesus is the Messiah' with 'crucifixion' in a way that is persuasive to his readers. In this sense, Mark appears to be addressing the problem encountered by Paul where the cross is 'a stumbling block to Jews' (1 Cor. 1:23; cf. Rom. 9:32–33; Gal. 5:11; 6:12–14; Phil. 3:18). Or the objection given by Trypho to Justin: 'It is just this that we

cannot comprehend . . . that you set your hope on one crucified'
(*Dial. Tryph.* 10). It is a problem that is quite understandable given
that Paul, Luke, Philo, and the Dead Sea Scrolls all link crucifixion to Deut. 21:23, which states that 'cursed is any man who
hangs upon a tree' (my trans.).[8] This would imply that Jesus was
'cursed' and therefore could not be the Messiah. It should be
borne in mind that the Messiah was meant to be the representative of Israel par excellence. Wright spells out a possible problem
that emerges: 'The cross is offensive to Jews because a crucified
Messiah implies a crucified Israel.'[9]

Additionally, in the Greco-Roman world crucifixion was the
antithesis of the noble death. Seneca writes, 'Can any man be
found willing to be fastened to the accursed tree, long sickly,
already deformed, swelling with ugly weals on shoulders and
chest, and drawing the breath of life amid long-drawn out agony?'
(*Lucil.* 101).[10] Josephus observed many crucifixions and said it was
'the most wretched of deaths' (*War* 7.203). Tacitus labelled crucifixion the 'punishment of slaves' (*Hist.* 4.11). The Alexamenos Graffito
depicts a figure on a cross with a donkey's head being worshipped
by a man, with the epithet beneath the picture reading 'Alexamenos
worships his god'.[11] This furnishes substantial proof of the derision
associated with worship of a crucified man.[12]

Jewish messianic expectations were well enough known
that Tacitus and Suetonius were familiar with the legend of a
Jewish king who would come and rule the world.[13] If Mark
was composed around the outbreak of the First Jewish Revolt
(c. AD 66–70), the Roman army was in the very process of dealing with royal pretenders such as Simon ben Giora and
Menahem in Judea.[14] Then any group named χριστιανοί
('Christians' = 'messiah followers')[15] which venerated a figure
known to have been crucified by a Roman official[16] was likely
to be viewed with suspicion.

Hence the scandal of the cross revolves around the cursedness
of Jesus as the reverse of messianic expectation, the stigma of
dishonour associated with crucifixion, and the association of crucified criminals with insurrection and disorder. The way in which
Mark addresses these objections can be seen by analyzing his
Gospel through different grids: narrative, linguistic, rhetorical,
social-scientific, and christological.

## Narrative: The story of the crucified Messiah

Mark's incipit begins, 'The beginning of the Gospel of Jesus the Messiah' (my trans.).[17] Though several translations render Ἰησοῦς Χριστός as 'Jesus Christ' (NRSV, NASB, ESV, CEB), the TNIV, NIV10, and NLT are probably correct to translate it as 'Jesus *the* Messiah'.[18] A titular meaning of Χριστός as 'Messiah' here is not only possible, but preferable. Mark uses the name Ἰησοῦς some eighty-two times and Χριστός is used sparingly only seven times, but on all but two occasions Χριστός possesses the article and is clearly titular as designating *the* Messiah (Mark 8:29; 12:35; 13:21; 14:61; 15:32; cf. without the article 1:1; 9:41). The subsequent usage of Χριστός eliminates a purely nominal meaning for Ἰησοῦς Χριστός in the incipit. What seems likely is that Ἰησοῦς Χριστός stands as an honorary designation for the central figure in the following story. As Adela Yarbro Collins states: 'The narrative of Mark as a whole evokes the titular sense, "messiah."'[19] Similar is John Donahue: 'The density of the key terms in 1:1 prepares the reader for the dramatic unfolding of the whole work, which revolves around the proper description of Jesus as Messiah and Son of God'.[20] Mark is not content to assert this title, but his subsequent narrative demonstrates precisely how Jesus is the Messiah and what kind of mission this Messiah will undertake.[21] The remaining question that dominates Mark's Gospel is: Precisely who is this Messiah and how will he be enthroned? There are cryptic hints along the way as to how this Messiah will be coronated. As the plot unfolds, it gradually becomes clearer that the cross dangles over the head of this Messiah like a sword of Damocles, unbeknownst to the disciples, but the reader is privy to it.[22]

In a dispute with the Pharisees, Jesus warns of a time when the bridegroom will be taken away from the disciples (2:20), which is a shockingly early intimation of his death. After the dispute in the synagogue concerning the healing of the man with the shrivelled hand on the Sabbath (3:1–5), it is reported in 3:6 that 'the Pharisees went out and began to plot with the Herodians how they might kill Jesus'. As the story progresses, the Pharisees and Herodians try to trap Jesus with a question about paying taxes to Caesar (12:13–17). Jewish readers might register the irony of this alliance, since the Pharisees and the Herodians had a long history of conflict between them, but are nevertheless willing to unite against a perceived common threat.[23]

The story of the death of John the Baptist at the hands of an impetuous king is sandwiched between the sending out of the disciples and their return in 6:6–31. This raises the question of what will happen to Jesus and his followers who, like the Baptist, are willing to announce the news of the kingdom despite the opposition building against them. What is clear is that God's kingdom very quickly draws human opposition of a violent order.

As the story moves along, tacit references to Jesus' forthcoming death dramatically increase. The huge turning point in the Gospel of Mark is about halfway through when Jesus is acknowledged as the Messiah by Peter at Caesarea Philippi (8:29). Yet the confession is met by a command to secrecy and the first of three passion predictions where Jesus announces the gruesome fate that awaits him in Jerusalem (8:31; 9:31; 10:33–34). This is not the beginning of the 'messianic secret' because 'inasmuch as the readers know from the very beginning that Jesus is the Christ, the Son of God, there is never any question of a Messianic Secret *for the reader of the gospel*'.[24] Rather, 8:29–31 is the summit of Mark's (and early Christianity's) messianic redefinition. Soon after, we learn that the restoration of Israel is intimately tied up with the sufferings of the end-time Elijah and the Son of Man (9:12).[25] The request of James and John to sit at the right and left hands of Jesus in his glory is met with invitations to share the same cup and undergo the same baptism, metaphors of the forthcoming passion (10:35–40). The imagery signifies that Jesus' passion will be his glory; his cross will be his throne.[26] After the provocative and explicitly messianic triumphal entry, it is reported that the chief priests and scribes were seeking a way to destroy him (11:18). The parable of the tenants, in which the son is killed and thrown out of the vineyard, further inflames the authorities in seeking to arrest Jesus (12:12).

The foreshadowing of the cross comes to an abrupt end in Mark 14, which accelerates towards the crucifixion scene. It is narrated that the chief priests and scribes 'were seeking how to arrest him by stealth and kill him' (14:1–2, my trans.); an anonymous woman anoints Jesus for burial, making a furtive connection between his messiahship and death (14:3–9);[27] Judas agrees to betray Jesus (14:10–11); Jesus conveys his awareness of the conspiracy (14:18–21); he institutes the new covenant through his death (14:22–25); predicts his resurrection and Peter's betrayal (14:26–31); and waits in Gethsemane for his captors to seize him (14:32–51). When the arrest and crucifixion ensue, the only persons caught off guard are the disciples. Jesus has foreseen the event and freely embraced it. This is precisely what the reader is supposed to do as well.

However, for Mark the cross is not a tragedy but is a part of the predetermined plan of salvation (see δεῖ ['necessary'] in 8:31 and γέγραπται ['it was written'] in 14:21). The divine imperative behind Jesus' death serves to soften the ignominy surrounding the crucifixion. For Mark, what is necessary is not merely that Jesus must die, but that he must die as 'king'.[28] Crucifixion becomes revelatory for Jesus' identity as Messiah and necessary for the salvation that God intends to provide through the Messiah.

The saving significance of Jesus' death is signified at several points. Jesus likens himself to a physician who has come to heal 'sinners' (2:17). His death will be the means through which the kingdom of God comes with power (9:1).[29] The ransom logion of 10:45 ('For . . . the Son of Man did not come to be served, but to serve, and to give his life as a ransom for many') does two things. First, it protests against Roman rulers and their Herodian clients, who were a dark and twisted parody of true kingship. Second, Jesus advances the notion of his death as 'ransom' (λύτρον). Jesus willingly endures the death of a 'slave' in order to redeem those who are themselves enslaved. What Mark means by ransom is not specified, but three things should be noted:

(1) The logion may evoke connotations of the Isaianic Suffering Servant who gives his life as a sin offering. To be sure, 10:45 is not a paraphrase of Isaiah 53:10–12 (LXX), and λύτρον never translates מָשָׁם ('guilt offering') in the Septuagint. Still, the intertextual echoes of Isaiah throughout Mark and the conceptual parallel of 'pour out his soul to death' (Isa. 53:12, my trans.) with 'give his life as a ransom for many', suggest

that Jesus embodies the Isaianic hope for a new exodus through redemption from sin.[30]

(2) λύτρον is probably meant in a sense analogous to Pauline redemption terminology which has an explicit connection with release from sin.[31]

(3) The best interpretation of Mark 10:45 is probably the Marcan account of the last supper (14:22–24). At the last supper Jesus tells his disciples that his blood is 'poured out for many' (14:24). Jesus interprets his death as heralding the new covenant of Ezekiel and Jeremiah where God forgives his people. Jesus' blood thereby becomes the sacrifice that enables a new covenant to be put into effect. Morna Hooker captures Mark's understanding of Jesus' death quite aptly: 'The death of Jesus is the beginning of something new: it is the ransom which creates a new people, the means of establishing the new covenant, the event which signifies the destruction of the temple and the beginning of a new form of worship'.[32]

Far from avoiding the scandal of a crucified Messiah, Mark in fact exploits the tension between the Jewish messianic traditions and Jesus' messiahship in his narrative.[33] Mark's christological project, if we may call it that, is to redefine the traditional category of messiahship along the lines of the reign of the crucified Son of God. According to Christopher M. Tuckett:

> It is almost as if Mark is aware that christological terms can be multivalent. Hence he writes his story to show what he regards as the true significance of words that can be spoken. Jesus is the Christ, the Son of God. But the nature of kingship, sonship, and of divinity, are all given new meaning by Mark's story, especially by his account of Jesus' death on the cross.[34]

The way that Mark does this is by drawing together Jewish traditions of a messianic deliverer with other Jewish traditions of suffering, sacrifice, and salvation.

The narrative of Mark is shaped by the persistent question, 'Who is this man?' while sewing into the fabric of the mystery of his person the dark and foreboding shadow of the cross

(1:27; 2:7; 4:41; 6:2–3). It is no coincidence that occurrences of Χριστός are concentrated in the second half of the book, where the shadow of Jesus' coming death looms large over the story.[35] The identity of Jesus reaches its chief clarification in the passion story. The revelation of his messianic identity as a suffering redeemer is clear in Jesus' affirmative answer to Caiaphas' question as to whether he is the Messiah/Son of the Blessed One. Jesus' answer incorporates a reference to the enthronement of the Son of Man, which is not a sequel to his suffering but defines the meaning of it: exaltation (14:61–62).[36] Thereafter the royal status of Jesus is underscored when he is tried, mocked, and crucified as the king of the Jews (15:6–12,26), and taunted as the Messiah and king of Israel (15:32). The centurion's confession of Jesus as the Son of God explodes the irony by heralding the true identity of Jesus *at the cross*, and the testimony is divinely confirmed by the tearing of the veil in the temple (15:38–39). The cross-confession-veil functions much like the heavenly voice at Jesus' baptism and transfiguration, namely, as a divine authentication of Jesus' divinely appointed messianic identity. Bringing us full circle, Mark defines Ἰησοῦς Χριστός (1:1) as the one crucified as ὁ βασιλεὺς Ἰσραὴλ ('the king of Israel'; 15:32). Viewed this way, the messianic nature of Mark's passion story puts him in close relationship with other Christian traditions that linked Jesus' identification as the Χριστός with his redemptive death (see Luke 24:26,46; John 12:34; Acts 2:36; 3:18; 17:3; 26:23; 1 Cor. 15:3; 1 Pet. 1:11; 2:21; 3:18; 4:1).

## Linguistic: The passion of the 'king'

The use of the word βασιλεύς ('king') in Mark's Gospel is illuminating. Prior to the passion narrative βασιλεύς occurs six times in contexts pertaining to confrontation with worldly rulers (6:14,22,25,26,27; 13:9). However, in Mark 15 it occurs six times (15:2,9,12,18,26,32) but is used exclusively in relation to Jesus. Paul Barnett suggests that Mark has deliberately interwoven the word βασιλεύς ('king') throughout the narrative because it is so close in sound to βασιλεία ('kingdom'). He writes: 'Mark wants us to understand that, incredible as it may seem, "the kingdom of God" actually begins with the crucifixion of "the king of Israel".'[37]

In Mark 15, Pilate asks three rhetorical questions about Jesus' kingship (vv. 2,9,12). The first, 'Are you the king of the Jews?' perhaps expresses the point of view that Mark is trying to combat. How could Jesus, led in chains before a Roman governor, be any type of king, let alone the anointed king of Israel's hopes? Jesus' enigmatic reply, 'You said so',[38] neither affirms nor denies the charge but invites further investigation. The second question, 'Do you want me to release the king of the Jews?'[39] allows Pilate to participate in what he thinks is a charade by referring to Jesus as king. Pilate already knows the answer and he elicits the petition for the release of Barabbas. This petition is in many ways symbolic of the Jewish rejection of Jesus' messiahship: the Jews preferred insurrection and brigandage over Jesus' message of the kingdom. Pilate asks thirdly, 'What shall I do with the man *you call* the king of Jews?' (15:12, my trans.). Pilate places the accusation of Jesus' kingship onto the lips of the Jewish audience. The crowd retorts with a bloodthirsty scream for violence in verses 13–14: σταύρωσον αὐτόν ('Crucify him!'). The tragedy is that what the Jewish leaders and the crowd want to do with *their* Messiah is hang him on a *Roman* cross.

The christological irony continues in the pseudo-worship of Jesus by the praetorian guard in 15:16–20. Jesus is enrobed in a royal purple garment, given a crown, and then mockingly worshipped: 'Hail, king of the Jews!' Mark writes that 'kneeling down, they began worshipping him' (vv. 18–19, my trans.). The word προσκυνέω ('I worship') is used earlier in 5:6 to describe what the Gerasene demoniac did in response to Jesus: he bowed down in reverent fear. Confession of Jesus as king and worship of him are entirely appropriate, but grotesquely reversed by the insatiable cruelty of Roman soldiers who instead mock Jesus and lead him out to be crucified.

It was customary in Roman executions to display the charge of the victim during the execution process.[40] The titulus 'THE KING OF THE JEWS' (v. 26) presents a stark irony. Jesus, in word and deed, preaches the kingdom of God and yet what comes is the kingship of the crucified.[41] This public declaration of Jesus' kingship on the titulus becomes a mocking jest and a clear warning of what Rome does with would-be messiahs. Yet the reader is invited to see the placard not as a punishment, but as a proclamation of a genuine reality.

The titles ὁ βασιλεὺς Ἰσραήλ ('the king of Israel') and ὁ Χριστὸς ('the Messiah') are correlated in verse 32 (see similarly *Pss. Sol.* 17.32,42). Jesus is mocked by the priests and scribes in verse 31 because he is οὐ δύναται ('not powerful') enough to save himself and therefore not a king. Yet it is Jesus' very act of powerlessness in giving his life as a ransom for many (Mark 10:45) that effects the salvation of others and proves his kingliness.[42] Overall, the passion story indicates that Χριστός is understood as a royal epithet that is equivalent to βασιλεύς ('king'). Resultantly if Χριστός and βασιλεύς are to be understood as synonymous, then it becomes clear that the passion narrative is permeated by messianic (i.e. royal) imagery.[43]

The narrative effect of the Messiah/king equivalency is striking: the cross is not disproof of Jesus' messiahship; rather, it is the primary line of evidence for it. The entire narrative web of Mark 15 possesses a kerygmatic irony.[44] What Pilate, the soldiers, and the priests say about Jesus' kingship turns out to be precisely the opposite of what they intended. They inadvertently confess him (Pilate), worship him (soldiers), and attest his saving power (priests and scribes). The cruel and pitiless actions of Jesus' opponents are conscripted by Mark into instruments of proclamation that herald forth the good news that Jesus is the royal Messiah and rightful king.[45] As Wilhelm Bousset stated: 'A look at the passion narrative shows us now how it is wholly dominated by the messianic idea and everything in it is placed under the rubric of the proof that this crucified Jesus is nevertheless the Messiah, the king of the Jews'.[46]

### Rhetorical: pointing to the triumph of the Messiah

If Mark's aim is to persuade Greco-Roman readers (Diasporan Jews especially)[47] that Jesus is the Messiah, he may appeal to beliefs, vocabulary, and ideas that he would expect his audience to have in their 'mental register'. I would suggest that the Roman triumphal procession and the notion of the ideal Hellenistic king may have been part of that background, which is used by Mark as a foil for his messianic agenda.

There are a striking number of parallels between Mark's passion narrative and a Roman triumphal procession.[48] A triumphal procession celebrated the conquest of kings and generals who returned victoriously from a campaign with booty and captives (see 2 Cor. 2:14–15; Col. 2:15). The triumphator would enter the city and lead a procession up the Sacra Via to the Jupiter Capitolinus, celebrating his conquest. From 20 BC onwards, the ceremony was the exclusive right of the emperor, and its procedure sometimes culminated in his deification. This procession possesses several points of contact with Mark's passion narrative: The gathering of the whole praetorian guard, the purple ceremonial dress and crowning of the triumphator, the accolades from the soldiers, the official who leads a sacrificial victim (a bull) and carries the weapon of execution (axe), the offer and refusal of a drink, the placard naming the conquered people, the accompaniment by two consuls or generals, and the confession as a 'son of god' are all paralleled in the *triumphus*. Schmidt summarizes the parallels:

> The Praetorians gather early in the morning to proclaim the triumphator. He is dressed in the triumphal garb, and a crown of laurel is placed on his head. The soldiers then shout in acclamation of his Lordship and perform acts of homage to him. They accompany him from their camp through the streets of the city. The sacrificial victim is there in the procession, and alongside walks the official carrying the implement of his coming death. The procession ascends finally to the Place of the (Death's) Head, where the sacrifice is to take place. The triumphator is offered the ceremonial wine. He does not drink it, but it is poured out on the altar at the moment of sacrifice. Then, at the moment of being lifted up before the people, at the moment of the sacrifice, again the triumphator is acclaimed as Lord, and his vice-regents appear with him in confirmation of his glory. Following the lead of the soldiers, the people together with their leaders and the vice-regents themselves join in the acclamation. The epiphany is confirmed in portents by the gods: 'Truly this man is the Son of God!'[49]

Jesus' death march along the Via Dolorosa is the anti-type to the triumphal procession along Rome's Sacra Via. The cascade of regal and triumphal imagery implies that what we have before us is no mere execution, but rather a coronation and epiphany of Israel's God. Schmidt comments: 'Mark designs this "anti-triumph" to suggest that the seeming scandal of the cross is actually an exalta-tion of Christ.'[50] This royal image of Jesus' crucifixion illuminates the reference to Jesus' death as an enthroned 'glory' in Mark 10:37. Similarly, Jesus' reply to Caiaphas in Mark 14:62 is perhaps a threat that Caiaphas will see him exalted and enthroned in a position reserved exclusively for God amidst his own execution. The cruci-fixion weaves together the golden threads of the Marcan narrative, so that the motifs of suffering, service, kingship, glory, and vindi-cation form a tapestry of poignancy and power.

Another feature that Mark's readers may have picked up on is how Jesus epitomizes and embodies the model of the ideal Hellenistic king. The shepherd metaphor is used at various points (6:34; 11:1–10; 14:27). In the Old Testament God promised to raise up a faithful Davidic shepherd to pastor God's people, and Greco-Roman literature sometimes described kings as shep-herds.[51] In 10:41–45 Jesus emerges as the exemplary servant-king who comes to serve and redeem his people and so fulfils the highest ideals of Hellenistic kingship. Plato stated that 'the man who has not been a servant (ὁ μὴ δουλεύσας) will never become a praiseworthy master (δεσπότης), and that the right way to gain honour is by serving (δουλεύω) honourably rather than by ruling honourably' (*Laws* 6.762e). Dio Chrysostom wrote of the 'kingly ruler who desires to serve all and has it in his power to do so' (*Disc.* 1.34).[52] When Mark's portrait of Jesus is read against this backdrop, Jesus' death is a regal triumph and Jesus emerges as superior to the self-deified monarchs of the first century who seek their own self-aggrandizement.

### Social-scientific: the shame of the cross and the honour of the Messiah

When Jesus' ministry and death are situated in the context of the cultural values of honour and shame, they take on new significance.[53] In the Greco-Roman world, honour is the claim to a certain status and the acknowledgement of that status by group consensus. Honour can either be ascribed by gender and rank, or acquired through social advancement in public accom-plishments and by excelling over others. Honour was a limited commodity in ancient societies and it was attained through the social competition of challenge and response. A challenge could be issued as an attempt to enter the social space of a competitor, or to dislodge him from his current status. This was how one excelled over others and increased one's own honour.

Jesus could be perceived as being dishonourable in Mark since he does not observe social boundaries. Throughout the Gospel, Jesus associates with lepers, women, tax collectors and the like, all of whom were of an inferior honour rating to himself. In one pericope he rejects, and therefore dishonours, his mother and brothers due to his allegiance to a fictive kinship shared with his disciples (3:21,31–35). More acutely, Jesus' crucifixion was the most reprehensible and ignominious of deaths. Yet despite this, Mark is convinced of the overall 'honour' of Jesus. Throughout the Gospel, Jesus enters into several encounters of the game of challenge and response and completely humiliates his opponents. Jesus' interlocutors frequently ask him a question designed to trap him. Jesus not only avoids the trap, but turns the tables on his opponents so that they are publicly shamed, and his honour rating thus increases *at their expense*.

In the conflict stories in the Gospel it becomes clear that Jesus has played the honour game better than his adversaries.[54] Jesus responds to the challenges of his rivals and publicly dishonours them in the process, which leaves them with the only 'honourable' option of plotting revenge. Jesus accumulates all this honour in the narrative and, by freely entering into death, does not have his honour taken from him. Instead, he freely surrenders it.

Jesus' death can be conceived as being 'honourable' on two fronts. First, Jesus represents the ideal ruler who saves his people and so advances his honour in the minds of Mark's readers. Epictetus asserts that Menoeceus, by dying to save Thebes, in fact gained honour (Epictetus, *Diss.* 3.20.5–6). Lycurgus tells the legend of the ancient king of Athens, Codrus, who 'thought it better to die for the salvation of his subjects' than to live himself (*Against Leocrates* 86).[55] Second, it was common for minority groups, who had countercultural (and therefore dishonourable) values, to compensate for this by appealing to a wider principle that approves of their practices, such as reason, nature, or divinity.[56] In Mark's account, God honours Jesus' death. It is immediately after the impassioned speech about the necessity of taking up the cross (8:34 – 9:1) that Jesus is transfigured in dazzling array (9:2–8). This not only vindicates Jesus' ambition to go to the cross, but also demonstrates that the path to divine glory begins with suffering.[57] In 16:6 the angel at the tomb tells the women followers, 'You seek Jesus of Nazareth, *the one having been crucified* (τὸν ἐσταυρωμένον); he has *been raised* (ἠγέρθη) and he is not here' (my trans.). The verb ἠγέρθη is a divine passive and amounts to 'has been raised *by God*'. The collocation of the substantive participle 'the crucified one' and the divine passive verb 'raised by God' removes the stigma of Jesus' death by appeal to a higher authority that honours Jesus. In this sense, the resurrection informs Mark's readers of what God thinks of the cross: vindication, honour, and glory.

### Christological: the messianic titles

Though limiting a christological investigation to the titles in the Gospels is about as effective as limiting an investigation of a political campaign to political headlines, the titles remain a significant part of the christological portrait of the Gospels, especially when located within the wider narrative, discursive, and intertextual materials. The paradox of Mark's Christology is that Jesus is depicted in disparate fashion. Jesus is portrayed as powerful and powerless, regal and rejected, victorious and victimized.[58] This paradoxical portrayal is discernible in Mark's juxtaposition of the christological titles 'Messiah', 'Son of Man', 'Son of God', 'Son of David', and 'King of the Jews/Israel'; titles which form a *mutually interpretive christological spiral where one defines the meaning of the others.*[59]

### Messiah

Explicit references to the Χριστός in Mark are actually quite limited (1:1; 8:29; 9:41; 12:35; 13:21; 14:61; 15:32).[60] However, the paucity of explicit references does not make the designation any less significant as it occurs at key junctures in the narrative. The appearance of Χριστός in the incipit in 1:1 suggests that readers/hearers are to understand the entire narrative as a messianic story, with the central character exemplifying a messianic role even in his death. It is the head term for the career of one venerated as Messiah, known to have been crucified, and believed to have been resurrected.

At the key turning point in the story Peter confesses Jesus as the Messiah (8:29–30). Given that the first half of Mark's Gospel focuses on Jesus' miraculous deeds, his power over spiritual and natural realms, and his liberating abilities, it is likely that Peter is convinced of this designation precisely by Jesus' miraculous powers. Matthew's reference to the 'deeds of the Messiah' (Matt. 11:2, my trans.) may reflect an expectation of such miraculous deeds and contain the same perspective of the Marcan Peter set out here. The designation is accepted by Jesus, but he makes two seemingly peculiar steps. First, he commands the disciples not to tell anyone about him (Mark 8:30) and, second, he proceeds to give the first of three passion predictions about the Son of Man being rejected and killed by the Judean leaders (8:31). Peter's rebuke to Jesus for this sombre remark regarding his messianic confession is counter-rebuked by the Marcan Jesus, who demands that discipleship be defined as joining him in his journey to the cross. For at the end of that journey, the disciples can expect to see the kingdom of God come with power (8:32 – 9:1). Peter's fairly conventional view of a messianic deliverer with miraculous powers and regal authority is unconventionally redefined as the suffering Son of Man by Jesus. It seems, then, that in this passage Jesus is indeed the Messiah, but his messianic identity cannot be properly understood apart from appreciation of his crucifixion as central to his messianic task.[61]

The next mention of Χριστός comes in the unit about competing exorcists in Mark 9:38–41. The conclusion of the story is given in the dominical words: 'Truly I tell you, anyone who gives you a cup of water in my name *because you belong to the Messiah* (ὅτι Χριστοῦ ἐστε) will certainly be rewarded.' Though Jesus does not explicitly name himself as the Messiah here, the fact that belonging to the Messiah is the grounds for giving water in Jesus' very name suggests a close relationship between Jesus and the Messiah. The story speaks to a situation, perhaps post-Easter, in which followers of Jesus are censured for their exclusionist attitudes. Perhaps the point is that those who are characterized by service belong in the family of the Messiah because they show their family likeness by the service rendered to those persecuted for the faith.

The messianic riddle that Jesus poses in his Jerusalem ministry, asking how the scribes can say that the Messiah is a Son of David when David calls him 'Lord', is an opaque passage.[62] Mark's interest in the story is that the standard 'Son of David' expectations are insufficient because messiahship must be defined according to the identity of the 'Lord'. The Messiah is a Son of David, but also more than a Son of David. As Larry Hurtado states, 'the reader is expected to see that Jesus "the Christ" is far greater than the commonly accepted notions of the Messiah'.[63]

The reference to false messiahs and competing messianic claimants appears in the Olivet Discourse (13:21–22). Mark warns against false messiahs because the title applies to Jesus alone. The performance of signs and wonders is no guarantee of messianic authenticity. That is the case because Mark defines messiahship along the line of a different string of values. Rather than a military leader, the Messiah is the coming Son of Man who gathers his people prior to the apocalyptic tribulation set to come upon the nation (13:26–27). In fact, I would add that we should take Mark 13 in unity with Mark 14 – 15 where the destruction of the temple and Jesus' death are part of the one eschatological act. The similarities are easy to spot: the portents of the temple's destruction occasioned by darkness (13:24) occur also at the crucifixion (15:33); disciples will be delivered up to rulers (13:9) while Jesus is delivered over to sinners and Gentiles (14:41,53–65; 15:1–15); the promise for one temple to be destroyed (13:2; cf. 15:38) is matched by one that will be rebuilt (14:58). In other words, Jesus' death is one of the first signs of the 'coming' of the Son of Man and the final judgement that will follow his enthronement.[64]

In the passion narrative Mark's use of Χριστός appears to define and influence the meaning of the other titles used for Jesus. This is seen quite explicitly where 'Messiah' is equated with the 'Son of the Blessed One' (14:61), 'Son of Man' (14:62), and the 'king of Israel' (15:32). As Mark's story of Jesus enters into its finale, the messianism of Jesus constitutes the controlling framework in which the other christological titles are to be understood.[65]

## Son of Man

The Son of Man designation is the most common title in Mark's Gospel and is Jesus' primary means of self-reference.[66] In Mark, and in the synoptic tradition more generally, the 'Son of Man' is portrayed in three main ways: an authoritative figure (2:10,28), a

suffering figure (8:31; 9:9,12; 9:31; 10:33–34,45; 14:21,41), and a
future judge (8:38; 13:26; 14:62).[67] The primary dichotomy is
between the Son of Man's role as a suffering figure in the present
and his apparent eschatological authority in the future. Yet this
dichotomy is not entirely without precedent in Jewish biblical
traditions. The simultaneous ascription of authority and suffering to a human figure is probably developed from Daniel 7.
Daniel's 'one like a son of man' is a heavenly figure who represents God, God's kingdom, God's people, and Israel's king over
and against the pagan kingdoms who ravage the saints. The cor-
respondence between the vision of Daniel and the Marcan Son of
Man is that the Son of Man, like the 'saints of the Most High'
(Dan. 7:18), goes through suffering before entering into his glory.
This mysterious 'man' suffers under the fury of the pagan beasts
but is vindicated on behalf of the saints, who in turn receive an
everlasting kingdom.[68]

Importantly, Mark also identifies the Son of Man as the
Messiah. According to George MacRae: 'The preference of Mark
for the title Son of Man over Messiah – or perhaps we should say
Mark's reinterpretation of the Messiah in terms of the Son of Man
– is at the heart of Mark's Gospel.'[69] At the big turning point in
Mark's Gospel, Peter confesses that Jesus is the Messiah, and the
sequel is Jesus' teaching that the Son of Man must suffer and be
killed (8:29–31). The messianic designation is not renounced by
Jesus (contra much scholarship that speculates about what real
dialogue hides behind Mark's account), but put into a different
narrative where the Messiah suffers for the redemption of God's
people. When Jesus is asked if he is the 'Messiah', the reply
Caiaphas gets from him is, 'you will see the Son of Man sitting at
the right hand of the Mighty One and coming on the clouds of
heaven' (14:62). According to Mark, then, Jesus is the Messiah,
and the allusion to the Danielic scene of divine enthronement
serves to make it clear that 'the Son of Man' rejected by the
Judean leaders will in fact be vindicated as the Messiah and the
divine Son with divine glory.[70] Taken together, these two episodes demonstrate that Jesus' self-designation as the Son of Man
is a virtual codeword for the secrecy and suffering of his messianic mission. Unique as Mark may be at this point by character-
izing Jesus in such a way, there was already a trend in Second

Temple Jewish literature of merging the roles of Messiah and Son of Man (see esp. *1 Enoch* 48.10; 52.4).[71] Mark is clearly within the orbit of a Jewish theology of mediators by identifying the Son of Man with the role of suffering, and by identifying the Son of Man as the Messiah. What is unique is how they are brought together so that Mark redefines the meaning of messiahship in terms of a suffering Son of Man who ransoms his people by his death and establishes the reign of God at his death.

*Son of God*

In the Gospel of Mark the designation 'the Son of God' (ὁ υἱὸς τοῦ θεοῦ) functions to signify Jesus' unique filial relationship to Israel's God and underscore his authority as a messianic deliverer. In the Old Testament 'Son' is frequently a designation for Israel's king (e.g. 2 Sam. 7:14; Pss 2:7; 89:26).[72] The title was also appropriate for the Messiah when those passages were linked to a narrative about an eschatological royal deliverer, hence, 'my son the Messiah' (*4 Ezra* 7:28) and '[I will be] his father and he shall be my son. He is the branch of David who shall arise with the Interpreter of the Law [to rule] in Zion [at the end] of time' (4QFlor 1.10–13). A messianic connotation to 'Son' and 'Son of God' appears elsewhere in the Qumran scrolls where it is proposed that the community meets for a meal 'when God begets the Messiah' (1QSa 2.11–12) and in the eschatological narrative about the advent of a kingdom brought by the 'Son of God' and 'Son of the Most High' (4Q246 2.1–10).

The messianic sense of 'son' appears in the Gospel of Mark in four ways.[73] First, in two divine declarations Jesus is commissioned and authenticated as the *messias designatus*. At Jesus' baptism there is a voice from heaven which says, 'You are my beloved son, in whom I am well pleased' (1:11, my trans.). The allusions to Isaiah 42 and Psalm 2 are hard to miss:

> Here is my servant, whom I uphold,
>     my chosen one in whom I delight;
> I will put my Spirit on him . . . (Isa. 42:1)

> He said to me, 'You are my son;
>     today I have become your father' (Ps. 2:7).

Perhaps also Isaiah 61:1:

> The Spirit of the Sovereign LORD is on me,
>     because the LORD has anointed me
>     to proclaim good news to the poor.

This intertextual allusion indicates a merging of the roles of Davidic king and the Servant of the Lord in the figure of Jesus according to Mark. God's royal emissary and redemptive agent become one and the same.[74] Thereafter, the climax of the transfiguration story is where a voice from the cloud speaks to the disciples: 'This is my Son, whom I love. Listen to him!' (9:7). This is the second heavenly voice in the Gospel, and it repeats the substance of Mark 1:11 – that Jesus is the Spirit-anointed figure who must be followed and obeyed. The significance of the transfiguration is that it points to an association of Jesus with two highly exalted prophets (Moses and Elijah), it confirms Jesus' divine commission as the Messiah, and most importantly, it constitutes a divine validation of Jesus' passion predictions previously given (see 8:32–33).[75] In the end, the first revelatory event of Jesus' sonship at his baptism marks his commission as the Davidic/Servant Messiah, while the second revelatory event at the transfiguration validates his mission to go to the cross.

Second, recognition of Jesus' messianic credentials may be intimated in Jesus' exorcisms. The unclean spirits who possess certain individuals recognize Jesus immediately as the 'Son of God' or 'Son of the Most High God' (3:11; 5:7), with due emphasis on his authority and power over them. On the one hand, the professions of Jesus' divine sonship by the spirits may be no more than admission that the superior divine Spirit is operative in him. On the other hand, we should keep in mind the tradition of David as an exorcist (1 Sam. 16; Josephus, *Ant.* 6.166–68; Pseudo-Philo, *LAB* 60.1–3; 11QPs[a] 27.2–5) and also Solomon (*T.Sol.* 1.5–7; Wis 7.17–21; *Ant.* 8.45-47; *Tg. Ps.* 91; 4Q11). Jesus stands in a line of royal Israelite rulers with supernatural powers over evil forces.

Third, in the parable of the wicked tenants (12:1–12; cf. Isa. 5; Ps. 118) Jesus is portrayed as the divinely commissioned messianic agent sent to a recalcitrant Israel. The climax of the parable is found in the citation of Psalm 118 at the very end, which narrates the vindication of the 'stone' despite its rejection. The parable is messianic because, first, in the original context of Psalm 118 the 'stone' mentioned in verse 22 is Israel's king. Second, 'stone' represents a possible word-play on 'Son' since they were natural rhymes in Hebrew (בֵּן [*ben*, 'son'] and אֶבֶן) [*eben*, 'stone']), which equates the messianic stone with the messianic son. Third, the mention of Jerusalem's rejoicing at her king returning to her on a donkey, in Psalm 118:25–26, seals the messianic significance of Jesus' entry into Jerusalem (11:8–10). In other words, Mark 12:1–12 is a microcosm of the whole passion story, where Israel's messianic king is rejected by the Judean leaders, and in the aftermath there is vindication for the rejected Son, and judgement waiting for the wicked leaders. I would go so far as to say that the use of psalms (esp. Pss 2; 22; 69; 110; 118) in Mark represents a consistent pattern of messianic exegesis.[76]

Fourth, the most obvious references to Jesus' messianic sonship in Mark are in the trial scene (14:53–65) and at the foot of the cross (15:39) where Jesus is the *suffering Messiah*. On the back of the messianic entry (11:1–10), the temple demonstration (11:15–17), and the riddle about David's son (12:35–37), Jesus is asked at the trial by Caiaphas, 'Are you the Messiah, the Son of the Blessed One?' (14:61). Jesus' point-blank answer, 'I am',[77] is then strangely qualified by way of reference to the enthronement of the 'Son of Man' in 14:62: 'And you will see the Son of Man sitting at the right hand of the Mighty One and coming on the clouds of heaven' (more on 'Son of Man' soon).[78] My suspicion is that 14:61–62 looks like a bit of a christological blender, with the major titles driven together and defined by each other. That is not to say that Messiah, Son of God, and Son of Man are entirely equated – they retain their specific Jewish-background, near-technical meaning within early Christianity – but they are pressed into the definition created by Mark's overarching narrative of the Messiah commissioned to enact God's reign and to die a martyr's death on the cross. To quote M. Eugene Boring again: 'Six streams of Markan christological imagery converge in this crucial scene: Messiah (Christ), Son of God, Son of Man, Suffering Servant of Isa 53, suffering righteous one of the Psalms and the Wisdom of Solomon, and true prophet of God'.[79]

Equally significant is the statement in Mark 15:39 where the centurion, in seeing how Jesus died, says: 'Surely this man was the Son of God (ἀληθῶς οὗτος ὁ ἄνθρωπος υἱὸς θεοῦ ἦν)'. Debates about the significance of the lack of the article do not seem to prove much either way. The remark is both ironic and iconic. It is ironic in the sense that a Roman centurion confesses Jesus with a title that a Roman soldier would normally attribute to the Roman emperor. In the early first century, Caesar Augustus was venerated as *divi filius* (son of God/divine one). According to ancient coinage Tiberius was 'the Son of the Most High Augustus'. Nero even arrogated for himself many divine roles and honours. In addition, the profession of Jesus as 'Son of God' in 15:39 functions as an *inclusio* with the trial scene in 14:61–62. Sandwiched in the middle are the proceedings before Pilate and the crucifixion sequence, where the dominant matter of marvel and mocking is Jesus as 'king of the Jews/Israel' (15:2,9,12,18,26,32) and the 'Messiah' (14:61; 15:32). The centurion's confession is meant to provide an alternative point of view to the horrendous events depicted. Jesus' death is not that of a messianic pretender but, as the story has been telling us, God's own Son commissioned in his messianic role to redeem the people and inaugurate a messianic kingdom. In Mark 15:39 the irony ends and the Messiah's iron rule is ratified by acclamation. As Adela Collins puts it: 'This scene, thus, is the climax of the reinterpretation by the author of Mark of the traditional understanding of the royal Messiah'.[80]

All in all, Mark insists that Χριστός receives its true and proper meaning as a designation of Jesus only in light of Jesus' mission to go to the cross, his divinely appointed suffering, and his transcendent power as the Son of God.[81]

*Son of David*
The reference to Jesus as the 'Son of David' (υἱὸς Δαυίδ) is limited to the second half of the Gospel. The background is evidently the hope for a resurgent Davidic kingdom (e.g. Isa. 11:1–5; Jer. 23:5–6; Amos 9:11–12; Zech. 3:8) that inspired Second Temple expectations for a new Davidic king who was uniquely empowered with God's Spirit (e.g. Isa. 11:2; *Pss. Sol.* 17:37; 4Q161). The prophetic and regal qualities of the Spirit-anointed leader are not mutually exclusive, as David was regarded as both a king and a prophet

(Mark 12:35–37; Acts 1:16,20–21). As the 'Son of David', Jesus exercises a prophetic ministry and possesses a royal status.

The messianic component of Jesus' identity becomes even more acute as Jesus nears his final destination in Jerusalem. The material running through Mark 10:46 – 12:44 can be regarded as a section that characterizes Jesus' Davidic activity.[82] In what bursts the bubble of the messianic secret, blind Bartimaeus appeals to Jesus for mercy by publicly lauding him as the 'Son of David' (10:47–48). Bartimaeus is the paradigm of discipleship in both his christological confession and his faith to receive healing from Jesus. He is a model of messianic faith.

In the 'triumphal' entry, Jesus is heralded as the one who comes in the name of the Lord. His coming to Jerusalem in fulfilment of Zechariah 9:9 occasions the chorus: 'Blessed is the coming kingdom of our father David!' (11:10). Thus, Jesus' entry into Jerusalem deliberately excites messianic enthusiasm among the crowds for a coming Davidic king to establish a new Judean kingdom. Yet, as the public element of the trial shows, Jesus disappointed those expectations in the end, which is why Barabbas was chosen over Jesus for amnesty (15:7–15). The redeeming mission of this Son of David did not curry favour with all segments of the Jerusalem population.

When teaching in the temple, the messianic riddle posed to his interlocutors does not claim that Jesus, though not a Son of David, is the Messiah, or that the Messiah is not a Son of David (12:35–37). Instead, the employment of Psalm 110 in the riddle indicates both the priestly function of the Messiah (hence the reference to Melchizedek in 110:4) and signifies the exaltation of the Messiah to sharing in God's own throne (hence the reference to the title 'Lord' in 110:1). What I take to be the primary point is that the Messiah is the Son of David plus a whole lot more.[83] Interesting also is that the preceding section has Jesus affirm the *Shema* of Deuteronomy 6:4: 'The LORD our God, the LORD is one' (12:29). This is as strong an affirmation of monotheism as one can imagine. Yet in the following section pertaining to the royal riddle, Jesus identifies the Messiah as 'Lord' (κύριος) and so binds together the messianic κύριος with the κύριος of Israel's monotheistic devotion. The Messiah is then invested with heavenly and divine authority, and such a claim stands in analogy to the

Son of Man who shares God's throne (14:62).[84] It seems that the Marcan Jesus' self-understanding embraces the terms υἱὸς Δαυίδ and κύριος in an eschatological sense. They are designations of who Jesus is and who he will be in his crucifixion-resurrection-exaltation.[85]

That Jesus is called 'Son of David' by Bartimaeus, celebrated as a Davidic deliverer in the triumphal entry, and engages in a game of biblical word-play about David's 'Lord' in Jerusalem is not to be missed. Messianic hopes in the Gospel of Mark have not been replaced by the passion predictions; rather the Davidic messianism becomes the needle that the material about a suffering Messiah must pass through.

## King of the Jews

Finally, we can consider the designation of Jesus as 'king' (15:2,9,18,26,32). The title is evidently a secularized version of messiahship. This, however, is not to deny that kings in antiquity were religious figures with religious roles in the cultus and priesthood. My point is, rather, that attribution of the title 'king' to Jesus affirms Jesus' royal claims apart from the web of hopes in Israel's sacred traditions and subsequent Jewish literature. The repetition of the title highlights the irony surrounding Jesus' death and the theocentric nature of the kingdom of God. The man mocked as king actually is king. The Roman political charge in fact announces a theological reality that God's kingdom comes proleptically in the death of Jesus. Strange as it sounds, Jesus' death is his coronation as king and the triumphal epiphany of the long-awaited kingdom. For this reason, Jesus' detractors rightly recognize the association of the mocking placard and his messianic claims (15:32). Their derision is overturned by the confession of the centurion who recognizes Jesus' valour and heroism in death and calls him a 'Son of God' (15:39).

## Summary

Mark's christological claims belong firmly within the aegis of Jewish messianic expectations. Mark's Christology is a revision rather than a rejection of Jewish messianic beliefs. The distinctive aspect in Mark's messianism is that the role of the Messiah, Son of Man, Son of God, and Son of David is redefined and reshaped by linking it with the passion narrative. Importantly, this redefinition of messiahship around Jesus is not a rejection of the messianic concept altogether, but Mark pins the hope for a Davidic deliverer to the fabric of Israel's Scriptures in a unique way by associating the messianic leader with the atoning value of the righteous sufferer.[86] Indeed, it was perhaps the early Christian view that the psalms pertaining to anguish and persecution were actually prayers of the Messiah that enabled the Christians to find a scriptural explanation for the association of the 'anointed one' with a pattern of suffering and rejection (see Pss 22:1–31; 89:38; 118:5–27). Identifying the Messiah with the 'biblical' script of the rejected righteous one – from Isaiah 53, Daniel 7, or the psalms of lament – enabled Mark (and perhaps even others before him) to resolve the oxymoron of a crucified Messiah.

For Mark, the cross is also a revelatory event that provides a divine clarification of Jesus' mission and identity. In the Marcan Gospel it is the cross that ultimately answers the question, 'Who is this man?' It is the cross that provides the epiphany of Israel's king, it is the cross that defines the nature of the kingdom, and it is the cross that constitutes the instrument of Israel's redemption.[87] According to Donald Senior, 'The death scene is the summit of Mark's narrative, the final resolution of the christological issues apparent throughout the Gospel.'[88] Similar are the words of Francis Moloney: 'Mark's understanding of Jesus' messianic status is entirely determined by the historical fact that Jesus of Nazareth was unjustly crucified. It is *on the cross* that Jesus is the Christ.'[89] In other words, it is Jesus as the crucified Messiah who provides the substance and meaning to the titles 'Son of Man' and 'Son of God'. The fundamental category that explicates Jesus' identity and story according to Mark is that of 'Messiah'.[90]

## Conclusion

Mark's theology of the cross is his leitmotif, but it comes to the fore as part of his literary project to tell the story of Jesus the Messiah for readers in the Greco-Roman world. In telling this story he anticipates the objections to the claim that a crucified Galilean peasant could be the Messiah. The idea was, in Pauline terms, foolishness to Greeks and a stumbling block to Jews. Mark is able to assuage these concerns through his narrative and rhetorical devices, which seek to undermine negative cultural dispositions to the cross. Mark's Gospel is not a cover-up about a failed messianic pretender.[91] Rather, Mark's Gospel is an attempt to persuade readers (especially Jews of the Diaspora) that Jesus is the Messiah. He prosecutes that task in several ways:

(1) The story culminates in the cross as a redemptive event.
(2) The Jewish hope for the arrival of the kingdom is fulfilled in Jesus' death and resurrection.
(3) Jesus epitomizes the true servant-king in his death.
(4) Jesus' crucifixion does not count him as accursed by God; rather, he is honoured by being resurrected.
(5) Israel's Messiah is the Son of Man and Son of God – roles that start with miracle-working glory, climax in suffering, and then conclude with a resurrection that vindicates his divine status.

These observations suggest that a significant purpose of Mark's Gospel is to be an apology for the cross.[92] The apology is necessitated by Jewish and Greco-Roman aversions to the veneration of a crucified figure. The momentum behind Mark's Gospel is to lead his readers to believe that Jesus is the Messiah – not despite the cross, but precisely because of it.[93]

# 2

# The Gospel of Matthew:
# The Davidic Messiah

## Introduction

The Gospel of Matthew is unique for a couple of reasons. First, it is the most Jewish of the Gospels. That is not to say that Mark, Luke, and John are not Jewish – far from it. The canonical Gospels are expressions of a messianic Judaism, composed for the benefit of audiences that are acquainted, in varying degrees, with the Jewish story as it was known in the wider Greco-Roman world. The Jewish nature of Matthew is, however, accentuated in his (though I dislike the term) *re-judaizing* of the Jesus tradition.[1] For instance, Matthew redacts Mark's wine-skins parable (Mark 2:22) by making clear that the new messianic wine still needs the wineskins so that 'both are preserved together' (Matt. 9:17, my trans.). Matthew's Gospel tries to hold together the 'old' and the 'new', or 'rupture and innovation'.[2] Similarly, Matthew adds a welcomed clarification to Mark's narration of Jesus and the purity laws (Mark 7:1–23) by making clear that the debate was about Pharisaic *halakah* concerning hand-washing and not the validity of the purity laws *in toto* (Matt. 15:20; and he omits Mark 7:19 about Jesus 'declaring all foods clean'). In that sense, Matthew is asserting the continuing validity of the Torah, in some sense, for Jewish Christians. For this reason, Matthew's Gospel, though at one level probably intended for a wide audience (at least as wide as that of Mark's Gospel), possesses the greatest utility for addressing Jewish Christians and non-Christ-believing Jews.[3]

Second, Matthew was the church's book. Matthew was the most popular book in the church fathers.[4] It was the most widely cited, copied, and remembered Gospel. There are more quotations and copies of Matthew's Gospel than any other Christian text from antiquity.[5] Matthew's placement at the head of the New Testament canon is not haphazard or insignificant. Matthew was the book perfectly suited to link the story of Israel (Old Testament) with the story of the church (New Testament). The Gospel of Matthew marks a canonical transition from the old to the new, and it is theologically significant because it places the faith of the church in the context of the hope of Israel. It assumes the social experience of Jewish Christians who are facing ejection from Jewish communities, while also trying to imagine a Gentile-majority future. Perhaps the Gospel of Matthew was even written as a bridge-building document between a Palestinian Jewish Christianity and a Jewish Christianity rooted in Diasporan culture, seeking to build a consensus around shared convictions about Messiah, Israel, law, and Gentiles.[6] Taking these points together, we can say that Matthew's Jesus stands as the embodiment of Israel's Davidic hope, while presenting him also as the leader of the messianic community of the new age.

## The Beginnings of the Messiah

From the outset of the Gospel of Matthew, the identity of Jesus is placed firmly within the story of Jewish history and the socio-political context of first-century Judea. The incipit, genealogy, and birth narrative underscore that Jesus is the messianic Son of David who has come to Israel at a crucial hour (Matt. 1:1 – 2:23). R.T. France rightly begins his comments on Matthew 1:1 – 4:11 with the words:

> The prominent repetition of the title 'Messiah' (or, in many English versions, 'Christ') in 1:1, 16, 17, 18; 2:4, together with the other related titles which recur in these opening paragraphs of the gospel ('Son of David,' 1:1, 20; 'King of the Jews,' 2:2), make it clear that Matthew is aiming to present an account not just of a historical figure (Jesus of Nazareth) but of the long awaited deliverer of

God's people of Israel. He will begin to tell the story of the Messiah's revelation to Israel, and of the way people respond to his coming in 4:17, where Jesus' public proclamation in Galilee begins.[7]

The incipit commences with reference to 'the scroll of the origins of Jesus the Messiah, the Son of David, the Son of Abraham' (my trans.). The 'scroll of the origins' (Βίβλος γενέσεως) is similar to the wordings given in Genesis 2:4 and 5:1 and so marks the origins of Jesus as a new beginning for Israel and the world.[8] What immediately follows in the genealogy is a survey of the history of God's people from its inception with Abraham, the progenitor of Israel, to the coming of the Messiah, the Son of David (Matt. 1:2–17). Despite all the debate about Matthew's source for the genealogy, why he chose 'fourteen' generations, and the significance of Gentile characters, the aim is clear: to locate Jesus within the story of Israel, as its ultimate climax, and to do so with a special focus on the Davidic dynasty as the proper context for understanding Jesus' origins, mission, and identity.[9]

The name 'Jesus' (Ἰησοῦς) is explained in Matthew 1:21 with reference to salvation based on the obvious etymology of יְהוֹשֻׁעַ (Yĕhôšûaʾ) in Hebrew or יֵשׁוּעַ (Yēšûaʾ) in Aramaic for 'Joshua', which means 'Yahweh saves'. The designation Χριστός is used in Matthew sixteen times (1:1,16,17,18; 2:4; 11:2; 16:16,20; 22:42; 23:10; 24:5,23; 26:63,68; 27:17,22). As Χριστός appears in the incipit as a qualification to Ἰησοῦς, one might think that Ἰησοῦς Χριστός is a proper name. Yet any restriction to a nominal sense for the designation disappears in light of verses 16–18, with the articular reference to Χριστός as 'the Messiah'. What is more, 1:16 and 27:17,22 both refer to 'Jesus who is called the Messiah' (Ἰησοῦς ὁ λεγόμενος Χριστός), which affirms the titular meaning of Χριστός in the genealogy and passion story.[11] As to the meaning of Χριστός in Matthew, Jack Kingsbury put it this way: 'As a christological title, Matthew understands the term Messiah as follows: the Messiah, the Coming One foretold by the prophets and awaited by Israel (11:2–6), is Jesus (1:16; 16:20; 24:5), that royal figure in the line of David (1:1,16,17) who brings the history of Israel (Abraham) to its culmination (1:1,17) and who, wielding the authority of God, means salvation or damnation for people (1:21; 3:11).'[12]

The additional descriptions of Jesus as 'Son of David' and 'Son of Abraham' indicate the pedigree and purpose of the messianic agent. David plays a central role in the forthcoming genealogy (1:6,17), while also appearing frequently in the Gospel (9:27; 12:23; 15:22; 20:30–31; 21:9,15; 22:41–45). Matthew's Christology is largely Davidic in a way analogous to, but with obvious differences from, Jewish literature and traditions from the first century.[13] Matthew locates his messianic story about an anointed figure in the trajectory of the Davidic tradition that looked forward to a new Israelite king to reign over a renewed Israel in the coming age. The mention of 'Son of Abraham' combines the particularism of the Jewish hope for a restored Davidic monarchy (reaching back to 2 Sam. 7:12–16) with the universalism of an equally Jewish hope for a restored Israel that embraces the nations (reaching back to Gen. 12:3).[14] Matthew ends the incipit with Abraham in 1:1, launches into the genealogy with Abraham at the head of it in 1:2, and recaps the David/Abraham link in 1:17. The opening sequence given in 1:1 is repeated in 1:17 with reference to the Davidic identity and Abrahamic scope of the Messiah's mission – bracketing Israel's exile and the plan for national restoration. In fact, there is a chiasmus that runs:

> Messiah . . . David . . . Abraham (Matt. 1:1)
> Abraham . . . David . . . Messiah (Matt. 1:17)

Thus, Matthew hooks his whole plot on Jesus, David, and Abraham (1:1) in order to show that Israel's history, running from the Abrahamic promises to the time of Israel's exile, comes to a messianic consummation through Jesus, who is the eschatological David.[15]

The Matthean genealogy is a maze of exegetical and historical-critical decisions that I have no time to navigate. Importantly, this genealogy is not a record composed for posterity interested in the dirt and grit of Jesus' family tree. If Jesus is born of the Holy Spirit through Mary (1:18–20), then he is not the biological son of Joseph and not of the Davidic line in that physical sense. Rather, we have here what Adolf Schlatter called 'the grafting of Jesus into the tribe of David'.[16] The overarching goal of the genealogy is the royal Davidic legitimation and the allusive articulation of

Jesus' christological vocation in light of Israel's story.[17] Indeed, the entire genealogy is a compressed summary of Israel's story with characters and events named in order to activate remembrance of a grander story behind the mere notice of physical lineage. The genealogy is a 'story whose plot may be summed up in the following narrative sequence: election, kingship, sin, exile, and messianic salvation'.[18]

Interpreters have long been concerned with the significance of the four patriarchs in the list (1:2), the exilic theme that appears in the centre and end (1:11–12,17), and the apparent 'annotations' in the genealogy including 'Judah *and his brothers*' (1:2), 'Jeconiah *and his brothers*' (1:11), and the four women Tamar, Rahab, Ruth, and Uriah's wife (1:3–6). Exploring these aspects of the genealogy elucidates the meaning of messiahship in the Gospel of Matthew.

First, following immediately from the incipit in 1:2, the author launches into a list of key patriarchs including: 'Abraham was the father of Isaac, Isaac the father of Jacob, Jacob the father of Judah and his brothers' (1:2). The big three patriarchs of Israel – Abraham, Isaac, and Jacob – figure prominently in key reminiscences of God's call of Israel and her election on the grounds of God's promise to the partriarchs (see Gen. 50:24; Exod. 2:24; 3:6,15–16; 4:5; 6:3,8; 33:1; Lev. 26:42; Num. 32:11; Deut. 1:8; 6:10; esp. 9:5,27; 29:13; 30:20). Israel's election, inheritance, and covenantal life rest on God's prior dealing with the patriarchs. Not only that, Matthew also adds 'Judah' to the list. Though Joseph was the key figure in the latter part of Genesis, it was Judah who received the promise of kingship in the oracle:

> The sceptre shall not depart from Judah,
>> nor the ruler's staff from between his feet,
> until tribute comes to him;
>> and the obedience of the peoples is his (Gen. 49:10 NRSV).

The oracle was crucially important in Jewish and Christian messianic hopes.[19] Significantly, then, the heading of the Matthean genealogy of the Messiah contains the topics of election and kingship.

Second, the first of two major annotations occurs in Matthew 1:2 with Judah 'and his brothers', and then the same for Jeconiah in Matt. 1:11. I am convinced by Jason Hood's thesis that the annotation 'and his brothers' for Judah and Jeconiah refers to their sacrificial actions on behalf of their brothers.[20] For Judah, this was his willingness to undergo slavery in place of Benjamin (see Gen. 44:17–34), and similarly for Jeconiah, who, in developing Jewish tradition, saved Jerusalem by voluntary captivity (see Josephus, *War* 6.103–6; amplifying 2 Kgs 25:27–30; Jer. 52:31–34). The point is that the Messiah, like ancestors and descendants of David, will sacrificially serve 'his brothers' and be God's agent of restoration in the aftermath of exile. The post-exilic restoration comes through the Messiah's suffering for his people.

Similarly, the inclusion of three women plus Uriah is not due to their association with sexual impropriety (foreshadowing Mary), or for being sinners (intimating Jesus' ministry), but because they are praiseworthy Gentiles in the ancestry of the Messiah.[21] They prepare readers/hearers for other praiseworthy Gentile characters in the Gospel of Matthew including the Magi (2:1–16), the Capernaum centurion (8:5–13), the Ninevites (12:41), the Queen of the South (12:42), and the Canaanite woman (15:22–28). That in turn sanctions a Gentile mission to bring the nations into the people belonging to the Messiah, for a transformed Israel will transform the world (see 12:18,21; 24:14; 28:19–20).[22]

Third, the 'exile' (μετοικεσία) is pivotal, as the entire genealogy is ordered around it (2:11–12,17), and it remains significant for the rest of the Gospel.[23] It might be an overstatement to say that most Jews considered Israel to be 'still in exile';[24] however, it is no stretch of the imagination to infer that for Matthew (and for other Jews, I suspect), the prophetic promises for the restoration of Israel had not been fully realized. Therefore, the effect of Israel's Assyrian and Babylonian exile still lingered, and there remained the hope for the eschatological exodus of which the prophets spoke. Thus, 1:17 uncovers the basic plot of the genealogy. From Abraham to David there was an ascent towards an ideal king. This ascent collapsed upon the ruin of Israel's sin that resulted in exile (1:2–11). Moreover, exile is traumatic because it is national death (hence Ezekiel 37 about the valley of dry bones!), it amounts to a covenantal divorce (hence the need for a new covenant spelled out in Jeremiah 31 and Ezekiel 34, and for a new covenantal marriage as nominated in Hosea 2), and it includes regicide (hence the need for a new David in Isaiah 7 – 16; Jeremiah 22 – 23; Amos 9; Micah 4; Zecheriah 12). Exile means that there is no king, the covenant relationship is broken, there is no temple worship, and there is no inheritance. Yet the story turns around after Matt. 1:11 and heads towards a new climax. Thereafter, what follows in Matt. 1:12–16 is a new ascent to kingship and national restoration that comes with the advent of the Messiah and a full and final end of exile.[25] In Deuteronomy 30 we read that God is able to bring the people out of exile even if they are suffering the covenantal curses for disobedience (Deut. 30:1–4). Afterwards, they will 'live in the land that the Lord swore to give to [their] ancestors, to *Abraham, to Isaac, and to Jacob*' (Deut. 30:20, my trans.). The reference to the patriarchs in Matt. 1:2 has instant connotations of restoration as those taken away by exile (1:11–12) are restored through the Messiah (1:17,21–23).

Taken together, this means that the genealogy sets up an expectation for those with such intertextual ears to hear an underlying story encoded in names. The people of Israel are the chosen sons of the patriarchs, and they are promised a king from Judah's line, in the house of David. The exile has interrupted the patriarchal promise for an inheritance for Israel and blessings for the nations. The Messiah is the leader of the people who will lead them out of exile. He is the sacrificial king who serves his brothers, and he fulfils the Abrahamic promises by including Gentiles in the purview of his messianic task. The genealogy sets up the story, hope, and mission of God's people, as executed through the Messiah.

Matthew switches from the 'origins of Jesus the Messiah' (1:1, my trans.) to the 'birth of Jesus the Messiah' (1:18).[26] Again, it seems clear that Ἰησοῦ Χριστοῦ in 1:18 is intended to be understood as 'Jesus the Messiah' in light of the articular 'the Messiah' (ὁ Χριστός) in 1:16,17 and 2:4 (see NRSV, TNIV, NIV10). The Messiah's origins have already been intimated with respect to the Abrahamic covenant, Israel's election and exile, the house of David, the rise and fall in the fortunes of Israel's kingship, and anticipation of the nation's forthcoming restoration. It falls now to the evangelist to indicate the circumstances of the Messiah's birth as a way of underscoring his divine mission, royal identity, and solidarity with Israel in the following birth narrative.

The virgin conception is narrated in Matt. 1:18–25 with special attention to Jesus' adoption into the Davidic line, his divine origins, and his conformity to scriptural pattern.[27] The vital information is what the angel announces to Joseph in 1:20. Joseph, a 'son of David', is commanded to take Jesus into his home. Novakovic comments: '[T]he crucial point is the continuity of the Davidic line. The adoption of Jesus by Joseph made him a legal descendant of David, the king.'[28] Joseph is expected to accept Mary and her child, as the conception is a work of the Holy Spirit. A further point we can note is that 'Jesus' is to be so named because he will 'save his people from their sins', and this deliverance is from the sin that occasioned the exile mentioned directly above (1:21). By naming the child, he legitimates the child as a Davidic heir. In addition, the title 'Immanuel' (Matt. 1:23 = Isa. 7:14) is fitting because it names the divinely given child to be born as a sign that the nation will be spared the perpetuation of exilic disaster that never fully ended despite the return of a remnant to Judea. It is not explicitly describing an incarnation per se, but, much like Ezekiel 34, it is about the coming of God in and through his Davidic king to shepherd the people. The Matthean Jesus undoubtedly contains and manifests the divine presence (see 18:20; 28:20). Krister Stendahl wrote: 'In Jesus' messianic deeds God visits his people and sets them free from the hardships which their sins have justly caused.'[29] Matthew's citation of Isa. 7:14 is typological rather than prophetic. Just as the child born during the time of King Ahaz was a sign of God's presence with his people in a time of national crisis, the same is true of another child born to a 'maiden' who carries in her womb the hopes of the nation.

The rest of the birth narrative from Matt. 2:1–23 constitutes Matthew's attempt to set up the pieces on the chessboard, as it were, in preparation for Jesus' campaign for national deliverance. That takes place only after he first reiterates Jesus' role as fulfiller of prophetic hopes and his identification with the Jewish people. First, the story of the Magi who come from the east to 'worship' the child appears to be an incipient fulfilment of the scriptural forecast that the end of Israel's exile would result in the nations streaming to Israel to worship God (e.g. Isa. 2:2–4; 66:20; Jer. 3:17; Mic. 4:1–4; Zech. 8:20-23).[30] The picture of foreign kings presenting gifts to an Israelite king is well enough known in scriptural traditions (1 Kgs 10:10; Ps. 72:10–11; Isa. 60:3), but more interesting here is that the Magi follow a 'star', which is an obvious allusion to the 'star out of Jacob' mentioned in Balaam's prophecy in Numbers 24:17–19. A messianic star was well attested in Jewish hopes for the Messiah (CD 7.18; *T.Levi* 18.3; *T.Jud.* 24.1), and Rabbi Akiba designated Simeon ben Kosiba as the Messiah by giving him the title 'Bar-Kochbar' or 'son of the star'. In Numbers, Balaam was a Gentile holy man summoned from the east to curse Israel (Num. 22:5; 23:7). The Magi, like Balaam, do not collaborate with a wicked ruler who wants to destroy God's people. The Balaam-Magi typology presents the first example of Gentile messianic faith in Matthew's Gospel. The inclusion of the Magi reflects the Abrahamic scope of salvation so that Matthew's Son of David actualizes the covenantal promises that God will bless the nations through his people (see 4:14–16; 8:5–13; 28:19–20).

Second, Jesus' birth in Bethlehem is also set forth as a further element on his messianic curriculum vitae. But more importantly, Jesus will be the messianic shepherd-king spoken of in Mic. 5:1–15. The Micaian prophecy about a new David has several interesting points of contact with Matthew's Gospel: birth in Bethlehem (Mic. 5:2; Matt. 2:1), a shepherd (Mic. 5:4; Matt. 9:36; 21:1–10; 25:32; 26:31), helping his brothers (Mic. 5:4; Matt. 1:2,11; 28:10), his greatness extending to the ends of the earth (Mic. 5:4; Matt. 28:18), and the raising of the remnant of Judah (Mic. 5:7–8; Matt. 10:5–6; 15:24). The Matthean Jesus is the rebuilding of the Davidic line so that the house of Israel will be rebuilt from the midst of national ruin in the face of the Assyrian exile.

Third, the flight of the holy family from Israel to Egypt provides occasion for Matthew's citation of Hos. 11:1: 'Out of Egypt I called my son' (2:14). As Kennedy observes, the citation is in fact logically and geographically out of place. It should appear not after verses 12–13, but after the departure from Egypt in verse 21. Far from being accidental, the placement of the quotation suggests that under Herod Israel has become a 'new Egypt'. This is affirmed by Herod's murderous actions against the children in Bethlehem (vv. 16–17), which re-enact Pharaoh's deeds given in Exodus 1 in killing the Hebrew infants. Also, the citation of Jer. 31:15 in Matt. 2:17–18 makes it clear that Israel is experiencing exilic conditions and pre-exodus-like oppression. Matthew identifies the land of Israel as a new Egypt, and Jesus' sojourn becomes a virtual new exodus.[31] The painful events of Jesus' infancy are to become the anvil on which God would forge the fulfilment of his promises to his people who experience everything from disease, to dislocation, to disempowerment, to near-destruction.[32] The return from Egypt to Judea and then on to Galilee is for the purpose of Jesus' ministry which, beyond the baptismal episode and temptation narrative, marks the beginning of a rescue of the covenant people from this 'exilic' condition. Notably Jesus' sonship means he stands in the place of Israel and assumes the filial relation to God predicated of the nation. Jesus is in solidarity with Israel who is also God's Son, and his exodus from a typological Egypt recapitulates the exodus of the nation (see Exod. 4:22–23; Jer. 31:20; Sir 36.17; Wis 18.13). According to John Nolland: 'The recapitulation of the nation in the life of Jesus is in some way, for Matthew, foundational for Jesus' significance in the purposes of God.'[33]

Another feature of the birth narrative is the irony surrounding King Herod's reign. The legal descendant of 'King David' (1:6) is Jesus on the grounds of his adoption into the Davidic line via Joseph and through the divine circumstances of his birth. Herod on the other hand was an Idumaean and called a 'half-Jew' by Josephus (*Ant.* 14.403). Even worse, in his actions against the children in Bethlehem he acts like a new Pharaoh, attempting to destroy the covenant family and their deliverer. The ethnically illegitimate and wicked ruler is made to suffer the insult as foreign guests come looking for the one born 'king of the Jews' (2:2). Though Herod was made king by Rome (Josephus, *Ant.* 14.385; *War* 1.284) and even called 'king of the Jews' according to Josephus (*Ant.* 14.311), the Magi come searching for another 'king of the Jews'. This king is an obvious rival to Herod. Though Herod was 'made' king by Rome later in life, Jesus is born king of the Jews by divine promise, which even foreign dignitaries recognize and bless.

Taken as a whole, the birth narrative and flight to Egypt in Matthew 1:18 – 2:23 could be read as a narrative expansion of the genealogy of Matt. 1:1–17. Matthew 1 – 2 constitutes a unity that deals with the question of the 'who' and 'where' of the Messiah.[34] Jesus is the Davidic king who brings deliverance to Israel in exile and encompasses Gentiles in the scope of the salvation that he achieves. The triangulation of Judea, Egypt, and Galilee is not a geographical merry-go-round as much as it touches upon the symbolic import of the geography in scriptural hopes for a new exodus, end of exile, and day of deliverance. Herod is, at best, a twisted parody of the true Davidic king who will restore and heal the nation, rescuing it from peril, as Micah and Isaiah laid out for the pattern of the Messiah. But it is more than that too. Jesus is the Son of David by adoption (1:20–21,25), but he is the Son of God from conception (1:18,20,23,25).[35] The angel tells Joseph that Mary will give birth to 'a son', not 'your son' (1:21), and he is thus the Son of God. As the Messiah, Jesus is not an earthly man raised up to the Davidic office; he is a divinely sent person commissioned to the messianic task who embodies the presence of God and executes God's plan of redemption. As Joel Willitts summarizes: 'When Jesus is born, the Messianic Shepherd-King arrives; he is the one who will deliver Israel and re-establish the Davidic Empire.'[36]

## The Son of David

One of the distinctive elements of Matthew's Christology is his amplification of the Son of David tradition. Matthew places the term at the head of his Gospel in the incipit to the genealogy (1:1). Thereafter Matthew explicitly nominates the kingship of David (1:6) and he defines David as the halfway point between Abraham and the exile (1:17). Joseph is a 'son of David', and Jesus is grafted into the Davidic line through Joseph, his paterfamilias (1:20). Matthew also retains Son of David material from Mark. This includes the healing of the blind men at Jericho (Matt. 20:30–34 [Mark 10:46–52]) and the riddle of the Messiah as David's son (Matt. 22:42–46 [Mark 12:35–37]). A story found only in Matthew pertains to the two men who are healed by Jesus at an early stage of his ministry (9:27–31). This is the first time in the Gospel that 'Son of David' is used as a form of address to Jesus. Later, after Jesus' healing of a blind and dumb man, the crowds are astonished at his actions and ask, 'Can this man really be the Son of David?' (my trans.). The Pharisees respond negatively to this by saying that Jesus casts out demons by the power of Beelzebul (12:22–24). The crowd draws the inference that Jesus wanted John the Baptist to make from observation of his healings. Matthew's account of the Canaanite differs from Mark's account of the Syro-Phoenician woman in several regards. In Matthew, she addresses Jesus as 'Lord, Son of David' and appeals for mercy for her demon-possessed daughter (15:22). The same appeal is used in 9:27 and 20:30–31 by the blind men. Jesus initially rebuffs her request, since his mission is focused on the 'lost sheep of the house of Israel' (15:24), but he acquiesces in the end, impressed by her witty reply. It is arguably the case that Matthew here wants to press the irony that it is a Gentile woman, of all people, who confesses Jesus as the Lord and the messianic king, and this is in contrast to his rejection within Israel. The receipt of her healing is likewise a marked contrast to the violent and nationalistic employments of the Son of David tradition, and Matthew believes that there is a place for Gentiles in a restored Davidic household (see esp. Amos 9:11–12 [LXX]). In the triumphal entry, Matthew develops the Marcan outline by pressing the Davidic theme all the more. Matthew adds the acclamation 'Hosanna to the Son of David' to 'Blessed is he who comes in the name of the Lord' (21:9). Immediately following, Jesus goes to the temple where he performs his symbolic act of judgement upon it. There he is assailed in the temple by those who want healing from him, and the chief priests and scribes become indignant towards the children, who repeat the celebratory cry of 'Hosanna to the Son of David' (21:15). For the crowd in the triumphal entry and for the children in the temple, Jesus was not just any king, but the expected 'Messiah' and 'coming one' that the prophets had foretold.

What is significant is that the title 'Son of David' is placed on the lips of those of lowly status who receive healing from Jesus – the blind, Gentiles, and children – and indicates a marked contrast between the humble and faithful acclamation of the marginalized and the proud arrogance of Israel's leaders who reject him at length.[37] Kingsbury even goes so far as to assert that 'Matthew utilizes the title Son of David in order to underline the guilt that devolves upon Israel for not receiving its Messiah'.[38]

Although Matthew seems to be quite aware of the connotations of the 'Son of David' as royal messianic deliverer (hence the amplification of 'Son of David' in the triumphal entry), it seems that his primary interest is in the new David's therapeutic ministry of healing and liberation for the vulnerable (9:27–31; 12:22–24; 15:21–28; 20:29–34; 21:15–16). This is strange because there was no clear expectation in associated literature for the Messiah to be a healing figure. One explanation for this is that Matthew is building on the tradition of David and Solomon as healers through exorcism (David: Josephus, *Ant.* 6.166-68; Pseudo-Philo, *LAB* 60.1–3; Solomon: *T.Sol.* 1.5–7; Wis 7.17–21; Josephus, *Ant.* 8.45–47; *Tg. Ps.* 91).[39] Another explanation is that the healings are rooted generally in the notion that Yahweh heals, especially in the aftermath of exile (e.g. Exod. 15:26; Deut. 32:39; Jer. 33:6; Hos. 7:1; 11:3; 14:4), or influenced by conceptions from Isaiah of the future age as one of healing and restoration (Isa. 30:26; 35:5–6; 57:18; 58:8–9; 61:1–2). In support of the Isaianic healing thesis, Matthew often quotes or alludes to Isaiah in connection with Jesus' healing ministry:

This was to fulfill what was spoken through the prophet Isaiah:

'He took up our infirmities
   and bore our diseases' (Matt. 8:17; see also 11:2–6; 12:15–21).[40]

A similar Isaianic motif appears in 4Q521 from Qumran, where the Messiah (or Yahweh?) will 'heal the wounded, and revive the dead and bring good news to the poor' (see Isa. 61:1). We have to remember that Jewish messianism was not an airtight dot-point list of expectations, but a tradition of exegesis of biblical texts, and it seems that some interpreters saw the healing ministry of the Servant in Isaiah as part of the job description for a Messiah.

For Matthew, the Son of David is defined by mercy rather than by massacres. He comes for compassion, not combat. Indeed, the concept of 'healing' arguably binds together the Isaianic message of good news with the nature of the kingdom, the authority of Jesus' teaching, and the appeal of Jesus to those in Judea, Syria, Decapolis, and Galilee (see 4:23–25). As such, the most analogous title to 'Son of David' in Matthew is not 'Messiah' or 'King' (though they are connoted), but 'Shepherd' (2:6; 9:36; 10:6,16; 15:24; 18:12–14; 25:31–46; 26:31). Shepherd was a role often assigned to kings in the ancient Near East (e.g. Ezek. 34), and David was the quintessential shepherd-king (2 Sam. 5:2; Ps. 78:70–72; Mic. 4:1–5). Matthew introduces the motif of compassion for the shepherdless sheep by the Shepherd in 9:36 and applies it broadly to the teaching and healing mission of Jesus. The metaphor of shepherding is also utilized in the description of the last judgement, where the righteous and unrighteous are separated much like a shepherd divides the sheep from the goats (25:32–33).[41] In effect, the function of judgement is delegated from God to Jesus who, as the Son of Man, acts as king and Lord (25:34,40).[42] Overall, the Matthean Jesus is the new Davidic Shepherd over the lost sheep of the house of Israel, who leads them in a new exodus where there is forgiveness of sins, healing, and restoration of the nation.[43]

## The Deeds of the Messiah

Though Matthew follows the Marcan outline, he supplements the story with unique material and often overlays his own theological emphases at key points.

Matthew has a unique reference to Jesus' ministry in the story of the delegation sent by John the Baptist to question Jesus about his real identity: 'When John heard in prison what [the Messiah] was doing, he sent his disciples to ask him, "Are you the one who was to come, or should we expect someone else?"' (11:2–3). The reference to 'the deeds of the Messiah' (τὰ ἔργα τοῦ Χριστοῦ) is unique to Matthew. The phrase is absent from the parallel version in Luke 7:18–19, and it is probably a Matthean addition to shared material. This is the first time that Χριστός has reappeared in Matthew's text since 2:4, and Matthew includes it to remind readers/hearers of the messianic theme with which he began. John's new uncertainty about Jesus is not unreasonable since he had pronounced the imminent end of the age involving the judgement of the wicked (3:12) and with some reluctance baptized Jesus as the one destined to bring the eschatological promises of salvation to fruition (3:14–17). If Jesus had not dealt with the enemies of

God, such as Herod, then was Jesus really the messianic figure about whom John had prophesied? John's question is not so much hostile, then, as it is uncertain, looking for confirmation and hope that Jesus is the one who John thought he was. When Jesus is asked if he is the 'Coming One'[44] – probably a descriptor for the Messiah (Ps. 118:26; Dan. 7:13–14; 9:25–27; Hab. 2:3; Mal. 3:1; Acts 19:4; Heb. 10:37; Rev. 1:4,8) – the question is harking back to Matthew 3:11 with John's prophecy about the 'coming' of the 'stronger one' who will baptize with the Holy Spirit and with fire.

Strictly speaking, John's question is not concerned with the signs of the Messiah, but with the person of the Messiah. Yet Jesus focuses on the former as the means of defining the latter. The 'what' and 'when' determine 'who' the Messiah is. It could be said, then, that it is not so much important *who* Jesus is as *when* Jesus is, when the Isaianic signs of salvation materialize.[45] According to Novakovic, Jesus' healings cannot of themselves authenticate the Messiah, but they facilitate human recognition that the messianic age has begun, and so, indirectly, contribute to the revelation of Jesus' messianic identity.[46] That is true to an extent. However, in Matthew it is clear that new age and divine agent are intricately interwoven. The messianic age arrives only because of the advent of the messianic deliver. By highlighting the signs of the messianic age (see 11:5), Jesus, in effect, declared his legitimacy as the messianic figure for whom John looked. Jesus invites John and his disciples to make the only inference possible, that the 'deeds of the Messiah' are performed by none other than the Messiah. John is urged not to mistake the reality of the kingdom with its reception. What is more, in the compassionate ministry of Jesus, God is visiting his people as he promised.[47] John's own private timetable, understandable as it is in his circumstance, is not the yardstick for determining messianic identity. His imprisonment may not feel like the messianic day of liberation (see 14:1–12 about John's death), but elsewhere the signs of redemption are happening. These signs are clear indicators that salvation has arrived and will culminate with judgement at a future juncture. The age of judgement has come and is yet coming still.

The Matthean account of Peter's confession at Caesarea Philippi has several unique traits that are illuminating for

Matthew's Christology (16:13–23). This section, just as in Mark and Luke, is the climax of the Galilean phase of Jesus' ministry (Matt. 4:17 – 16:20). It provides a lucid and unequivocal declaration of Jesus' messiahship and summarizes the meaning of Jesus' deeds and words in the preceding section. (The repeated questions about Jesus' identity anticipate Peter's confession: 'What kind of man is this?' [8:27]; 'Are you the one who is to come, or should we look for another?' [11:2]; and 'Can this be the Son of David?' [12:23]; my translations.) Jesus has already been confessed as the 'Son of God' by demons (8:29) and the disciples (14:33). A unified profession of Jesus' identity is proffered by Peter in the more sedate and serene environs, and he draws the careful and reasoned conclusion: 'You are the Messiah, the Son of the living God' (16:16).[48] Notably Matthew expands Mark's 'You are the Messiah' (Mark 8:29) with 'Son of the living God' (ὁ υἱὸς τοῦ θεοῦ τοῦ ζῶντος). Thus Matthew underscores the link between messiahship and sonship. The expression 'the living God' is from the Old Testament (e.g. Deut. 5:26; Pss 42:2; 84:2; Isa. 37:17; Jer. 10:10; 23:36; Dan. 6:20,26; Hos. 1:10) and designates Israel's God as the true God of the world as opposed to the false gods of the pagan nations. This is all the more relevant since Caesarea Philippi held a shrine for the god Pan and the area was the most northern frontier of Galilee, where Judaism and paganism met. Nolland contends that 'to refer to God as the "living God" is to point to him as the one to be reckoned with, who has all the powers of deity to bring to bear on the situation.'[49] To define the Messiah as the 'Son of the living God' means that he is more than a human figure. He is uniquely bound up with God's will and workings in the world, for in his person one encounters the presence and power of God.[50]

Jesus' response to Simon Peter is twofold. He begins with a beatitude that Peter has received this insight through a revelation from Jesus' heavenly Father (16:17), and this is followed up with a promise that 'on this rock I will build my church, and the gates of hades will not overcome it' (16:18, my trans.). Protestant paranoia about papal legitimacy has led many to insist that it is Peter's confession rather than Peter himself that constitutes the 'rock' upon which the church is built. But it is quite simply Peter to whom the Matthean Jesus refers. To this we must add that it is the confessing Peter who is the rock-solid foundation of the church and the representative of Christ. That Jesus anticipated a community that would endure after him is hardly impossible, since other religious leaders of the day established movements that survived them, such as John the Baptist, Banus the Ascetic, and the Teacher of Righteousness. That Jesus came to establish the eschatological people of God is a plausible motive for his actions, and the statement assigns Peter a prominent place in the new eschatological community.[51] Furthermore, 'rock' (πέτρα; כֵּיפָא) could be an image of the renewed people of God as it is in Isa. 51:1–4.[52] In context, the promise is a mission statement for the restored Israel: a rebuilt temple, standing on the foundations of a confessing Peter. The 'church' known to Matthew (see 18:17) does not find its identity and purpose in a shared socio-ethnic or religio-historical association with other Jews, nor in adherence to the nexus of Torah-temple-territory. Although it may share these and uphold them to some degree, it is around Jesus as the teacher, prophet, Messiah, and Son of God that the messianic community is born, bounded, and brought into the new age.

Within the discourse of Matthew 23 that denounces the Pharisees and scribes, Jesus presses his audience about their loyalty to their instructor. Just as they are to call no man 'Rabbi' because '[they] have only one Master and . . . are all brothers' (23:8), so too: 'Nor are you to be called "Teacher", for you have one Teacher, the Messiah' (23:10). The problem is that there was not, as far as we know, any widespread expectation for the Messiah to be a didactic figure.[53] Nils Dahl thinks that Matthew regarded Jesus as both '*christos* and *didaskalos*'.[54] It is perhaps the case that Matthew presents Jesus, in his identity as Messiah, as coming to teach God's will, and it is by virtue of his messianic authority that he demands to be honoured as the 'only Teacher'.[55] Matthew's conception of the messianic office is that of a teaching figure who exposits the true meaning of the Torah, explains the mystery of the kingdom, and exhorts people to avoid judgement. As commentators have long since suspected, the five major discourses of Matthew are like a *new Torah* for the *new age*. Jesus' giving of the Sermon the Mount is an intertextual allusion to Moses' giving of the law to Israel. Dale Allison states: 'Just as philosophers wore clothing of a certain king in order to advertise their office, similarly did Matthew drape the Messiah in the familiar mantle of Moses, by which dress he made Jesus the full bearer of God's authority.'[56] It is the messianic catechesis that is to be passed on to new disciples (5:19; 10:24–25; 13:52; 23:34; esp. 28:20).[57] In Matthew's situation this means that followers of Jesus owe their adherence not to apostles, church founders, or even Gospel writers, but to the Messiah, who instructs in the way of life under God.[58]

A further distinctive feature of Matthew's Gospel occurs in the trial before the Sanhedrin (26:57–68). The high priest is drawn to ask Jesus whether he is the 'Messiah'. This is a plausible question in light of his entrance into the city as the messianic king of Zech. 9:9, the resultant 'Hosannas' that followed and which he refused to repudiate (21:1–9,15–16), his demonstration in the temple (21:12–13), his parable of the king and wedding banquet (22:1–13), his engagement in scribal debates about the Messiah and David's Son (22:42–46), and the parable of the tenants which posits God's 'son' as standing over and against the Judean leadership (21:33–46). The high priest's question in Matthew 26:63 differs from Mark 14:61 because in Mark the high priest asks Jesus if he is 'the Messiah, the Son of the Blessed One', whereas in Matthew the high priest asks if Jesus is 'the Messiah, the Son of God'. The questions are similar, but Matthew's version reflects the co-ordination of 'Messiah' and 'Son of God' given earlier in Peter's confession (16:16). There is also a difference in Jesus' answer. The Marcan Jesus responds, 'I am' (Mark 14:62), while in Matthew Jesus replies, 'You have said so' (Matt. 26:64; cf. again in Mark 15:2/Matt. 27:11 to Pilate).

Matthew's conjunctive πλήν ('nevertheless') marks a contrast, as the Matthean Jesus intends to explain his messianic identity on his own terms. Jesus is the Son-of-Man-type-Messiah as one destined for heavenly glory and invested with divine authority after his sufferings. Matthew, more than the other evangelists, heavily freights Jesus' teaching and works with a divine authority (see 7:29; 8:9; 9:6–8; 10:1; 21:23–24,27, esp. 28:18). In any case, Jesus expects the tables to be turned, and his enthronement beside God (hence the echoes of Ps. 110:1 and Dan. 7:13) will mean the imminent collapse of the regime as a prelude to the universal sovereignty of the Son of Man.[59]

At the end of the trial, Jesus is then brutally treated by the members of the council (in Mark it was 'some people' [Mark 14:65] and in Luke it was 'men guarding Jesus' [Luke 22:63–64]; my translations), who proceed to slap, strike, and spit on him, and do so with the mocking words, 'Prophesy to us, Messiah. Who hit you?' (Matt. 26:68). In contrast to Luke and Mark, Matthew adds that Jesus was scoffed at as 'Messiah'. The mocking and abuse of Jesus as 'Messiah' (Matt. 26:68) is paralleled by the derision and cruelty of the Roman soldiers who mock him as 'king of the Jews' (Matt. 27:27–31).

Though Luke is the evangelist who, more than others, narrates Jesus' story in simultaneously messianic and prophetic categories, it cannot be forgotten that Matthew shares the same viewpoint, albeit less acutely. Matthew combines a royal messianism (Jesus as Son of David) with a prophetic messianism (Jesus as Isaianic miracle worker).[60] The only time that Jesus is hailed as a prophet in Matthew is after his royal entry into Jerusalem where the Jerusalemites enquire about who Jesus is and the crowd accompanying Jesus answers with the words, 'This is Jesus, the prophet from Nazareth in Galilee' (21:11). The response of the crowd to the royal procession is to underline his divine authority as one who speaks for God. A point accentuated later as Jesus himself provocatively elaborates David's prophecy about the Messiah in 22:42–46. In the trial scene there is also a sharp irony as the council violently mocks Jesus' prophetic abilities. In so doing they confirm his prophetic powers, because Jesus predicted the very violence and rejection that he is now undergoing (see 16:21; 20:19). Furthermore, the abuse inflicted upon Jesus is reminiscent of that committed against the Servant of the Lord in Isaiah (50:6; 53:7). The redemptive mission of Jesus to bring the forgiveness of sins (1:21) was later elucidated at the last supper as transpiring through his blood being shed (26:26).

Hence the Messiah's redemptive mission is executed as the suffering Servant of the Lord, for which he was commissioned at his baptism (3:16–17), and confirmed by Matthew's citation of Isa. 42:1–4 (12:18–21). The trial scene then highlights Jesus as the suffering yet soon-to-be-exalted Messiah, the Son of God, and Servant of the Lord, who redeems people by his death.

The Matthean passion sequence in its own way emphasizes Jesus' messianic identity. Pilate twice refers to '*Jesus who is called Messiah*' (τὸν λεγόμενον Χριστόν) and he asks what the people want him to do with Jesus (27:17,22); their answer is clear: 'Let him be crucified' (σταυρωθήτω) (my trans.). However, Jesus dies as the Son of God as the climax to his messianic mission. Matthew intimates Jesus' sonship at several key places. The temptation narratives could be described as 'The Temptation of God's Son', since the satanic temptations are prefaced with challenges beginning, 'If you are the Son of God then . . .' (4:3,6). Jesus is confessed as the Son of God by demons who believe that he has come to destroy them (8:29). After the stilling of the storm the disciples worship him and confess, 'Truly you are the Son of God' (14:33). The 'Son of God' is identified with the messianic designation in Peter's confession and at Jesus' trial (16:16; 26:63). All of this is preparatory for the manifestation of Jesus' divine sonship at the cross. During the crucifixion, the passers-by reprise the satanic temptation: 'You who are going to destroy the temple and build it in three days, save yourself! Come down from the cross, *if you are the Son of God!*' (27:40), and the 'Son of God' reference is unique to Matthew (see Mark 15:29–30).

An analogous jibe is repeated in Matthew 27:42 by the chief priests, the teachers of the law, and the elders, where Jesus, as the 'king of Israel', is invited to get himself down from the cross as proof of his power. A further insult is added, again found only in Matthew: 'He trusts in God. Let God rescue him now if he wants him, for he said, "I am the Son of God"' (27:43).[61] The irony is that Jesus' sonship is being tested, though not by coming off the cross but by remaining upon it! Jesus' kingly power is not located in his self-defence, but in his self-giving. Jesus is the humble shepherd-king who leads God's people through tribulation (11:29) and will therefore be exalted by God (23:12). Jesus loses his life so that he can save the life of others (10:39; 16:25). He gives his life as a ransom for many (20:28). The shepherd king is struck so that the flock may survive (26:31). Nolland comments: 'To save himself would be to abort his mission, to undercut all that his ministry has represented. The drawn-out horror of dying on a cross must have frequently provoked a revery of breaking free from the cross to which one was pinned. This is what Jesus is being mockingly challenged to do.'[62]

Matthew knows that the cross is about two things: salvation and the Son of God. In Matt. 27:39–44, Jesus' ability to 'save others' is mocked with his seeming inability to 'save himself'. He trusts in God to rescue him as he called others to trust in him (8:10; 9:28; 11:28; 18:6). Yet the reader/hearer knows that salvation has been the task of Jesus since his birth (1:21), that it was exercised across his ministry (9:2–6), and that mission culminates at the cross where his blood is shed for the forgiveness of sins (26:28). Matthew lifts out Mark's reference to Jesus as 'Messiah' from the crucifixion scene (Mark 15:31), replaces it with 'Son of God', and amplifies it in order to show that Israel's 'Messiah', Israel's 'Son of David', and the 'king of the Jews', must be understood in light of the mission of the Son of God to save people from their sins. At the end of the crucifixion, the centurions (rather than a singular centurion who observes the manner of his death in Mark 15:39) behold the portentous events surrounding Jesus' death and confess, 'Truly he was the Son of God!' which repeats the words of the disciples uttered in Matt. 14:33. The one impression that Matthew wants to create by the crucifixion story is that Jesus fulfils the role of the Messiah as the Son of God.[63]

Afterwards, in the resurrection, Jesus rises to be the Lord of the church who is worthy of worship (28:17) and is invested with all authority (28:20). Matthew thus emphasizes that Jesus is the crucified Messiah, yet he shows the church that the crucified one is also its exalted Lord to whom it owes obedience and whom it must follow.[64] Terence Donaldson writes:

> Jesus' apparent defeat turns out to be his victory. Precisely because he followed the path of humble obedience to the end, refusing to use the power at his disposal to extricate himself from the consequences of his obedience (e.g. 26:53–54), Jesus is vindicated in resurrection and endowed with 'all authority in heaven and on earth' (28:18). Sovereignty is won through suffering. It is precisely his faithfulness as the humble, obedient Son that makes possible in the divine scheme of things, his exaltation as the royal, sovereign Son. And as Son, who shares a name with the Father and the Holy Spirit, he is the teacher and baptismal means of identity for a new people drawn not only from Israel but from all nations (28:19–20).[65]

## Conclusion

The Matthean portrait of Jesus is hardly monochrome. Jesus is depicted in various ways and with various titles such as the Son of David, a new Moses, a charismatic rabbi, the Suffering Servant, the eschatological prophet, Son of God, and Son of Man all rolled into one. Matthew is a fairly conservative redactor of Mark. He amplifies the Son of David tradition inherited from Mark and provides further material to anchor Jesus' story in the messianic hopes of Israel's Scriptures, principally Isaiah 40 – 55. He probably writes at a time when debate and division between Jewish Christ-believers and non-Christ-believing Jews has become increasingly intense.

In sum, Matthew's Jesus is the Davidic Messiah sent for Israel's salvation, though the circumference of his reign encompasses the nations too. He is the healer and exorcist par excellence, the ultimate teacher and prophet, and the harbinger of a new age, a new kingdom, a new Torah, and a new people of God oriented around the Messiah. Although a major christological focus is on Jesus as the Son of God, this need not be played off against Jesus as Messiah; both are integral to his identity, ministry, and death.[66] Jesus is the divine Son who has become on behalf of Israel in his vocation as the Messiah.

It is not the case that Matthew insists on Jesus' messianic credentials in the genealogy, and then interprets the role of the Messiah purely by way of reference to his 'spiritual qualities' all because Matthew omits reference to Israel's liberation from foreign domination.[67] On the contrary, Matthew places the ministry of Jesus within the range of fully orbed expectations for a Jewish Messiah to reign over a Jewish kingdom that encompasses Jewish territory. Thereafter, Matthew envisages a Jewish mission to the nations to herald the work of the Jewish Messiah.[68] Matthew moves Jesus away from nationalistic expectations of a violent warrior king and instead presents Jesus as the shepherd king who brings eschatological healing to all the nations. Matthew places the identity of Jesus within a story of Israel's election and exile, telling the story of how the resolution to those two poles comes through the ministry of the Son of God, who operates as the Messiah and heralds the day of deliverance for both Jews and Gentiles.

# 3.

# The Gospel of Luke (and Acts): The Prophetic Messiah

## Introduction

There is a whole host of possible reasons why Luke penned his διήγησις ('narrative account') about Jesus and a subsequent historiography on the beginnings of the church. In reading through his two-volume work 'Luke–Acts', one gets the impression that those purposes included both apologetic and kerygmatic intentions. Luke goes to great lengths to set out Jesus' identity and to defend the place of the χριστιανοί ('Christians') within the religious context of Judaism in the wider Greco-Roman world. As Luke does this, we observe that there are several features unique to the depiction of Jesus in Luke–Acts. For a start, Jesus is 'Messiah the Lord', 'the Lord's Messiah' (Luke 2:11,26; see Acts 2:36) and 'Messiah of God' (Luke 9:20; 23:35; see Acts 4:26). The Lucan Jesus is also the 'leader and saviour' of Israel, the Jewish 'Messiah' (Acts 5:31,42), and the 'Lord' of all who believe in him, including the Gentiles (Acts 10:36; 19:10,17; 20:21). That is coupled with his identity as a prophet, indeed the prophet par excellence, who comes to Israel with a message of redemption (see Luke 4:18; 7:16,39; 13:33; 24:19; Acts 2:30; 3:22; 7:37,52). Prophetic themes loom prominently in Luke–Acts to the point that E. Earle Ellis described Luke's portrayal of Jesus with the words: 'His whole life, death, and resurrection are one continuing fulfilment of prophecy.'[1] Accordingly, Luke wishes to show the continuity of the church with the promises of Israel and to demonstrate how the work of Jesus and his followers represents the fulfilment of those promises. That continuity could be understood in terms of believing in the prophetic Messiah of Israel's hope and receiving the Spirit of prophecy sent by Israel's Davidic Lord. In light of this, the aim of this chapter is to explicate the significance of Jesus' messiahship in Luke–Acts in its various narrative and theological horizons.

## The Story of Jesus in Luke's Gospel: The Prophet–Messiah

In the prologue to Luke's Gospel (1:1–4), the things that have been 'fulfilled', 'handed down', and 'investigated from the beginning' pertain to the messianic identity of Jesus and his prophetic vocation. He is God's agent to bring the long-awaited time of salvation to its divinely appointed climax: a salvation that encompasses Israel and Gentiles.

Jesus' messianic identity is vitally important in the birth narratives, as seen in the angelic announcements.[2] The angel Gabriel announces to Mary that she will give birth to a son, he will be called 'Son of the Most High', and he will be given 'the throne of his father David' and will 'reign over the house of Jacob forever; his kingdom will never end' (1:32–33). After Mary's question to the angel, Gabriel responds by speaking of Mary being overshadowed by the Holy Spirit and giving birth to a child called 'the Son of God' (1:34–35). The title 'Son of God' is correlated with Jesus' Davidic enthronement (cf. 2 Sam. 7:14; Ps. 2:7), but the title ultimately goes beyond the conventional messianic understanding of the designation by redefining the nature of Jesus' mission and person in language that espouses Jesus' unique filial relationship to God.[3] Still, Jesus' Davidic lineage and his being heir to the Davidic throne cannot be divorced from messianic ideas. The Davidic theme looms large, and Jesus' Davidic quality is emphasized at key christological sections in the two-volume work.[4] Davidic messiahship is co-referential with royal messiahship, as Jesus' enthronement as king is the accession to the throne of David.[5] Later, an 'angel of the Lord' makes an announcement of good news to the shepherds: 'Today in the town of David, a Saviour has been born to you; he is Messiah the Lord' (2:11, my trans.). Jesus has already been designated as κύριος earlier ('mother of my Lord' [1:43]), and he is defined in 2:11 (see v. 26) as 'Messiah, the Lord' (χριστὸς κύριος). The double title χριστὸς κύριος is rare and occurs elsewhere only in Lam. 4:20 (LXX) and *Pss. Sol.* 17.32. C. Kavin Rowe comments: 'In fact, the χριστὸς κύριος juxtaposition in 2:11 is so immediate that it creates a problem for the translator. Jesus is not simply χριστός; he is Christ–Lord'.[6] Thus, Jesus is not the heavenly Lord; he is the messianic Lord. It is the nature of Jesus' identity as 'Messiah' and 'Lord' that will feature in the messianic riddle in 20:41–44. In any case, the titles of Saviour, Messiah, and Lord compressed in 2:11 are indicative of Jesus' identity, authority, and mission. He traverses the heaven/earth divide as Lord, he is fulfiller of Israel's hopes as the Davidic Messiah, and he executes deliverance as the appointed saviour.

The coming of God's Messiah is situated against the backdrop of divine saving actions announced in the three major hymns of the Lucan infancy narrative. In the 'Magnificat' of Mary (1:46–55), echoing Moses' song in Deuteronomy 32, Mary celebrates the 'mighty deeds' of God who exalts the poor, scatters the proud, brings down rulers, helps his Servant Israel, and remembers to be merciful to Abraham's descendants. Similarly, the 'Benedictus' of Zechariah (1:67–79) describes this agent of salvation in terms reminiscent of the exodus where the God of Israel has appeared in his agent, has 'redeemed his people', and has 'raised up a horn of salvation for us in the house of his servant David'. The goal is to bring salvation, to effect a rescue, show mercy, and demonstrate his faithfulness to the promises made to Abraham. The coming of this Davidic son is placed in the context of God fulfilling the promises made to the patriarchs, and effecting a new and dramatic redemption of Israel, which will include the 'forgiveness of sins' and 'salvation' (1:77). Luke also introduces the unique title ἀνατολή, which is translated varyingly as 'dayspring' (KJV), 'rising sun' (TINV, NJB), 'dawn' (NRSV, CEB, NET), 'morning light' (NLT), and 'sunrise' (ESV, NASB). We read:

> By the tender mercy of our God,
>> the ἀνατολή from on high will break upon us,
> to give light to those who sit in darkness and in the shadow of death,
>> to guide our feet into the way of peace (1:78–79 NRSV).

The designation ἀνατολή is used messianically in the Septuagint ('Behold, the days come, says the Lord, when I will *raise up* to David a *rising dawn*, and a king shall reign' [Jer. 23:5]; 'I lead my servant the *rising dawn*' [Zech. 3:8]; 'The Lord Almighty says to him, "Behold, a man whose name is *rising dawn* and he shall *rise up* from his stem and he will build the house of the Lord"' [Zech. 6:12]; my translations).[8] Philo seems to understand ἀνατολή as 'east' and 'dawn'. Philo cites Zech. 6:12 (LXX) and sees it as designating a special figure in Israel's heritage (*Conf.* 62). The east could be associated with the direction from which deliverance comes for God's people, and so is a natural designation for God's deliverer of the people (see Isa. 41:2; Matt. 2:2; 24:27; *Bar.* 4.36; *4 Ezra* 1.38). In Luke 1:78–79, ἀνατολή may be epexegetical and will give light to those in darkness.[9] The fact that the ἀνατολή comes from on high or heaven might even indicate pre-existence,[10] intimate a divine visitation that is messianic in character (see 19:44),[11] or perhaps point to the approaching *dawn* of the Davidic *horn* of salvation.[12] Moreover, in the 'Nunc Dimittis' (2:29–32), the saviour of Israel will have national and universal significance. Simeon, the righteous man upon whom the Holy Spirit rested, was waiting for the 'consolation of Israel' and 'the Lord's Messiah' (2:25–26). The latter designation, 'the Lord's Messiah' (τὸν χριστὸν κυρίου), indicates God's specially chosen instrument akin to Old Testament references to God's anointed leader (e.g. 1 Sam. 24:6,10; 26:9,11). There it is probably meant as messianic in light of Luke 2:11, and the same (though anarthrous) phrase appears in *Psalms of Solomon* 18.7. The theme of Davidic messianism joined with national restoration is cued at this point and will reappear later in the two-part narrative (Luke 24:21–26; Acts 3:18–21; 15:15–18). Simeon also declares that the child Jesus will bring salvation 'for all peoples' and be a 'light for revelation to the Gentiles'. This replays Isaiah 42:6 and 49:6 and delineates a universal dimension to messianic hopes.

The infancy narratives, especially in the angelic announcement and hymns to salvation, highlight in scriptural language Jesus' identity as a Davidic deliverer, prophetic leader, and Son of God. The royal messianic categories of the birth narratives, spelled out here, will eventually occupy a key role in the unfolding narration of Luke's story (see Acts 2:25,29,31,34; 13:22,34,36; 15:16). Mark

Strauss rightly avers: 'This might suggest that Davidic messiahship is programmatic and definitional for Luke's christological purpose in Luke–Acts. Jesus is *introduced and defined* as the one who will fulfil the Old Testament promises made to David.'[13]

In the 'Nazareth Manifesto' (Luke 4:16–30), Jesus enters a synagogue at Nazareth; he reads from Isaiah 61 and pronounces its fulfilment, which is followed with his rejection by the crowd. Jesus responds to his rejection by quoting the proverbs of the sick physician and the rebuffed prophet. This riposte continues with allusions to the biblical stories of the widow of Zarephath and Naaman the Syrian. This unit is programmatic of Jesus' ministry, and overtures the various motifs of Luke–Acts: Spirit, mission, Christology, Israel's rejection, and God's acceptance of outcasts.[14] The word 'anointed' has obvious messianic connotations, and when Jesus declares that God has anointed him with the Spirit, he is making a *de facto* messianic claim.[15] It is entirely plausible that we have in this section echoes of a royal Davidic figure, the final eschatological prophet, the Suffering Servant, and the Messiah all put into one compressed presentation of Jesus.[16] Some may wish to see the significance of Jesus' claim to an anointing here as purely prophetic rather than messianic.[17] Yet this is unlikely for several reasons. First, the Isaianic Servant displays both prophetic and royal traits.[18] Second, 11Q13 and 4Q521 provide a messianic reading of Isaiah 61 similar to Luke. Third, it must be observed that a messianic reading of Isaiah 61 is found elsewhere in Luke. In response to the delegation sent from John the Baptist, Jesus replies: 'Go back and report to John what you have seen and heard: The blind receive sight, the lame walk, those who have leprosy are cured, the deaf hear, the dead are raised, and the good news is preached to the poor' (7:22). Put together, Jesus answers the Baptist's question by way of reference to a messianic reading of Isaiah 61. The signs of national renewal associated with the messianic age are present, thus the divine design for the sending of the messianic deliverer is indeed taking shape. If John can look past his incumbent situation and identify Jesus within the story of the anointed one and his deeds, then the question that John asks is easily answered.[19]

Consequently, the Nazareth Manifesto sets up the mission of the Messiah, and 7:22 has Jesus claiming, with the support of

Luke's narrative, that he is implementing the Isaianic mission of the anointed one. The most analogous contemporary text is the Messianic Apocalypse of the Dead Sea Scrolls (4Q521), where the Messiah will 'heal the wounded, raise the dead, and proclaim good news to the poor'. The significance of this is that for Luke, the Messiah is the exemplary redeemer who saves the poor and outcasts. The 'poor' are not only those impoverished economically, or those who have low status in society, but also those devoted to God in their lowly estate, for they have no hope but God. The positive reception of the poor, along with the acceptance of the outcasts, and even Gentiles, is indicative of the fact that this Messiah is redrawing the boundaries of Israel's election around himself. Jesus is both a messianic deliverer but also a prophet calling Israel back into true covenant fellowship with God. It is those who respond in faith and repentance towards him who are constituted as the true 'children of Abraham' (see 3:8; 13:16,28; 16:22; 19:9). The advent of Israel's Messiah results in a radical reversal, since the rich and self-righteous are cast out, while the poor and oppressed experience divine mercy (e.g. 16:19–31). Much of this is intimated in the Nazareth Manifesto, as James Sanders writes: 'By this enriching juxtaposition of Elijah, Elisha, and Isaiah 61, Jesus demonstrates that the words meaning poor, captive, blind, and oppressed do not apply exclusively to any in-group but to those to whom God wishes them to apply.'[20]

Luke's redaction of Marcan material often makes implicit messianic themes more explicit. This is certainly the case in Luke's version of Jesus casting out demons after the healing of Simon Peter's mother-in-law. Whereas Mark reports that 'he also drove out many demons, but he would not let the demons speak *because they knew who he was* (ὅτι ᾔδεισαν αὐτόν)' (Mark 1:34), Luke explains, 'Moreover, demons came out of many people, shouting, "You are the Son of God!" But he rebuked them and would not allow them to speak, because *they knew he was the Messiah* (ὅτι ᾔδεισαν τὸν χριστὸν αὐτὸν εἶναί) (4:41). Luke takes Mark's fairly innocuous reference to the demons' knowledge of Jesus and turns it into a statement of messianic testimony to 'the' Messiah.

In Luke's account of Peter's confession, Jesus is the 'Messiah of God' (Luke 9:20), which stands in contrast to Matthew (16:16: 'the Messiah, the Son of the living God') and Mark (8:28: 'the

Messiah'). Luke's phrase is a genitive of origin, that is, the Messiah who has come from God. The genitive expresses Jesus' special relation to the Father and clarifies the origin of his anointing for Gentile audiences.[21] Like the other Synoptics, Luke relates this confession to the suffering and resurrection of the Son of Man and the necessity of taking up one's own cross (9:22–23). Luke also conjoins with it the transfiguration episode where the temporary glorification of Jesus in the manner of Moses and Elijah is a glimpse of the heavenly enthronement of the Messiah that will transpire after his 'exodus', which is 'about to be fulfilled in Jerusalem' (9:31). In Luke's literary tapestry the messiahship of Jesus then follows a pattern of suffering and glory. Jesus' authority and glory as Messiah is not inconsistent with the crucifixion that is soon to follow.

The Lucan travel narrative enhances Luke's Christology in several ways:

(1) Jesus is the *prophetic Messiah*[22] who journeys to Jerusalem with a profound awareness of his messianic destiny (9:51; 13:31–35; 18:31–34).
(2) Jesus is the *preacher of the kingdom* who understands his unique role in relation to God's purposes (10:23–24; 11:29–32) and summons Israel to repent (Luke 13:1–9).
(3) Jesus is the *compassionate Messiah* who extends salvation to sinners and those in need (13:10–17; 15:1–32; 17:11–19; 18:35–43).
(4) Jesus is *faithful to Moses and the prophets* in fulfilling the divine will (10:25–28; 16:16–17,29; 18:18–23).
(5) Jesus is the *Son of Man* who will return to restore Israel and gather the elect (17:22–37; cf. Acts 3:21).[23]

In the travel narrative (Luke 9:51 – 19:27) Jesus enacts the ministry of liberation, redemption, and eschatological fulfilment, with his messianic identity always on the horizon. Jesus' response to a would-be disciple (9:57–58) is to say that: 'foxes have holes and birds of the air have nests, but the Son of Man has no place to lay his head.' 'Fox' is quite likely a symbol for Herod Antipas (cf. Luke 13:32) whose father, Herod the Great, was an Idumean and regarded as a half-Jew (ἡμιιουδαίῳ).[24] The phrase 'birds of the air' is most probably a symbol for Gentiles (see Ps. 104:12,16–17; Ezek. 17:22–24; Dan. 4:12; *1 Enoch* 90.30; *4 Ezra* 5.26). The title 'Son of Man' is drawn from Daniel 7, and in contrast to the preceding imagery, signifies Israel. The Son of Man, then, is the messianic representative of the Jewish nation. The point of the contrast is to say that everyone, even Gentiles like the Romans, even half-Jews like the Herodians, are making themselves at home in Israel, while the people of God are oppressed by the greed of these pagan beasts. If you wish to join in the Messiah's mission, then you have to join the ranks of the disinherited and dispossessed.

The messianic connotations of 'the Son of Man' are more transparent elsewhere in Luke's narrative. On the road to Jericho, a blind man addresses Jesus as 'Son of David' (Luke 18:38–39), which is a clear messianic epithet. The following pericope in 19:1–10 concludes with Jesus announcing that 'the Son of Man came to seek and to save what was lost'. The language here is indicative of the Davidic shepherd in Ezekiel 34. The intertextual echoes of Ezekiel's shepherd-king in 19:10, taken together with the blind man's confession of Jesus' Davidic lineage in Luke 18:38–39, indicate that 'the Son of Man' is a veiled reference to Jesus' messianic mission to make the hopes of Luke 1 – 4 a reality.

Some less-than-subtle messianic imagery pervades the sections immediately following Luke 19:10. The parable of the ten minas (19:11–27) is arguably a parody of the real accession of Herod the Great's son Archelaus, who went to Rome to be appointed king of Judea despite opposition from a delegation of his future subjects that tried to prevent his appointment.[25] In Luke's retelling, the 'king' is a cipher for Jesus, and the parable is employed by Luke to indicate the possibility of delay in the king's return. The story underscores the imminent opposition faced by the king, and urges subjects of the king to remain loyal and industrious in his absence. Luke's edition of the triumphal entry (19:28–44) portrays Jesus as the shepherd-king riding on a donkey rather than a warhorse. Tragically, Jerusalem, the city of David, does not see the things of peace or recognize that in Jesus they are experiencing the divine visitation (19:41,44). In fact, Luke has Jesus extolled as 'the king who comes in the name of the Lord' (19:38), as opposed to Mark's 'the one who comes in the name of the Lord' (Mark 11:9).

Luke's account of the messianic riddle poses the question of how the Messiah can be a Son of David in light of his elevated status in Psalm 110. Rowe avers: 'At this point in the narrative, the irony is all but directly signalled: ὁ κύριος himself quotes the text of the psalm and asks the question – how can the κύριος be David's son? – that leads to a reappraisal of the nature of χριστός. Κύριος is thus the word by which Luke elevates χριστός to signify much more than υἱὸς Δαυίδ.'[26] That accords with the pattern in Luke–Acts, where Jesus is both the Davidic Messiah and (in some greater sense) the divine Lord.[27] Thereafter Jesus cleanses the temple and teaches Israel with messianic authority. Yet the Davidic 'king' is accused (23:2; cf. Acts 17:7), mocked (23:36–37), and put to a dishonourable death. In sum, Matera is right when he says that Luke's presentation of Jesus' ministry in Jerusalem presents a kaleidoscope of christological images that are rooted in his messianic theology.[28]

However, the death of Jesus in Luke's Gospel comes as no surprise. Beyond the Lucan passion predictions (9:22,43–45; 18:31–34) we have the personification of Jerusalem as the one who kills the prophets and stones those sent to her (13:34–35), the call to carry one's cross and follow Jesus (14:27), the parable of the wicked tenants, which depicts Jesus as a son murdered by the tenants of the vineyard (Luke 20:9–19), and at the last supper the words of Jesus to his followers that the bread is his body 'given for [them]' and the cup is 'the new covenant in my blood which is poured out for [them]' (22:14–23). For Luke, Jesus' death is not redemptive in and of itself, but is part of the movement from suffering to exaltation that will effect the forgiveness of sins and the divine dispensing of the Holy Spirit.[29] Strauss notes: 'Jesus' death does not negate the claims of the birth narrative that Jesus is the Christ but rather confirms them. The prophet-like suffering of the messianic king was prophesied in Scripture and was a necessary stage on the "way" to his glorious enthronement at God's right hand.'[30]

The resurrection of Jesus marks the beginning of a world now partially reborn, but also denotes the noetic transformation of the disciples from misunderstanding Jesus to fully comprehending the contours of his prophetic and messianic identity. The resurrection not only completes the passion predictions, but also brings Jesus' followers to a point of perception that they did not possess before Easter (24:8,31,45). Grundmann stated: 'For Luke this disclosure [of Jesus as Messiah] was understood and accepted as a gift of the risen Lord.'[31]

In the Lucan narrative, the more Jesus repeats his impending fate, the more perplexed and confused the disciples become. Up to a point this is not entirely the disciples' fault, since the meaning of his words 'had been hidden from them' (9:45; 18:34), and the perfect passive periphrastic constructions (παρακεκαλυμμένον and κεκρυμμένον) are a divine passive, that is, God kept them from understanding. The resurrection appearances are revelatory in that they impart a cognitive change in the disciples to finally grasp who Jesus is: the Messiah of Israel. The angel at the empty tomb announces to the women: 'Remember how he told you while he was still in Galilee: the Son of Man must be delivered into the hands of sinful men, be crucified, and on the third day be raised again.' The impact this has upon the women is that 'they remembered his words' (24:6–8). The Son of Man who suffers and is raised is identified explicitly as 'the Messiah' in the Emmaus story (24:25–26). The two travellers opine that with the death of Jesus, a great prophet, their hope for Israel's redemption has been waylaid. The risen Jesus, as yet unrecognized by the sojourners, goes on to explain 'all the Scriptures concerning himself', that the Messiah had to suffer and to enter his glory. Jesus' words, 'beginning with Moses and all the prophets', explain how the Scriptures point to himself (24:27). The logic of Jesus' exposition is based on the correlation of the rejected prophets with the rejection of the Messiah, so that the Scriptures 'presage the eschatological king who would suffer before entering his glory'.[32] In the room with the disciples, Jesus appears once more, and 'he opened their minds so they could understand the Scriptures', specifically as they relate to the Messiah suffering and rising on the third day (24:45–46). Thus, Luke builds a paradox into his narrative, insofar as Jesus both acted and spoke as Messiah, and followed the biblical script for the Messiah to the (Mosaic) letter, and yet his identity as Messiah is only grasped through a revelatory experience of faith and transformation.

In the final scenes of the Gospel of Luke there is a missionary commission to the disciples with the words, 'This is what is written: The Messiah will suffer and rise from the dead on the third day, and repentance for the forgiveness of sins will be preached in his name to all nations, beginning at Jerusalem. You are witnesses of these things' (24:46–48). The orientation of Jesus' messiahship towards Israel has been clear from the beginning (1:16,68; 2:25,34) and is continued at the resurrection and even after his exaltation (Luke 24:21; Acts 1:6; 3:21). At the same time, the movement towards the Gentiles, which Luke has mostly restrained given the omission of Gentile stories present in Mark, has seeped out already (Luke 2:32). The missionary commission indicates that Messiah, witness, forgiveness of sins, and Spirit all belong to the one story of God reaching out to the world through Israel's Messiah. As Larry Hurtado puts it: 'Clearly it is an important Lukan emphasis that Jesus is the Messiah of Israel, and precisely as such also brings universal redemption.'[33] God's mission to the world flows through the prism of the fulfilment of Israel's messianic hopes. That is the presupposition of the book of Acts and the catalyst of the early Christian mission.

## The Story of Jesus Continued in the Church: Christ and Christians in the Acts of the Apostles

Whereas the Christology of Luke's Gospel is essentially narratival, in Acts the vehicle for Luke's Christology is largely titular.[34] In Luke's second volume Jesus' identity and achievement are explicated in the apostolic proclamation *about Jesus* and through the actions of the witnesses who continue the work *of Jesus*.

One could easily get the impression that Luke's Gospel is the story of Jesus' mission to Israel, whereas Acts is the story of the church's mission to the Gentiles. Yet this is far from the case. We have already noticed points at which Luke hints about the salvation of the Gentiles in his Gospel (e.g. 2:32; 4:25–27; 7:1–10; 11:29–32; 24:47). Furthermore, the messianic proclamation of Acts is made principally towards the Jewish people. Much has been written about the Jews in Luke–Acts and whether or not Luke is anti-Semitic.[35] Addressing this, Lloyd Gaston goes so far as to say that: 'Luke–Acts is one of the most pro-Jewish and one of the most anti-Jewish writings in the New Testament.'[36] To this I only wish to say that I find it most probable that Luke is drastically concerned about the economic, political, and spiritual state of the Jewish people. He is simultaneously excited by the fact that it is the Jewish Messiah who has brought salvation to the world; he is deeply pained by the Jewish rejection of Jesus and the apostles; he is angered by the treatment of Jesus and Christians at the hands of the Jewish leadership in Palestine and the Diaspora; and he continues to hold out hope that Israel will yet respond to the good news, and that they will experience 'times of refreshing' (Acts 3:19) and discover in Jesus the 'hope of Israel' (Acts 28:20).

To begin with, the very name 'Messiah' or 'Christ' (Χριστός) has a salvific and a quasi-sacramental function. There is repentance, baptism, and reception of the Holy Spirit in the name of 'Christ' (Acts 2:38; 8:12; 10:48), and power for miraculous healings or exorcisms (Acts 3:6; 9:34; 16:18). Israel's long-awaited hope for redemption and restoration has been and will be effected through Jesus, the messianic agent of salvation (Luke 24:21; Acts 1:6; 3:21; 26:7). In Peter's Pentecost speech in Acts 2, there is a remarkable parallelism between David and Jesus, in terms of their office and anticipated fate. King David was a prophet who looked forward to escaping the grave (Ps. 16:10–11), yet this scripture was obviously not about David, who had died, so it must therefore refer to one of his descendants, the prophet Jesus whom God had raised up (Acts 2:22–33). This is a clear accentuation of Jesus' role as the Davidic and prophetic Messiah.

Luke's conviction about Scripture is not only that Moses, the Law, and the Prophets point to Jesus as Messiah, but also that they can only be properly understood when viewed through the lens of Jesus as the appointed messianic deliverer (Luke 18:31; 24:25,27,45; Acts 3:18,24; 10:43; 24:14). The followers of 'the Way', or 'Nazarenes', are even given the name 'Christians' to signify their distinct socio-religious identity (Χριστιανοί [Acts 11:26; 26:28]). In Acts 15, James sides with Peter in relation to the inclusion of Gentiles, for the reason that Peter's actions correspond to the words of the prophets, specifically Amos 9:11 (LXX) which testifies that the restoration of David's tent (i.e. the Davidic dynasty) will result in a remnant of Jews and Gentiles bearing God's name (Acts 15:16–18). Thus, salvation, initiation, healing, identity, Scripture, and the inclusion of the Gentiles are all inextricably bound up with 'Messiah'.

Jesus as 'Messiah' is at the heart of Christian preaching to the Jews in Acts.[37] In Acts 2, Peter's Pentecost speech is addressed to 'men of Judea and those who live in Jerusalem', 'Israelites', and 'brothers' (Acts 2:14,22,29, my trans.). The speech includes a summation of Jesus' ministry and passion (Acts 2:22–24), the assertion that Jesus' death was divinely ordained (Acts 2:23), and a citation of Psalms 16 and 110 concerning his resurrection and exaltation (Acts 2:25–28,34–35). The 'signs' of Jesus' ministry probably allude to his messianic acts of preaching good news to the poor, healing the lame, and raising the dead (see Luke 4:18–21; 7:22). The reference to Jesus' death as being according to the 'purpose and foreknowledge'[38] of God is designed to anticipate the objection that the Messiah was not to be crucified, and to show that on the contrary the surprising revelation of the Messiah was divinely determined (see Luke 9:22; 22:22) and according to the Scriptures (see Luke 18:31; 24:27,44–45). Hence the appeal to Psalm 16, which refers to the Davidic king who would not experience 'decay', but since David died, it cannot properly apply to him. Instead Psalm 16 refers to Jesus as the one who could not be subjugated by the power of death indefinitely. Similarly, Psalm 110 identifies the 'Lord' with Jesus the exalted Messiah who is now enthroned as God's vice-regent. The use of Psalm 110 here brings to resolution Jesus' own citation of the psalm in Jerusalem (Luke 20:41–44), where the riddle of how the Messiah can be both David's 'son' and also the 'Lord' is solved in Jesus' exaltation to God's right hand. Peter's conclusion is: 'Therefore let the entire house of Israel know with certainty that God has made him both Lord and Messiah, this Jesus whom you crucified' (Acts 2:36 NRSV). This is based on the tripartite proofs of (1) Jesus' messianic ministry, (2) his death as divinely foreordained, and (3) his fulfilment of the scriptural pattern for the Messiah. The whole speech builds on prophecies and patterns of Scripture that indicate to the evangelist that God's oath to David to seat a descendant on his throne forever is made good in Jesus.[39]

A similar model emerges elsewhere in Acts 3:11–26 (Peter's speech in Solomon's Portico, esp. Acts 3:18,20) and Acts 4:8–12 (Peter's speech before the high priestly family; see the interpretation of the rejection of the messianic message in Acts 4:25–26 in terms of Ps. 2:1–2). The speech includes a statement of culpability for Jesus' death, Jesus' vindication by God, the fulfilment of scriptural prophecy, and a call for faith and repentance. The Jerusalem phase of Acts closes with the following summary of the apostles' activities: 'And every day in the temple and at home they did not cease to teach and proclaim Jesus as the Messiah' (Acts 5:42 NRSV). The burden of the speeches in the initial chapters of Acts is to claim that 'the suffering Messiah is not an invention of the church, but the testimony of old from God himself.'[40]

Outside of the Jerusalem environs, Luke's story has messianic proclamation strewn throughout the larger narrative, including the story of Philip who proclaimed 'the Messiah' to Samaritans (Acts 8:5). When Apollos came to Ephesus, he was instructed more accurately about 'the Way of God' by Priscilla and Aquila, and in moving to Achaia, Luke reports that Apollos 'powerfully refuted the Jews in public, showing by the scriptures that the Messiah is Jesus' (Acts 18:27–28 NRSV). Even Saul, after his conversion, has his initial ministry in Damascus described in similar terms: 'Saul became increasingly powerful and confounded the Jews who lived in Damascus by demonstrating that Jesus was the Messiah' (Acts 9:22, my trans.). In his preaching at Pisidian Antioch, Paul (i.e. 'Saul') underscores Jesus' Davidic lineage, as he is the Saviour who fulfils the promise made to David about a descendant being on the throne of the ancestor (Acts 13:22–34). The same thing happens when Paul enters a synagogue with Silas in Thessalonica, where he sets about 'explaining and proving that it was necessary for the Messiah to suffer and to rise from the dead, and saying, "This is the Messiah, Jesus whom I am proclaiming to you"' (Acts 17:3 NRSV). Again in Corinth 'Paul was occupied with proclaiming the word, testifying to the Jews that the Messiah was Jesus' (Acts 18:5 NRSV). In Paul's speech before King Agrippa, Paul can say that he has declared his message to 'those in Damascus, then in Jerusalem and throughout the countryside of Judea, and also to the Gentiles, that they should repent and turn to God and do deeds consistent with repentance . . . that the Messiah must suffer, and that, by being the first to rise from the dead, he would proclaim light both to our people and to the Gentiles' (Acts 26:20,23 NRSV). When Paul finally arrives in Rome, he calls together the local Jewish leadership, and they prove to be a relatively receptive audience. Luke narrates:

> After they had fixed a day to meet with him, they came to him at his lodgings in great numbers. From morning until evening he explained the matter to them, testifying to the kingdom of God and trying to convince them about Jesus both from the law of Moses and from the prophets. Some were convinced by what he had said, while others refused to believe (Acts 28:23–24 NRSV).

While the response from Paul's Jewish Roman audience is not categorically negative, it is sufficiently disconcerting to prompt Paul to quote from Isaiah 6:9–10 that the mind of this people is closed to things of the gospel (Acts 28:25–28; cf. 3:17). Despite Luke's emphatic and repetitious plea that Jesus is the Messiah of Israel, does he at the end write them off or consign them to perdition? I think not. While the Jewish response is arguably disappointing from Luke's perspective, put more positively, it has provided occasion for Gentiles to gain a share in salvation (Acts 13:46; 18:6; 28:24–28). Luke is glad that Gentiles have a place in the kingdom, but their place in the kingdom does not exist despite the Jews, but because of them. Neither the influx of Gentiles into the church, nor the recalcitrance of the Jews to the apostolic preaching, is able to dissuade Luke from believing that the gospel is that Jesus is the Messiah of Israel. In the words of Michael Wolter: 'Luke thus seems to envision a new epoch of the Christian mission beginning in Rome, and not a word suggests that this mission will not reach Jews as well.'[41]

We should also pay attention to the pattern that Luke has developed in his account of Paul's ministry. Twice before, Paul has abandoned the Jewish mission (Acts 13:46; 18:6) only to return to it again. Is that a pattern that Luke sets for Paul to emulate once more in the future? We are, of course, speculating, but we can hardly be faulted for thinking so. In fact, this habitual return to Jewish mission after a period of rejection shows that the Lucan Paul resembles, in many respects, the apostle Paul's own perspective in his letters. Paul experienced persecution from his own countrymen (e.g. 2 Cor. 11:24–27; 1 Thess. 2:15–16); yet in Romans 9 – 11, Paul could still agonize over Israel's failure to believe the gospel (9:15). He uses vitriolic language to describe their hardness of heart (9:6 – 10:13), pleads for a continuing mission to Israel despite their disobedience (10:14–21), affirms God's commitment to a remnant within Israel (11:1–10), notes how Israel's disobedience resulted in the in-grafting of the Gentiles (11:11–24), and holds out a hope that 'all Israel' will yet be saved (11:25–36). Also, the prospects for the Jews at the end of Acts 28 are not entirely negative. Luke's final words are that Paul 'welcomed all who came to him, proclaiming the kingdom of God and teaching about the Lord Jesus Christ' (Acts 28:30–31). Not only is the audience's identity, the 'all', left open (quite deliberately, I believe), but also the 'kingdom' is something that is yet to be restored to Israel (Acts 1:6) and is what Paul previously proclaimed to Jews (Acts 19:8; 28:23). Elsewhere in Luke–Acts, the response from the Jewish people to Jesus or the message of Jesus is positive: they recognize Jesus' authority and power (Luke 4:36), they glorify God on behalf of him (Luke 5:26), they acknowledge Jesus as a great prophet and claim that God has visited his people (Luke 7:16–17), the church grows exponentially among the Jerusalemites (Acts 2:41,47; 5:14–16; 6:1), the church in Judea, Galilee, and Samaria multiplies (Acts 9:31), and even though Paul experiences rejection among Jews of the Diaspora, he still makes a number of Jewish and Gentile converts (Acts 14:1; 16:2,5,11–15; 17:4,10–12; 18:8; 19:10; 28:24). Overall, the results may be mixed, but they are not entirely negative. Moreover, Israel's lack of understanding and their dullness is no more problematic than that experienced by the disciples. What is left for Israel then is not judgement, but waiting for the revelation of the Messiah, and having their minds opened as was done for the disciples on that first Easter Sunday.[42]

## Conclusion

According to Matera, in Luke–Acts 'the central concept for identifying Jesus is *messiahship* . . . Of the many terms that Luke employs to identify Jesus, then, "Messiah" is among the most important. Indeed, one could argue that it is *the* title in reference to which all others are to be understood.'[43] Jervell is of a similar opinion when he states that 'Christ' is the most significant title in Luke–Acts.[44] Finally, Stanton asserts that 'there can be no doubt that one of [Luke's] primary aims in both his writings is to stress that Jesus is the promised Davidic Messiah'.[45] I find myself in agreement with these claims, since Jesus' identity as the Davidic Messiah is not, in Luke–Acts, a residue of early christological tradition that Luke has blandly perpetuated. Jesus is a prophetic agent who is anointed with the Spirit in order to carry forward the promises for a Davidic deliverer.[46] He is a new David, but is more than David *redivivus,* in that he is also the Messianic Lord of whom David spoke about in the Psalms. This significance of Jesus' messianic identity manifests itself on at least two levels.

First, Luke–Acts can be said to have an apologetic and kerygmatic function. Luke expresses a clear apologetic urgency in the sense that he wants to make a resolute defence of Jesus' messiahship, which is called into question by the crucifixion and the failure of national Israel to respond in faith to his messengers. This type of apologetic (as with most apologetics) is probably written for internal consumption by insiders, and it gives Luke's readers a sense of assurance or certainty about the things that they have been taught (see Luke 1:4). What is also plausible, however, is that Luke has constructed a rhetorically powerful and imaginative narrative that seeks to persuade audiences that Jesus is the Messiah, to urge them to respond in faith with repentance, and to identify with the people who bear his name. Viewed this way, Luke–Acts could easily be used as a form of *Missionsschrift.* In the words of Rebecca Denova: 'Luke–Acts, we may conclude on the basis of a narrative-critical reading, was written . . . to persuade other Jews that Jesus of Nazareth was the messiah of Scripture and that the words of the prophets concerning "restoration" have been "fulfilled".'[47] In order to do that, Luke must redefine the meaning of messiahship somewhat, so as to accommodate the contours of Jesus' life and exaltation.[48] It is not the case that the redefinition is so drastic that, in Christopher Tuckett's words, 'Luke's Jesus seems to be at most a Christ figure in name only.'[49] The similarities between Luke 7:22 and 4Q521 dispel that view with remarkable ease. At any rate, the fulcrum of Luke's Christology lies not in an anti-Gnostic tendency, not in correcting a prophet/Messiah/servant Christology with a κύριος Christology, not in an absentee Christology, not in advocating subordinationism; rather, at its hub, it is a messianic proclamation with the Messiah redefined to include much more than often thought, but certainly not any less.

Second, Luke–Acts imparts assurance to its readers that those who express faith in Jesus and join 'the Way' are constituted as the people of God in the messianic age. In other words, Luke–Acts is concerned with group identity and self-definition.[50] Beneath the Lucan narrative lurks the probing question: Who are the people of God? Followers of the Jesus movement are assailed by pagan authorities and Jewish crowds alike. They are an obscure 'sect' (Acts 24:5,14; 28:22) whose relation to Judaism remains ambiguous (even to Luke), and they have not established an independent identity in the Greco-Roman world. Luke does not see the church as superseding Israel, but believes that Israel's Scriptures find their fulfilment in Jesus and the church (Acts 13:33–34). Luke does not think that Christians pose a threat to the imperial order, but they are most certainly an alternative to it, as they knowingly pay homage to a king other than Caesar (Acts 17:6–7). According to Luke, allegiance to Jesus as Messiah and Lord is what establishes and secures the identity of the people of God and places them in a bond of solidarity that reaches through Israel all the way back to Abraham. They are part of a movement that will lead to the full restoration of Israel and will reach to the ends of the earth (Acts 1:6–8).

# 4.

# The Gospel of John:
# The Elusive Messiah

## Introduction

According to Mark Stibbe, in the Gospel of John, 'Jesus is an elusive figure. Even when Nicodemus finds him, Jesus proves opaque to his understanding. When the crowds seek Jesus, he only allows them to find him when he is ready for them. And as for the Jewish authorities, I am reminded of Baroness Orczy's Scarlet Pimpernel: "they seek him here, they seek him there, those Jews seek him everywhere."'[1] One of the things that makes the Johannine Jesus so elusive is that he is unequivocally the Messiah according to the testimony of the author (John 1:41; 11:27; 20:31), yet the make-up of Jesus' messianism is somewhat different in texture from that of the Synoptic Gospels, while also diverging in some degree from contemporary Jewish sources. In the Gospel of John, Jesus is *more* of a 'heavenly revealer' sent by God the Father than an eschatological deliverer demonstrating himself to be the king of God's coming kingdom. Over a hundred years ago, Charles Briggs suggested: 'The Gospel of John gives us a Messianic ideal that is beyond the conceptions of the synoptic evangelists, and which may be summed up under the title, the *Messiah from heaven*.'[2] That is all well and good, but it does not explain why John's Christology is different from the other evangelists at this point, nor does it clarify the narrative function of Jesus' messianic claims in the Gospel; and we are still left with the issue of how John's christological portrait relates to Jewish hopes about messianic figures.

Wayne A. Meeks said: 'The uniqueness of the Fourth Gospel in early Christian literature consists above all in the special patterns of language which it uses to describe Jesus Christ.'[3] How the messiahship of Jesus functions within the symbol-laden language of John's Gospel is particularly intriguing, as Jewish messianism is put in service to a particular Christian conception of Jesus as the Son of God. The messianic identity of Jesus in the Fourth Gospel constitutes a crucial motif in the plot, but also an *entrée* into the christological claims being made by the author. The great Bishop J.B. Lightfoot commented: 'Among friends, among foes, among neutrals alike, it [i.e. Jesus' messianic identity] is mooted and discussed. The person and character of Jesus are tried by this standard. He is accepted or he is rejected as he fulfils or contradicts the received idea of the Messiah.'[4] C.H. Dodd noted that the messiahship of Jesus is a persistent theme in the Gospel of John, as it constitutes a key point of contention between Jesus and the Judean authorities.[5] Rudolf Schnackenburg similarly observed that the question about whether Jesus is the Messiah dominates the Fourth Gospel (see 1:20–25; 4:29; 7:26–27,31,41–42; 10:24; 12:34).[6] C.K. Barrett affirms that 'the synoptic language of the messianic hope is not abandoned; on the contrary it is more common in John than elsewhere'.[7] John Painter sees the Gospel as based around the 'Quest' for the Messiah, specifically to answer the questions: 'Who is the Messiah?' and 'What he is like?'.[8] Accordingly, John raises the question as to 'who' exactly the Messiah is, and 'what' kind of Messiah Jesus is. John's answer to the 'who' is obviously Jesus, and the 'what' is defined by way of reference to his signs and glory. Yet a vexing issue for commentators is that John has chosen to explicate Jesus' messianic identity in a manner that is, in many ways, quite dissimilar from the messianic discourse of the Synoptics, Paul, and Revelation. The question is: Why?

Many also object that the Johannine Jesus is so christianized that he has lost all vestiges of Jewish messianism in his identity and mission. As such, George MacRae states: 'The Johannine church wants to insist that Jesus qualifies as Messiah without fulfilling the requirements. The concept has become a radically transcendent one . . . The Johannine Messiah, however, shares relatively little with the Jewish and even other Christian concepts of Messiah in that the eschatological dimension of the messianic role is diminished, if not eliminated.'[9] Perhaps Justin's Jewish dialogue partner Trypho was right that Christians 'invent a Christ for yourselves'.[10] But in violent contrast, C.H. Dodd declared: 'As for the title Messiah itself . . . no other New Testament writer shows himself so fully aware of the Jewish ideas associated with it as does the Fourth Evangelist.'[11] Whether John's Jesus is an authentically *Jewish* Messiah seems to be up for debate.

In light of those disputed points of interpretation, the aim of this chapter is to plot the basic contours of John's messianism and to situate it in the wider sway of messianic hopes in first-century Judaism and in early Christianity.

## The Incarnation of the Pre-Existent Messiah

The prologue of the Fourth Gospel raises a labyrinth of issues concerning its structure, background, sources, redaction, integrity, length, meaning, and purpose. My own view is that the prologue functions much like an operatic overture, as it highlights the themes and motifs in the dramatic performance that follows. Jesus as the Word, Light, Truth, Life, and Glory of God are all embryonic in the prologue and sprout forth in the rest of the story. The prologue may correctly be called 'John's Gospel in a nutshell': it stands firmly in the context of Jewish monotheism, but in such a way as to identify the Creator and covenant-making God with his action in Jesus the Son.

The first category through which Jesus' identity is explicated in the prologue is the *Logos* or 'the Word' (λόγος). The verb ἦν ('was') in 1:1 implies pre-existence, relationship, and divinity.[12] The Word *was* there in the beginning and precedes the created world. The Word *was* with God in a relational sense of sharing prerogatives with him. The Word *was* God, and divinity is predicated of the Word, so that what is true of God is also true of the Word. The background to the Logos concept lies in Hellenistic thought reaching back to Heraclitus, who regarded the Logos as the rational principle that guides all things – the pilot of the universe, so to speak. For later Stoic philosophers, the Logos was the account that governs all things and sustains them. Philo attempted to mediate between Jewish and Hellenistic traditions by making the Logos an intermediary between God and the world, one that was embodied in the wisdom of the Torah. Christians from John the evangelist to Justin Martyr took up the notion of the Logos and identified it with Jesus. The Logos was the creative word of God issued in creation (Gen. 1:1), the wisdom that dwelt among Israel (Proverbs 8; Sirach 24; Wisdom 10; 14), and this wisdom is now identified with Jesus Christ. Jesus, as the Logos, is the pre-existent self-expression of God, and therefore he is uniquely fitted to 'tabernacle' (σκηνόω) among the people as a human being in much the same way that wisdom tabernacled in the Torah as a means of instruction for Israel.

The relationship of this Logos Christology to the messianism of the Gospel of John is debated. According to J.A.T. Robinson: 'It has been said by no less a Johannine scholar than E.F. Scott that "in the Fourth Gospel the Messianic idea is replaced by that of the Logos". But this is precisely what does not happen. The word λόγος never recurs as a title, and the dominant christology of the Gospel is expressed rather in terms of "the Christ, the Son of God"' (see 20:31).[13] Robinson is quite correct. The prefatory remarks about Jesus as the Logos do not deny, eclipse, or supersede any messianic faith known to the evangelist. The purpose of John's literary work is declared at the end: 'these are written that you may believe that Jesus is the Messiah, the Son of God, and that by believing you may have life in his name' (20:31). Evoking (or encouraging) faith in Jesus as the Messiah is the goal of the Gospel. Reading the prologue through that lens sheds considerable light on what John is trying to set up in the prologue.

The implicit messianism of the prologue is apparent in at least four ways. First, John is amplifying his messianic testimony by placing the person of the Messiah within the orbit of the divine identity. One way that John does this is by identifying Jesus as pre-existent. The pre-existence of Jesus in the Gospel is clear in several units, not only in the prologue with 'in the beginning', but elsewhere too, such as Jesus' retort to the Pharisees: '"Very truly I tell you . . . before Abraham was born, I am!"' (8:58). Moreover, the pre-existence of the Messiah seems to have been debated within Judaism. The concept of a pre-existing Messiah is implied, to varying degrees, in several Jewish texts,[14] yet the late-second-century Christian author Hippolytus knows of a Jewish tradition that disputed such a claim since the Messiah is the one 'who as yet has no existence'.[15] Such an objection might be raised against specifically Christian notions of a pre-existent Messiah. However, the discussion among the Jerusalem crowd about whether Jesus is the Messiah at the Feast of Tabernacles ('But we know where this man is from; when the Messiah comes, no one will know where he is from' [7:27]) and Trypho's remark to Justin ('But Messiah – if He has indeed been born, and exists anywhere – is unknown, and does not even know Himself' [*Dial. Tryph.* 8.4]) seem to amount to a clear affirmation of an established view within Judaism that the Messiah was a person concealed and then climactically revealed (see further *1 Enoch* 46.1–2; *4 Ezra* 7.28). The pre-existence of the Messiah was not a consistent aspect of messianic hopes, but a deployable one for some. A pre-existent Messiah was not, then, a Christian innovation. John's two cents about the pre-existent Messiah debate was given in his affirmation that Jesus the Word is the king of Israel.

Second, a further intimation of Jesus' messianic vocation is made in the prologue by the emphasis on the Word as 'coming' (ἔρχομαι) to his people. There are three 'coming' statements in the prologue pertaining to Jesus. To begin with, he is the light coming into the world (1:9); and the Baptist testifies about him with the words, 'This is he of whom I said, "He who comes after me has surpassed me because he was before me"'(1:15). In-between these verses is the statement: 'He came to that which was his own, but his own did not receive him' (1:11).

The notion that Jesus as Messiah is the 'coming one' is firmly embedded in the Gospel tradition. Jesus is the stronger one/coming one in the witness of the Baptist (Mark 1:7/Matt. 3:11/Luke 3:16/John 1:15,30). Jesus is asked by John's disciples if he is the 'one to come' (Luke 7:19–20/Matt. 11:2–3). In the triumphal entry, rich with messianic overtones, Jesus is the one who 'comes in the name of the Lord' (Mark 11:9/Matt. 21:9/Luke 19:38/John 12:13). This is more than a movement from A to B, as 'the coming one' was rich with eschatological and messianic significance. The Septuagint version of Hab. 2:3 is messianic, and refers not simply to a coming age, but to a coming person. That is not to make the substantive form of 'coming one' (ὁ ἐρχόμενος) a technical term for a messianic advent, but the description fitted the royal deliverer who would arrive in the coming age. At Qumran, the verb 'to come in' (בוא) can refer to the coming eschatological age, the coming of God, and also to the coming of the Messiahs or the eschatological prophet (4Q252 5.3; CD [B] 19.10–11; 1QS 9.11).[16] Not all 'coming' figures are the Messiah, yet the Messiah is a coming figure.

Furthermore it is the rest of the Gospel that informs us that this 'coming' is of a messianic nature. John's witness to Jesus in the prologue – 'He who comes after me has surpassed me because he was before me' (1:15) – is repeated in John 1:30. Interestingly, in the second occurrence of this description, the evangelist adds several features:

(1) The witness of John is prefaced with a delegation of Judean priests and Levites asking John about who he was, and John explicitly denies being the Messiah, meaning that messianic hopes provide the context for John's witness to this 'coming' man (1:19–28).
(2) The purpose of the Baptist's ministry was so that this unknown person who was before him would be revealed to Israel – again hitting the theme of the mysterious and pre-existent Messiah revealed at the appointed time (1:30–31).
(3) Immediately before and after John's testimony to Jesus, this coming figure is described with what I will soon argue are messianic titles: 'Lamb of God' and 'God's Chosen One' (1:29,34,36).

If that were not enough, in the rest of the Gospel there are explicit references to the 'coming Messiah'. The Samaritan woman gives a one-sentence summary of Samaritan messianic hopes: '"I know that Messiah" (called Christ) "is *coming. When he comes,* he will explain everything to us"' (4:25). After the feeding miracle in Galilee, the crowds extol Jesus as the messianic prophet: 'Surely this is the Prophet *who is to come* into the world' (6:14). The grieving Martha confesses to Jesus, 'I believe that you are the Messiah, the Son of God, *who was to come* into the world' (11:27). The pilgrims who accompany Jesus in his triumphal entry sing the words,

'"Hosanna!" "Blessed is *he who comes* in the name of the Lord!" "Blessed is the king of Israel!"' (12:13). Finally, the exchange between Pilate and Jesus accents Jesus' messianic coming: '"You are a king, then!" said Pilate. Jesus answered, "You say that I am a king. In fact, the reason I was born and *came into the world* is to testify to the truth"' (18:37). The coming of Jesus in the prologue is not simply the coming of a heavenly redeemer. No, in light of the rest of the Gospel it is the coming of the Messiah, the prophet, and the king of Israel. Jesus is sent by the Father and comes from the Father, hence the ubiquitous sayings about Jesus being 'sent' (5:23,36,37; 6:44,57; 8:16,18,42; 10:36; 12:49; 14:24; 17:21,25; 20:21). The sending of Jesus is the execution of his messianic role. As the coming one, he transcends the heaven/earth divide (see 1:1–13,51; 3:13,31). Ironically, his advent causes a divide within Israel (1:11; 7:43; 9:16,22; 10:19; 12:42; 16:2). The division relates fundamentally to his identity as the Messiah sent as the Son of God to bring light and life into the world.

Third, the prologue explicitly nominates Jesus as μονογενής ('the one and only Son' [1:14,18; see 3:16,18; 1 John 4:9]). The exclusiveness of being the one and only Son is not that of an only child, but of a 'one-of-a-kind Son'. By way of an *inclusio*, the 'one and only Son' serves as a commentary on what is meant in 1:1 by the 'Word was God'. The Word was God, and thus Jesus is unique and divine, though in the flesh.[17] The Son-language is not strictly ontological, then, for, just as in the Synoptics, references to Jesus as the Son in the Gospel of John cannot be wrested from connotations of messiahship. In fact, John is more explicit than the Synoptics in making 'Son of God' a messianic title. Nathanael declares Jesus to be the Son of God and king of Israel (1:49). Martha confesses Jesus as the Messiah and Son of God (11:27); and climactically the purpose of the evangelist is to lead readers to faith in Jesus as Messiah and Son of God (20:31). The Johannine Son is the Messiah sent to Israel.

Fourth, while the structure of the prologue is difficult to map – such as whether it ends in verses 5, 14, or 18 – by the time we reach 1:17, the Word and Son are explicitly identified as 'Jesus Christ' ('Ιησοῦς Χριστός). It is quite possible that 'Jesus Christ' functions as a proper name here, especially in light of Jesus' high-priestly prayer where he states, 'Now this is eternal life: that they know you, the only true God, and Jesus Christ, whom you have sent' (17:3). However, in the scene immediately following the prologue, Χριστός is used with the article in the Baptist's denial that he is *the* Messiah (1:20,25). In fact, fourteen out of eighteen uses of Χριστός possess the article. A quick shift from a nominal to an articular usage of Χριστός from 1:17 to 1:20 is plausible only on the assumption – one validated by what we've seen elsewhere – that even as a name, Ἰησοῦς Χριστός never lost its titular significance as 'Jesus is the Messiah'.

The Johannine prologue provides a paranoramic display of the pre-existent and eternal Word of God who is enfleshed as the Son of God. He comes to his people as the Messiah, radiating God's glory, and inviting people to faith and sonship. The story and symbols of Israel's sacred traditions are reconfigured around Jesus-the-Word, who is also the Messiah whom Israel must receive. The advent of the messianic deliverer effects a redefinition of the God who sends him, because the 'sender' and the 'sent' are drawn so closely together. Thus, the prologue of John's Gospel sets up the messianic story that follows: Jesus [the] Christ, as testified by the Baptist, is the Word of God revealed to Israel. He is the coming one, the Son of God who brings the full measure of the scriptural qualities of grace, glory, wisdom, and truth.

## The Signs of the Messiah

Unlike Mark, appearance of the word Χριστός occurs mainly in the first half of the Gospel of John (see 1:17,20,25,41; 3:28; 4:25,29; 7:26–27,31,41–42; 9:22; 10:24; 11:27; 12:34; the exceptions are 17:3; 20:31). By sheer linguistic statistics the 'messianic question' dominates the first half of the Gospel. Even so, in this section it is not simply titles that indicate who Jesus is, but it is also Jesus' teachings, confrontations, interaction with others, tensions in the plot, Old Testament allusions, and internal dialogue among the crowd that provide pieces to the puzzle of who this elusive figure is. This first half of the Gospel, John 1 – 12, is often called the Book of Signs. In this section, specifically 1:19 – 12:50, Jesus' miracles and encounters with several persons demonstrate his messianic work and validate his unity with the Father. The 'signs' (σημεῖα) function as an additional witness alongside John the Baptist and the Scriptures to indicate Jesus' unique role as God's agent of revelation and salvation (5:31–47). The purpose of these signs is to explicate Jesus' identity as the heaven-sent Messiah who reveals the Father's glory.[18] Unlike Jesus' mighty deeds in the Synoptic Gospels, which are primarily demonstrations of the in-breaking kingdom, the signs in the Fourth Gospel contain a heightened christological focus. The signs foster division over Jesus' person as they demand a response of either faith or rejection. At a crucial point the people in the crowd ask of themselves, 'When the Messiah comes, will he perform more signs than this man?' (7:31). The 'signs' are analogous to Matthew's 'deeds of the Messiah' (Matt. 11:2), in that the Johannine signs bring a crisis of messianic belief in the audience, in Jesus' own day and among John's contemporaries, as the work of Jesus forces individuals to decide who he is.

### Could this be the Messiah? (John 1:19–51)

John 1:19–51 constitutes a prelude to Jesus' public ministry that features the witness of the Baptist (1:19–34) and the calling of the first disciples (1:35–51). Importantly both subsections hinge on Jesus' messianic identity, which is the core of the Baptist's testimony, and the amazing news that magnetically attracts the disciples to Jesus. In this section we find the beginning of the 'Quest for the Messiah', which starts with John pointing his interlocutors to Jesus, whom the disciples soon find.[19]

The Baptist was explicitly nominated as a μαρτυρία ('witness') to Jesus in the prologue (1:7), and now he undertakes to flesh out that witness further. When confronted with a delegation of Jerusalem priests and Levites concerned to know who he is, the Baptist immediately responds, 'I am not the Messiah' (1:20). The Messiah here is the royal Davidic Messiah as he is elsewhere in the Gospel (see John 7:42). The Baptist also denies being 'the Prophet' or 'Elijah' (1:21). The 'Prophet' is obviously the eschatological prophet like Moses (Deut. 18:15–19), and the evangelist also believes that this designation is true of Jesus, not the Baptist (4:19; esp. 6:14; 7:40,52; 9:17). The expectation of the return of the prophet Elijah is based on Mal. 4:5–6 and figures in many Jewish expectations for the future (Sir. 48.10–12;

*Eupolemus* 2.1; 4Q558; cf. Matt. 17:10–11; Mark 9:11–12; Luke 1:16–17). Interesting is that some Jewish sources appear to have identified the returning Elijah as an eschatological high priest. In the Targum of Pseudo-Jonathan to the Pentateuch, Elijah is identified with Phinehas, the grandson of Aaron.[20] Justin's *Dialogue* with the Jew Trypho contends that it will be Elijah's role to anoint the Messiah.[21] As Richard Bauckham concludes: 'Therefore, it is very possible that in John 1:19–21 the three eschatological figures represent the three roles of king, high priest and prophet.'[22] The *triplex munus* of Christian Christology (Jesus is prophet, priest, and king) owes its roots to Judaism, since the Community Rule at Qumran refers to the regulations that must be obeyed 'until the prophet comes, and the Messiahs of Aaron and Israel' (1QS 9.11), and Josephus says that John Hyrcanus 'was accounted by God worthy of the three great privileges, the rule of the nation, the office of high-priest, and the gift of prophecy' (*Ant.* 13.299).[23] In other words, the Baptist denies being any of the anointed figures that had currency in contemporary eschatological hopes. As such, his symbolic actions are not identifications of his anointed status, but preparations for the coming anointed deliverer. That is made clear by the subsequent exchange of dialogue in John 1:22–28.

Not content with returning to their masters with a series of denials by the Baptist, the members of the Judean delegation continue to pester the Baptist to reveal who he is if he is none of those anointed figures. The Baptist's response takes the form of a quotation of Isaiah 40:3, as he is preparing the way of the Lord. Notably, what is an editorial addition in the synoptic account is here found on the lips of John the Baptist. His response speaks directly to the priests' concerns about the appearance of a messianic leader. They were interested in the authority behind John's baptism and were curious if the Baptist could be one of the anticipated eschatological figures. The Baptist affirms his authority to baptize as divinely bestowed; but he subordinates this preparatory role to a coming figure (the coming of the 'Lord', no less) who follows after him, whom he considers himself unworthy to serve in even the most menial of tasks. The Baptist's words continue the theme of his redemptive-historical inferiority from the prologue (1:6–8,15) and define his relation to Jesus the

Messiah in a way that anticipates his self-confessed weakness in comparison to Jesus in 3:30–36.[24]

The real answer to the priestly delegation is given in the Baptist's words, uttered the next day, when he sees Jesus coming towards him. To the question of why John is baptizing (1:25), the answer is: 'the reason I came baptizing with water was that he might be revealed to Israel' (1:31), and his water baptism is an anticipation of the 'one who will baptize with the Holy Spirit' (1:33). Also, the 'one who comes after me' (1:27) is explained further with the words, 'A man who comes after me has surpassed me because he was before me' (1:30). The real purpose of the Baptist's non-messianic actions is to prepare for the revelation of the Spirit-anointed, Spirit-dispensing Messiah. This again is an enhancement of the prologue as the Messiah's revelation to Israel (1:9–14,17–18), and his pre-existence (1:1–3,15) is placed within the historical testimony of John the Baptist.

The Baptist provides a testimony to Jesus that explains how he identified the Coming One. Referring to Jesus' baptism, he testifies to having seen 'the Spirit come down from heaven as a dove and remain on him' (1:32). In the Synoptic Gospels, the descent of the Spirit as a dove was something witnessed only by Jesus himself (Matt. 3:16; Mark 1:10; Luke 3:22), a parabolic act of anointing reinforced by the voice from heaven. In the Fourth Gospel, however, the dove assumes a different role: it identifies the Coming One to the Baptist. He had been told by God himself who the Coming One would be: the one who receives the Spirit will be the one who baptizes with the Spirit.[25]

Jesus' reception of the Spirit is transparently messianic. Isaiah identified anointing with the Spirit as a mark of the selection of a new Davidic king and the means for empowering the Lord's Servant (Isa. 11:1–2; 61:1–2). What is more, the Baptist's account of Jesus' baptism is bracketed with two messianic titles: 'Lamb of God' (1:29) and 'Elect One' (1:34). When the Baptist identifies Jesus as 'the Lamb of God' (ὁ ἀμνὸς τοῦ θεοῦ), who takes away the sin of the world, the primary reference should not be an atonement theology (though the evangelist undoubtedly has one [John 10:15–18; 11:51–52; 12:24; 15:13]).[26] More probably the intended referent is the apocalyptic lamb, the warrior lamb, found in several Jewish and Christians texts (1 *Enoch* 90.9–12;

*T.Jos.* 19.11; *T.Benj* 3.8) and taken up in the Apocalypse of John (Rev. 5:6,12; 7:17; 13:8; 17:14; 19:7,9; 21:22–23; 22:1–3). The Baptist's acclamation 'Behold the Lamb of God' (1:29, 36) appears to be parallel to Andrew's announcement to Simon, 'We have found the Messiah' (1:41).[27] In this light, what the Baptist meant by 'one who takes away the sin of the world' may have had more to do with judgement and destruction than with expiatory sacrifice; it is 'God's Messiah who makes an end of sin'.[28] The second title ascribed to Jesus, 'the Elect One' (ὁ ἐκλεκτός τοῦ θεοῦ), comprises the conclusion to John's witness about Jesus' reception of the Spirit. If 'elect one' is the correct reading,[29] then John is probably alluding to Isaiah 42:1, where God promised to pour out his Spirit on his servant, his 'chosen one' (ὁ ἐκλεκτός; LXX). The designation 'elect one', or 'chosen one', features prominently in *1 Enoch* as a messianic title.[30] Carson comments: 'In John's Gospel, the theme that the disciples of Jesus are his elect, his chosen ones, is extremely strong (e.g. 6:65,70; 13:18; 15:16,19). But this privilege of believers is ultimately grounded in the fact that Jesus himself is God's chosen one *par excellence* – chosen as the suffering servant, the Lamb of God who takes away the sin of the world.'[31]

The material in verses 19–34 and 35–51 are linked together with the theme of the messianic Lamb. In the second 'next day' (ἐπαύριον), John's testimony to Jesus as the Lamb of God, the Spirit-receiving and Spirit-baptizing Elect One, is delivered to the two disciples (Andrew and an unnamed disciple). They in turn start following Jesus (1:37). The fact that they ask where he is staying means they want to commit themselves to his teaching and perhaps join his school. Jesus responds favourably to their request, and they are invited to come and see where he is staying (1:38–39). What follows in verses 40–51 contains the disciples' apprehension of Jesus' messianic identity and their compulsion to share it with the members of their immediate family.

Andrew's enthusiasm for his new teacher is given with the narration of his actions: 'The first thing Andrew did was to find his brother Simon and tell him, "We have found the Messiah" (that is, the Christ)' (John 1:41).[32] Strictly speaking, there is nothing in the narrative that would itself lead Andrew to infer Jesus' messianic identity. The mere acceptance of a disciple for teaching by a rabbi was hardly out of the ordinary. Instead it was the

Baptist's testimony combined with Jesus' individual charisma that led to Andrew's conclusion. The excited profession 'We have found the Messiah' was also the testimony of the Johannine network, and reflected the central and uncompromising christological affirmation of the evangelist and his fellow believers. They have found the one to whom the Scriptures pointed for deliverance. An article of faith not shared with their fellow Jews and one which caused their eventual exclusion from some aspects of Jewish life (a tension reflected in the dis-synagoguing in John 9:22; 12:42; 16:2; see 1 John 2:22; 5:1; Rev. 2:9; 3:9). For the first time in the Gospel (see 4:25), the evangelist transliterates the Aramaic מְשִׁיחָא (*Mĕšîḥaʾ*) as Μεσσίας, and in a parenthetical remark translates it as Χριστός ('Christ'). The sequel to Andrew's confession is Simon's call to be a disciple and his renaming as 'Cephas' or 'Peter'.

The following material centres on the calling of Philip and Nathanael (1:43–51). The scene moves from 'Bethany beyond the Jordan' (1:28) to 'Galilee' (1:43). The call of Philip is immediate and abrupt ('Finding Philip, he said to him, "Follow me"' [1:43]). Just like Andrew, he is compelled to go and immediately inform his brother of his discovery. Philip tells Nathanael: 'We have found the one Moses wrote about in the Law, and about whom the prophets also wrote – Jesus of Nazareth, the son of Joseph' (1:45). Philip's description arguably provides the scriptural justification and definition of Andrew's previous declaration that Jesus is the 'Messiah'. In the Fourth Gospel there is a strong theme of the Scriptures witnessing to Jesus, especially through Moses and the prophets (2:22; 5:39,45–47; 6:45; 7:38,42; 10:34–36; 12:38; 19:24,28,36–37; 20:9). Unlike the other disciples, Nathanael does not meet the news with enthusiasm but with scepticism. The notion of a messianic deliverer coming from Nazareth was a stumbling block, as it probably was to other Jews known to the evangelist (1:46). The origins of the Messiah are a point of division among the crowds (7:27,42), and the prevailing opinions are either that the Messiah's origins will be mysterious, or that he'll come from Bethlehem. Nathanael, like other Jews whom the evangelist probably has in mind, is simply ignorant of Jesus' origins in eternity past. But Nathanael's mind changes upon his encounter with Jesus. Philip answers Nathanael's question in the affirmative 'Come and see', which is tantamount to 'Come and see that the Messiah does in fact hail from Nazareth' (1:46). As Nathanael approaches, Jesus says of him, 'Here truly is an Israelite in whom there is no deceit' (1:47). Nathanael is perhaps bemused at Jesus' presumptuous comment and inquires how the Nazarene can know such things. Jesus' reply catches his attention and frees his unbelief: 'I saw you while you were still under the fig tree before Philip called you' (1:48). Exactly what Nathanael was doing under a fig tree is a mystery to us, and a guesstimate is all one can offer (perhaps praying, meditating, fasting, or experiencing a vision).[33] At any rate, Nathanael is so impressed with Jesus' mysterious knowledge of his whereabouts that he confesses: 'Rabbi, you are the Son of God; you are the king of Israel' (1:49). As in 1:41, the expressive outburst of confession of Jesus as the Messiah does not seem to follow from the evidence. A mysterious knowledge hardly necessitates a messianic identity. However, for Nathanael (and the evangelist) there is no other category comprehensive and full enough to explicate who Jesus is. He is a rabbi, but also 'Son of God' and 'king of Israel'. 'King of Israel' in fact defines 'Son of God' as messianic and avoids purely pagan associations with the designation 'Son'.[34] Here 'king of Israel' in 1:49 stands as a messianic title conceptually similar to 'Messiah' in 1:41.[35] The final two titles are equivalents, and define the Messiah as a special son and a special ruler. Reference to Jesus as the 'Son' and 'king' will appear again in the Gospel, often in a context of unbelief and confrontation.

Attached to the excited effusion of messianic faith from Andrew, Philip, and now Nathanael is Jesus' enigmatic response to Nathanael: 'Jesus said, "You believe because I told you I saw you under the fig tree. You will see greater things than that." He then added, "Very truly I tell you, you will see 'heaven open, and the angels of God ascending and descending on' the Son of Man"' (1:50-51). The scriptural background is Genesis 28:12-17: Jacob's vision of the heavenly ladder in the Bethel narrative. My understanding of this text is that as Jacob inherits the Abrahamic promises as the representative of Israel, so the Son of Man inherits them as the representative of a new Israel. The 'greater things' pertain to the signs in the rest of the Gospel, signs designating Jesus as the inheritor of these promises, and the guarantor of a divine promise of eternal life. These signs constitute the opened heavens, the apocalyptic revelation of Jesus as Son of Man, and the glory of his passion and resurrection. The fulfilment of the promise pertaining to the Father's attestation of the Son and the privilege of seeing the glory of the Son of Man – these emerge throughout the Gospel of John and attain their zenith in Jesus' death and resurrection.[36]

The Johannine Son of Man combines elements of Jesus' self-reference, a new Israel, a renewed humanity, a mediator between heaven and earth, and a messianic vocation. The full extent of his messianic task is exercised in his role as the Son of Man who shows forth divine glory in his signs and sufferings, and transcends the division between God and humanity. As such, the full weight of 'Son of Man' encompasses all of Jesus' ministry, including his life, resurrection, and exaltation. All in all: 'The identification of the heaven-sent Son of Man with Jesus the Messiah and Son of God is at the centre of John's gospel.'[37] Therefore, the 'Son of Man' designation functions to qualify the other designations – Messiah, Lamb of God, Elect One, Son of God, and King of Israel – in line with an equally Jewish hope for a restored Israel, a renewed humanity, and a revelation of the Messiah. As Benjamin Reynolds concludes:

> The apocalyptic nature of the Son of Man highlights the unique Christological meaning of 'Son of Man' as a heavenly pre-existent figure who is the Messiah, brings judgment and salvation, is similar to God, is recognized, and gathers the righteous. The title 'Son of Man' functions alongside 'Son of God' and 'Messiah' to present a richer portrait of Jesus in the Gospel of John's Christological bouquet.[38]

The preparations for Jesus' public ministry are now complete in the witness of the Baptist, the messianic profession of the disciples, and Jesus' own affirmation of his person as the 'Son of Man'. Placed on the narrative table are Jesus' pre-existence, his unique relationship to the Father as Son, the co-ordinates of his scriptural work as 'Messiah', his royal authority as king, and his being the arch-representative of the new Israel. In 1:19–51 we find language about seeking, coming, finding, following, staying, and confessing. This episode invites readers/hearers to respond in discipleship like the first followers. To respond properly means having a right view of Jesus' person. The opening scenes of John's Gospel anticipate the conclusion that 'Jesus is the Messiah' (John 20:31), and the rest of the story becomes a demonstration of the divine glory that is bound up with the sending of the Son of God and the lifting up of the Son of Man.[39]

### The signs of the Son: meetings with the Messiah (John 2:1 – 13:38)

In the unfolding narrative of the first half of the Gospel, John develops his theological purposes primarily through Jesus' signs and the various encounters that Jesus has with several persons. What loiters around the episodes, signs, and encounters is the pressing question of Jesus' identity in light of the robust messianic affirmation of the prologue, John the Baptist, and Jesus' first followers. Thus, the reader has insider knowledge of who Jesus is, while the tension in the story is created by the other characters in the plot who fail to grasp the significance of the signs and don't understand that they are meeting the Messiah. The messianic identity of Jesus remains hidden from them, whether through ignorance, indecision, or unbelief. When the messianic cat gets let out of the scriptural bag, it is the occasion for faith – faith that finally grasps the meaning of Jesus' testimony that he was sent by the Father. Viewed this way, John has his own version of the messianic secret.[40] Jesus' identity is openly mooted by the characters, but the secret of his messiahship and origins is known only to select characters (and to the reader). These people know, however imperfectly, that despite all objections he *is* the Messiah, and despite doubts and conjectures, he is *from* God. The secret identity of Jesus is manifested in his sign miracles and discourses, and in his conversations with individual characters. The eyes of faith enable one to penetrate the veil of secrecy.[42]

The signs elicit faith, albeit at times a superficial faith, but they also constitute a large part of the testimony to Jesus' glory. Several of these signs contain allusions and echoes of messianic themes. The first sign, that of turning the water into wine at Cana (2:1–11), climaxes in the complaint of the master of the banquet to the bridegroom: 'Everyone brings out the choice wine first and then the cheaper wine after the guests have had too much to drink; but you have saved the best till now' (2:10). The remark functions on a number of levels. Jesus rescues the honour of the bridegroom, and his own honour accordingly increases. Jesus, though a wedding guest, fulfils and exceeds the role of the bride-groom in what he provides. In many ways he is the ultimate bridegroom. The Baptist will provide further testimony to this when he again denies that he is the Messiah and accepts his role of waiting for the bridegroom, who is the Messiah (3:28–29). The picture of Jesus as the bridegroom is indebted to the Old Testament imagery of Israel as the bride of Yahweh (Isa. 62:4–5; Jer. 2:2; 3:20; Ezek. 16:8; 23:4; Hos. 2:19–20), and several New Testament texts designate the church as the bride of Christ (2 Cor. 11:2; Eph. 5:25). We find Jesus portrayed explicitly in Revelation as the Messiah who is the bridegroom of the messianic commu-nity (Rev. 19:7–9; 21:2; 22:17). Although no extant Jewish writing equates the Messiah with the bridegroom of Israel,[43] that is argu-ably the assertion that is made in both the Gospel of John and the Apocalypse of John.[44]

In John 2:1–11 is the introduction of Jesus as the true bride-groom (of Israel) who supplies (new) wine for the (messianic) wedding feast. John 3:29 again identifies Jesus as the bridegroom of a new Israel.[45] That would imply an innovative tradition of messianic exegesis of Old Testament texts describing Yahweh's marriage with Israel, taken up to describe the relationship of Jesus to his followers.[46] Furthermore, the parabolic and terse comment of the banquet master builds on the comment made at the end of the prologue: 'the law was given through Moses; grace and truth came through Jesus Christ' (1:17). The best comes last; the good wine of the messianic age has been saved 'until now'! At Qumran, the messiahs of Aaron and Israel would preside over a banquet with the covenanters where 'new wine' would be served (1QSa 2.17–21). Note also the biblical promise that at the restoration of the Davidic monarch, God would pour out his favour on Israel so that:

> New wine will drip from the mountains
>> and flow from all the hills,
>> and I will bring my people Israel back from exile
>>> (Amos 9:13–14).

What must also be noted is that depiction of Jesus as the bride-groom and new wine in close order is found in the synoptic tradi-tion (Mark 2:18–22/Matt. 9:14–17/Luke 5:33–39). Thus in the wedding at Cana, John the evangelist amplifies the synoptic tradition that Jesus is the messianic bridegroom of the people of God, and he is the new wine of the new age, symbolic of the joy associated with the messianic banquet.

A second sign rich with messianic significance is Jesus' demon-stration in the temple in John 2:12–25. The synoptic tradition treats the temple demonstration as a symbolic act of judgement against the temple and its leadership for its fermentation of vio-lent nationalism and exclusion of the Gentiles from worship (Mark 11:15–17/Matt. 21:12–13/Luke 19:45–46).[47] In the Johan-nine version, Jesus comes to Jerusalem from Capernaum for the Passover (2:12–13), enters the temple precincts where merchants are selling animals and exchanging currencies, and responds by violently driving the sheep and cattle from the temple and over-turning the money tables (2:14–15). In John's telling, Jesus appears to identify the error of the temple's operation as chiefly economic, by turning a sacred space into a place of commerce and a means of financial exploitation: 'Get these out of here! Stop turning my Father's house into a market!' (2:16). A legitimate point, since the temple and its establishment were linked with economic oppression. During the Jewish War, when the zealots took over the temple, the first thing they did was burn the records of debt kept in the temple.[48] Josephus also noted that priests sent their servants, who 'would go to the threshing floors and take by force the tithes of the priests; nor did they refrain from beating those who refused to give.'[49] The temple was long associated and remembered in Jewish sources as an instrument of corruption and ill-gotten gain.[50]

In a post-resurrection cameo, the Evangelist comments that this incident in the temple later reminded Jesus' disciples of Psalm 69:9 about 'zeal' for God's 'house' (2:17). The response of Judean leaders to his provocative action is to ask Jesus, 'What sign can you show us to prove your authority to do all this?' (2:18). Jesus accordingly responds: 'Destroy this temple, and I will raise it again in three days' (2:19). The Judean leaders' reply is that Jesus' belief in rebuilding the temple in merely three days is ridiculously unrealistic: 'It has taken forty-six years to build this temple, and you are going to raise it in three days?' (2:20). Unbeknownst to them, 'the temple he had spoken of was his body', and the disciples remembered this after he was raised from the dead (2:21–22). The fulcrum of the pericope is Jesus' climactic pronouncement, 'Destroy this temple, and I will raise it again in three days' (2:19). The same words appear in the synoptic tradition, but as a charge by 'false witnesses' at Jesus' trial (Mark 14:58/Matt. 26:61) and as a mocking taunt at his crucifixion (Mark 15:29–30/Matt. 27:39–40). It also appears in the *Gospel of Thomas* (71), and Stephen is accused of teaching that Jesus would 'destroy this place and change the customs Moses handed down to us' (Acts 6:14). In my mind the saying is undoubtedly authentic[51] and it reflects the view that Jesus saw himself as the 'architect, sponsor and representative' of the new temple, to the point that Jesus 'was the temple' and he saw himself as 'its extension into the future'.[52] The statement is pregnant with messianic significance. The Davidic covenant announced in 2 Samuel 7:12–14 makes the 'offspring' of David the builder of the temple ('He . . . will build a house for my Name, and I will establish the throne of his kingdom forever'). This point is repeated elsewhere in the Old Testament where the 'shepherd' of Isaiah will rebuild the temple (Isa. 44:28 – 45:1), as will the 'branch' announced in Zechariah (Zech. 6:12–13). The coming anointed figure is a temple-builder, a point that is emphasized in various Jewish traditions.[53] This is not the mere protest of an agitated reformer, but rather it is a sign of the advent of the Messiah. The action proceeds from a messianic vocation.[54] We must grant the intramural Jewish debates over what kind of new temple would be erected and acknowledge that some believed that God alone would build it. Even so, there was a vibrant tradition that closely identified the task of building the temple as that of the Messiah.[55] Nick Perrin perfectly captures John's appropriation of this saying of Jesus:

> The early Christians had a post-Easter vantage point from which at a very early stage they correlated Jesus' messiahship and resurrection. Retrospective reflection on Jesus' messianic claim to rebuild the temple, followed by sightings of the risen Jesus and the empty tomb, must have quickly led the post-Easter community to

conclude that Jesus' self-representation as the final temple-builder was now vindicated by his rising from the dead. The risen Jesus had proven himself to be the true and everlasting cornerstone for the true and everlasting temple. In attaching themselves to the risen Christ, the early Christians had declared their union with the unfolding eschatological temple.[56]

Thus, for John, Jesus is both the messianic temple-builder and the embodiment of God's glory as the new temple itself.

Out of the various encounters that Jesus has with key figures, the encounter that makes the most of the messianic theme is the exchange that takes place between Jesus and the Samaritan woman (John 4:1–42). The substance of the dialogue focuses on 'Living Water' (4:4–14), 'The Woman's Husbands' (4:15–19), 'Worship True and False' (4:20–26), and 'The Woman's Witness' (4:27–30). In terms of the christological affirmations of this section, the woman affirms that Jesus is a prophet because of his knowledge of her circumstance (4:19). This leads to her pressing question – the one that divided Jews and Samaritans – about the proper place of worship: Jerusalem or Mount Gerizim (4:20). Jesus' response is that what matters is not the place of worship, but worship performed 'in the Spirit and in truth' (4:23–24). The 'Spirit' here is not the human spirit, but the Holy Spirit who inspires the worship of the believing community. It is the believer's experience with God's Spirit that can replace the Jerusalem temple and Mount Gerizim as the place of worship.[57] Furthermore, the co-location of 'Spirit' and 'truth' is a hendiadys, as in 3:5, for 'water and Spirit'. 'Spirit and truth' stands for 'Spirit of truth' (14:17; 15:26; 16:13). Given that in the Fourth Gospel Jesus epitomizes 'truth' (1:14,17; 8:32; 14:6; 18:37), the experience of the Spirit is grounded in experience of Jesus in worship.[58] Jesus' remarks about worship and Spirit lead the woman to move to a new subject, namely, the Messiah. 'The woman said, "I know that Messiah" (called Christ) "is coming. When he comes, he will explain everything to us." Then Jesus declared, "I, the one speaking to you – I am he"' (John 4:25–26). It is not a radical turn to a new topic, as C.K. Barrett observes: 'The woman is not merely catching at a straw to divert the argument; she grasps the messianic bearing of the reference to worship in Spirit and truth'. In a parenthetical remark, John once more translates Μεσσίας as Χριστός (see 1:38,41). Evidently, Jews and Samaritans both expected a messianic figure (ὅταν ἔλθῃ ἐκεῖνος ['when that one comes'] might hint at a general concept of a 'coming one').[60] Yet sources indicate that the Samaritans had a specific conception of a Messiah as the 'Taheb' (תהב), who would be a prophet like Moses, as described in Deuteronomy 18:15, one who would return and restore all things. In the Samaritan woman's view the Messiah would 'explain everything to [them]'. The verb for 'explain' is ἀναγγέλω which means 'to announce' or 'declare' (which is also used to described the ministry of the *paraclete* in 16:13–15). The notion of a Messiah who teaches is virtually non-existent in Jewish sources, though what John has to say here can be correlated with Matthew's Jesus, who is revered as the 'only teacher' (Matt. 23:10). The concept of a Messiah with a didactic office is indebted primarily to the Johannine (and perhaps more generally early Christian) claim that the Messiah is a revealer of truth. Jesus' response makes a clear affirmation, just as explicit as his words in the trial before the Sanhedrin (Mark 14:62 and parallels), that he is the Messiah. The words Ἐγώ εἰμι ὁ λαλῶν σοι ('I the one speaking to you am he', my trans.) are the first of the absolute 'I am' sayings in the Fourth Gospel (see 6:20; 8:23,28,58; 13:19; 18:5,6,8). On the surface Jesus' affirmation means no more than 'I am the Messiah you just mentioned.' Yet as one reads on, it is clear that Jesus is claiming not just messiahship but divine identity.[61] The self-description is significant because of its biblical background in Hebrew (אני הוא) and in the Greek translation (ἐγώ εἰμι) as a stated profession of divine identity and strict monotheism (e.g. Deut. 32:39; Isa. 41:4; 43:10; 46:4). Just as the 'I am [he]' statements in the Hebrew Bible sum up what it is to be truly God, so in the Gospel of John, the 'I am' sayings identify Jesus as truly God in the fullest sense.[62]

After this conversation, the Samaritan woman leaves and testifies to her townspeople: 'Come, see a man who told me everything I ever did. Could this be the Messiah?' (4:29). Her action mirrors that of Andrew and Philip, who testify to Jesus' messianic identity to others shortly after meeting him. The result of her testimony speaks for itself: 'Many of the Samaritans from that town believed in him because of the woman's testimony' (4:39).

Then, after hearing Jesus' many words for themselves, the people in turn tell the woman: 'We no longer believe just because of what you said; now we have heard for ourselves, and we know that this man really is the Saviour of the world' (4:42). The Samaritans come to recognize that Jesus, Israel's Messiah, is the 'saviour of the world' and are enlisted as witnesses to Jesus' *Jewish* and *messianic* status as the God-sent saving agent. This is part of a theme that has been seen before in John's Gospel: faith comes from testimony, and the testimony is that Jesus is the Messiah – a Messiah of God, from God, who is God!

A close link between prophecy and kingship has been made at several places in the Fourth Gospel (see 1:20–25,45–49; 4:19,25) and is stated again in 6:14–15.[63] We are told that after the feeding miracle by the Sea of Galilee, 'the people saw the sign Jesus performed [and] they began to say, "Surely this is the Prophet who is to come into the world." Jesus, knowing that they intended to come and make him king by force, withdrew again to a mountain by himself.' The 'signs' that Jesus performed for the sick (6:2) led the crowd to follow after him. Then, after experiencing the 'sign' that Jesus did in multiplying the loaves and fishes, the people are even more excited about his miraculous abilities and intend to make him king by force. Jesus is a regular moveable feast, and who better than him to provide for the people as their king? In the crowd's estimation, he is 'the Prophet', which is undoubtedly the figure denoted in Deuteronomy 18:15: 'The LORD your God will raise up for you a prophet like me from among you, from your own people. You must listen to him.' The reader knows by now that Jesus is aligned with Moses (1:45; 5:46), but also exceeds Moses as a revealer from God (1:17) and saviour of the people (3:14–15; 6:32). The coming prophet-like-Moses is the figure whom the Baptist denied being (1:21,25–26), the person implied in Philip's recognition of Jesus as 'the one Moses wrote about in the Law' (1:45), and the same prophetic figure the Samaritan woman regarded as the Taheb (4:19). Specifically, the crowd believes that he is the 'coming' prophet (ὁ ἐρχόμενος, which coheres with the theme of Jesus as *the* 'coming one' as far back as the prologue. Jesus comes to the world (3:17,19 and later 9:39; 10:36; 11:27; 12:46; 16:28; 17:18; 18:37) as he is the 'Saviour of the world' (4:42).

The switch from 'prophet' to 'king' might seem abrupt and out of place. However, the same switch has already occurred in Philip's testimony to Jesus as the one about whom Moses wrote and Nathanael's confession that Jesus is 'the king of Israel' (1:45,49). On top of that, Philo spasmodically described Moses as a kingly figure. Philo goes so far as to say that through God's providence Moses became 'king and lawgiver and high priest and prophet' (Philo, *Vit. Mos.* 2.3) and that 'he did not become king in the ordinary way by the aid of troops and weapons or of the might of ships and infantry and cavalry. It was God who appointed him by the free judgement of his subjects, God who created in them the willingness to choose him as their sovereign' (Philo, *Praem. Poens.* 54). The evangelist also places Jesus in this Mosaic tradition of a prophetic king or kingly prophet. Though the people are right in their profession of Jesus' kingship, they are desirous of Jesus to reign over them without understanding the proper nature of his kingship, and their kingly aspirations are based inadequately upon the signs rather than upon faith. Though Jesus is king and Messiah, he is such on God's terms, not theirs.[64] It will be the passion narrative that shows the true nature of Jesus' kingship.

The developing tension in the Gospel of John centres on the Judeans' failure to believe that Jesus is the Messiah and on their rejection of his claims to have been sent by the Father. The point where this tension comes to a head is in John 7:25–44 at the Feast of Tabernacles. Following Jesus' teachings in the temple during the feast (7:14–24), a number of reactions are attributed to the people (i.e. pilgrims) in Jerusalem in their subsequent deliberations about Jesus' identity. The people are perplexed by two things. First, that Jesus is speaking in public when the authorities have privately condemned him. Does this refusal to act against Jesus suggest that the rulers have changed their mind because they know or suspect that he actually is the Messiah after all (7:26)? Second, the Jerusalemites wonder whether Jesus should logically be disqualified as the Messiah because they 'know' where Jesus is from, yet no-one is supposed to know where the Messiah is from. They answer their own question when they collectively profess: 'We know where this man is from; when the Messiah comes, no one will know where he is from' (7:27). In the background here is the view that the Messiah will be hidden until he is revealed (see Isa. 32:1–2 [LXX]; Amos 4:13; *1 Enoch* 48.3; 62.6–7; *4 Ezra* 12.32; 13.26,32,52; *2 Bar.* 29.3; 30.1; 39.7; Justin, *Dial. Tryph.* 8.4; 49.1; 110.1). The problem is that although they claim to 'know' Jesus' origins – that he is probably from Nazareth of Galilee and is a son of Joseph (see 1:45; 6:42) – they don't really know where he is from. In fact, later, the man born blind who has his sight restored is amazed that the Pharisees do not know where Jesus is from (9:30).

For the reader, Jesus' origins are inscrutable and mysterious since he is 'from above' (3:31) and 'from heaven' (3:13,31; 6:32–33,38,42,50–51). The logical response of Jesus should have been to say: 'No, you don't know where I am from. You only think you do. I am from above. Consequently, I am the Messiah.' But that's not what he says.[65] While teaching in the temple Jesus cries out: 'Yes, you know me, and you know where I am from. I am not here on my own authority, but he who sent me is true. You do not know him, but I know him because I am from him and he sent me' (7:28–29). We are probably meant to hear a note of irony regarding what the crowds *claim to know* and what they *should know* about Jesus' origins. Jesus avoids confrontation on the messianic issue and focuses on his mission from the one who sent him, namely, the Father. If the crowds 'know' Jesus' origin as they think they do, then they will know that his origin is not a place but a Person.[66] Jesus' words bring division, as some (presumably the authorities) tried unsuccessfully to seize him (7:30); but we are told that as a result, 'many in the crowd put their faith in him. They said, "When the Messiah comes, will he perform more signs than this man?"' (7:31).

Though Jesus' origins may prove inconsistent with their default messianic ideas, Jesus' signs are compelling demonstrations of his messianic identity. It is not the case that a link between miracles and messianism shows that what 'we have here is not Jewish but Christian messianic dogma'.[67] A link between miracles and messianism was plausible in Jewish hopes because there was a Jewish tradition of David and Solomon as healers/exorcists, Matthew refers to Jesus' miraculous feats as the 'deeds of the Messiah' (Matt. 11:2), 4Q521 2.1–10 from Qumran associates a messianic figure with Isaianic workings such as healings, and the Olivet Discourse in the Synoptic Gospels identifies false messiahs and false prophets who perform 'signs' (Mark 13:22/Matt. 24:24). Jewish messianism was a developing and fluid tradition of exegesis, and some persons seem to have attributed miracle-working abilities to the Messiah in his role.[68] In any case, among the Jerusalem pilgrims it is the signs that evoke belief in Jesus as the Messiah, though their faith is expressed in little more than 'whispering', which does not strike confidence in the reader that their faith is sufficiently rooted in Jesus' testimony (7:32).

The people in the crowd think that the authorities are trying to kill Jesus (7:25), and their suspicion is confirmed when the chief priests and Pharisees dispatch temple guards to arrest him (7:32). It is assumed that Jesus eludes the guards, and we are given only his allusive words about going away and not being found, prompting confusion about where he is going (7:33–36). The fact that they don't recognize his messianic coming means that they have even less chance of understanding his glorious departure to be with the Father. Then, Jesus makes a dramatic appeal, on the final day of the Feast of Tabernacles, concerning the promise of 'living water', which is the Spirit for those who believe in him. Jesus is the Spirit-baptizing and Spirit-birthing messianic agent who dispenses the Spirit to the people (7:37–39; cf. 1:32–33). The response of the people to Jesus' words is mixed: 'On hearing his words, some of the people said, "Surely this man is the Prophet." Others said, "He is the Messiah." Still others asked, "How can the Messiah come from Galilee? Does not Scripture say that the Messiah will come from David's descendants and from Bethlehem, the town where David lived?" Thus the people were divided because of Jesus' (John 7:40–43).

The coming 'prophet like Moses' and the Messiah are separate individuals in the questions posed to John the Baptist (1:19–21) and for the Qumranites (e.g. 1QS 9.11). Yet it is unlikely that two types of eschatological expectations are being played off against each other. For a start, the evangelist regards Jesus as the climax of the Law and the Prophets, which contain prophetic and royal figures in their hopes. On top of that, Philip's confession, 'We have found the one Moses wrote about in the Law', that is, the Mosaic prophet (1:45), is matched by Nathanael's confession that

Jesus is Son of God and king of Israel, i.e. the Messiah (1:49). In the banter of the people, Jesus' messianic status, featuring the categories of Messiah and prophet, belong and blend together.[69] It is probable that Christian interpreters were among the first to equate the Mosaic prophet with the Messiah.[70] In any case, the Mosaic 'prophet' and Davidic 'Messiah' equivalency is stated rather than explained. Although the roles of prophet and Messiah are not strictly synonymous, they evidently overlap in the sense of being eschatological deliverers anointed by God who 'come' to Israel at an appointed time. Since Moses was the means by which God gave the people water to drink in the wilderness (Exod. 17:1–6; Num. 20:1–11; 1 Cor. 10:4), Jesus' claim to be able to provide 'living water' convinced them that he was Moses' prophesied successor. Concerning the eschatological successor to Moses, *Eccles. Rab.* 1.9 declares of this figure, 'As the former redeemer made a well to rise [Num. 21:17–18], so will the latter Redeemer bring up water [Joel 3:18]'.[71] In addition, some strands of messianic expectation associated the Messiah with springs of wisdom from which the people were to drink (*1 Enoch* 48.1,10; 49.1). Jesus, then, is a new Moses and an anointed dispenser of the refreshing waters of the Holy Spirit.

A critical rejoinder is raised by others, who object to describing Jesus in such terms, on the grounds that the Messiah does not come from Galilee, but from Bethlehem (7:41). A similar objection was canvassed earlier by Nathanael, who was incredulous at the notion that the prophet Moses spoke about would hail from the backwater rustic town of Nazareth (1:45–46), though Nathanael soon changed his tune and confessed Jesus as 'king of Israel' (1:49). The expectation of a Davidic Messiah coming from Bethlehem derives from Micah 5:2 and is affirmed as a Jewish hope here in John 7:42 and in Matthew 2:1–16.[72] Most likely, though John does not explicitly mention Jesus' birth in Bethlehem, the evangelist and his readers are aware of the traditions behind Luke and Matthew concerning Jesus' birth in Bethlehem. The episode is ironic, because what some regard as an objection to Jesus' messiahship is for John and his readers actually an affirmation of it, because they know that Jesus was born in Bethlehem and that he comes from David's line. The objectors misunderstand Jesus' true origins – both his heavenly origins and the circumstances of his earthly birth – since if they knew from where Jesus hailed, they would have grounds, not grievance, for Jesus' messianic claim.[73]

Taken together, 7:25–27 and 7:40–43 concern the question of where the Messiah is from. We have a window here into Jewish speculations about the question of 'whence cometh the Messiah', and it is evident that Jewish views were polarized around Bethlehem for a Davidic Messiah and mysterious origins for a transcendent Messiah. The pilgrims in Jerusalem see Jesus' signs and are seemingly led to infer his messianic status, but then shrink from doing so since his origins are neither mysteriously shrouded nor prophetically plum in their estimation. Unbelief is fostered by two mutually exclusive objections: no-one knows where the Messiah is from, and the Messiah comes from Bethlehem. By their own criteria Jesus could not satisfy both objections. If it was known that he came from Bethlehem some could protest that the Messiah's origins are meant to be unknown, and vice versa. The content of the objections is actually true. The Messiah *is* mysterious in origins and Davidic in pedigree, but the problem is that the Jerusalemites do not know where Jesus comes from. No-one understands his heavenly origins, and in the tradition known to the evangelist he is obviously from Bethlehem and David's line. If the Judeans knew that he was sent from God and born in Bethlehem, as narrated in Christian testimony, then they would have no objection to his messianic claims. Thus Jesus' identity creates a division in Israel between those who accept the testimony to Jesus' origins, and those who reject it and the messianic claims that go with it.

The rejection is cemented by the warning from the Judean authorities that followers of Jesus will be 'dis-synagogued', that is, expelled from the synagogues, if they confess that Jesus is the Messiah. After Jesus heals the man born blind, an investigation is launched by the Pharisees because of concern that Jesus had broken the law pertaining to the Sabbath (see John 9:1–41). This would constitute a serious infringement of the Jewish law according to Pharisaic interpretation and so warrants an informal inquiry. The man who was blind is interrogated at length and so are his parents. His parents, fearing for their welfare before the pharisaic inquest, deny any knowledge of how their son was cured – admitting only that he was indeed born blind (9:19–21).

The reason for their concern is explained in 9:22: 'His parents said this because they were afraid of the Jewish leaders, who already had decided that anyone who acknowledged that Jesus was the Messiah would be put out of the synagogue' (ἐάν τις αὐτὸν ὁμολογήσῃ Χριστόν, ἀποσυνάγωγος γένηται). A similar warning about being expelled from the synagogue on account of faith in Jesus, specifically faith in him as Messiah, is issued later in John 12:42 and 16:2.

Often, these warnings of being expelled from the synagogue are regarded as anachronistic intrusions of events from the life setting of the Johannine community that are projected back into Jesus' life. The fact of the matter is that Jewish-Christian relationships in the late first century were volatile and even vitriolic, depending on the location (e.g. see Rev. 2:9 and 3:9 about the 'synagogue of Satan' referred to by John the Seer, nominating Jewish groups in Smyrna and Philadelphia). Much of the polemic and in-fighting seems to be that of species of insiders haggling over how to be Israel in the post-70 AD era. But there is no evidence for a widespread and universal expulsion of Jewish Christians from the synagogues in the late first century (the so-called *Birkat ha-Minim* or 'Benediction against the Heretics' supposedly promulgated by a pharisaic council at Jamia). Allegiance to a Messiah was not considered grounds for temporary expulsion in sources, as far as is known. More likely, expulsions against Christians were spasmodic, caused by local pressures, due to individual temperaments, and perhaps even meant to be temporary. There is no doubt in my mind that Jewish Christians and their clientele of Gentile adherents suffered social ostracizing from their Jewish contemporaries, and the synagogue expulsion passages found in John reflect such experiences. After all, all story-telling imports something of the situation of the storyteller into the act of storytelling itself!

But let us remember that Jesus excited debate and division in his own day, and already his followers were confronted with criticism and warned about punitive action because of their decision to follow him (see Matt. 10:23; 24:9; John 15:20; Acts 22:4). In the synoptic tradition, Jesus warned them about interrogation in synagogues for their faith and anticipated punishments like floggings (Matt. 10:17; 23:34; Mark 13:9; Luke 12:11; 21:12). On top of that, tensions between followers of Jesus and the leadership of the temple and the Diaspora synagogues went back to the earliest days of the Jerusalem church and extended to Paul's missionary endeavours.[74] Opposition to Christians, their theology and their practices, did not begin in AD 90—in which case, the best way to understand the synagogue expulsion passages in John is that they conflate the memory of Jesus and his first followers as rejected by their audiences with the subsequent experiences of his followers as ejected from Jewish assemblies on account of their faith. Profession of Jesus as the Messiah was just as controversial and contentious in Jesus' day as it was at the time of John's readers. Given the temptation of many to deny such a confession, the importance of confession of Jesus as the Messiah is clearly accentuated (see 1 John 2:22; 5:1). What links followers of Jesus, both pre- and post-Easter, is the belief that Jesus is the Messiah, the king of Israel, and Son of God.

John 9 – 12 narrates and nominates the identity of Jesus as Israel's Messiah despite the opposition that mounts against him. In each case, the messiahship of Jesus is both affirmed and enhanced by the addition of new information as to what kind of Messiah he is. The revelation of Jesus as Messiah is defined by way of the Messiah as healer (John 9), the Messiah as shepherd (John 10), the Messiah as life-giver (John 11), and the Messiah as king (John 12). There is a repetition of themes related to signs, blindness, testimony, unbelief, and Jesus as the Son of Man. These provide the christological context in which Jesus' death and resurrection are to be understood in John 13 – 21. The passion and resurrection of Jesus will provide testimony to the glory that God has revealed in Jesus the Messiah.

John 9 concerns Jesus' healing of the man born blind. The whole chapter is largely symbolic of the spiritual blindness of the Pharisees who refuse to believe in Jesus. They reject the authenticity of the miracle and Jesus' authority because he does not keep the Sabbath so is not from God (9:16), he is a sinner (9:16,24–25), and they do not know where he is from (9:29). Their opposition reaches the point where the Jewish leaders decide that anyone who acknowledges that Jesus is the Messiah is to be put out of the synagogue (9:22). The man born blind has a clever rejoinder to his interrogators: 'Now that is remarkable!

You don't know where he comes from, yet he opened my eyes. We know that God does not listen to sinners. He listens to the godly person who does his will. Nobody has ever heard of opening the eyes of a man born blind. If this man were not from God, he could do nothing' (John 9:30–33). The point is that the power of Jesus' actions speaks louder than the depth of the Pharisees' objections. The signs demand that he is sent from God and that he be acknowledged as such. Later, Jesus finds the man and asks, 'Do you believe in the Son of Man?' (9:35). Whereas one might expect to find the title 'Son of God' or 'Messiah' used, the title 'Son of Man' is employed for two reasons. First, as with Nicodemus in 3:13, the author wants to emphasize Jesus' origin 'from God' (9:33). Second, the Son of Man, Jesus, has all authority to judge (5:25–29), which squares neatly with the subsequent exchange that Jesus has about the susceptibility of the Pharisees to judgment because of their claiming to see (John 9:39–41).[75] Taken together, the sign of healing signifies Jesus' messianic identity, proves his origins as one sent from God, and demonstrates his judicial authority as the Son of Man.[76]

There is no shift in location or context from John 9 to John 10. The subsequent 'good shepherd' discourse is a continuation of Jesus' response to the Pharisees. Whereas John 9 focuses on Jesus as authorized by God on account of his signs, John 10 centres on the singular suitability of Jesus to be the leader of God's people on account of his self-giving actions. The climax of the discourse is obviously the 'I am' statement: 'I am the good shepherd' (10:11,14). The shepherd metaphor concerns the intimate care and sacrificial protection that Jesus gives to the sheep as their leader. However, no-one can escape the regal imagery, because in the ancient Near Eastern sources and in Greco-Roman traditions a 'shepherd' was primarily an image for kings. The Egyptian monarch Amenhotep III (1411–1374 BC) was called 'the good shepherd, vigilant for all people, whom the maker thereof has placed under his authority'. The Homeric phrase 'shepherd of the hosts' referred to a commander of military forces.[77] In the Old Testament, the metaphor of a shepherd is applied both to Yahweh and to ancient kings. To give a few examples, first, concerning Yahweh, Isaiah contains the words:

See, the Sovereign LORD comes with power,
and his arm rules for him.
See, his reward is with him,
and his recompense accompanies him.
He tends his flock like a shepherd:
He gathers the lambs in his arms
and carries them close to his heart;
he gently leads those that have young (Isa. 40:10–11).

The Lord of the nations guides them into the pastures of a restored land like a shepherd directing a flock. Second, it is interesting that Cyrus is labelled as 'my shepherd' in Isa. 44:28 and '[my] anointed' in Isa. 45:1. He was the anointed shepherd used by Yahweh to end the exile of the remnant in Babylon. Third, the quintessential shepherd-king was David, the shepherd boy who became a king. At Hebron, the tribes reminded David that the Lord had said to him: 'It is you who shall be shepherd of my people Israel, you who shall be ruler over Israel' (2 Sam. 5:2, my trans.). The hope for a new Davidic king was the hope for a new shepherd-king to guide Israel into its day of restoration (Jer. 23:1–6; Mic. 5:1–9). In fact, Ezekiel 34 depicts the coming of Yahweh as Shepherd in and through the raising up of a new Davidic shepherd-king (Ezek. 34:16,23–24).[78]

The upshot of this is that when Jesus says, 'I am the good shepherd', we are not confronted with merely a claim pertaining to his quality of pastoral care-giving. It is a royal and even messianic claim. Jesus will be the restorer of Israel, exactly as is attributed to him elsewhere in the Gospel (1:11–12; 10:16; 11:47–52), and precisely what the Messiah was supposed to do. As Painter concludes: 'The shepherd parable is a parable concerning the rulers in Israel and it is right to conclude that the Good Shepherd is a messianic image.'[79] Furthermore, John 10 is analogous to the Animal Apocalypse found in *1 Enoch* 89 which focuses on shepherding as a key metaphor for national restoration. In *1 Enoch* the 'Lord of the sheep' leads Israel, brings them into pasture (89.42; 75; 90.29,33), and also gathers them into a new Jerusalem (90.32–36). In imagery reminiscent of Jeremiah 23 and Ezekiel 34 – 37, Jesus as the Good Shepherd is the true and benevolent shepherd who leads Israel into the pastures of restoration. Building specifically from Ezekiel 34, Jesus seems to take on the shepherding roles of both Yahweh and David. Jesus the Shepherd is contrasted with the false shepherds or the 'hirelings' – the Judean leaders and the Pharisees – who should have led people to their Messiah rather than hindering their faith and attempting to thwart Jesus' ministry at every turn. What will prove the true nature of Jesus' shepherding is when he lays down his life for the flock (10:15–18).[80]

Proof that Jesus' divine identity and messianic role is the presenting issue – not two issues, but two aspects combined of one debate about who Jesus is – is that the subsequent unit in John 10:22–39 explicitly raises the question of his messianic claims and his claims to equality with God. During the Feast of Dedication, whilst in Solomon's Colonnade, a cohort of Jews gather around him and demand from him: 'How long will you keep us in suspense? If you are the Messiah, tell us plainly' (10:24). This has been the dividing issue among the crowd (7:40–44), the Pharisees (9:16), and the Jews (10:19–21). Despite the surface issues of whether Jesus is demon-possessed, a sinner, or sent from God, there is the underlying matter of whether he is claiming to be the Messiah (see 7:26–27,31,41–42). The Jews confronting him want a plain answer, one not veiled in parabolic speech about bread, light, doors, and shepherds, but a straightforward answer. Jesus' response is that he has indeed told them directly (see too 18:20) because his signs speak for him. The problem is not the clarity of Jesus' discourse and deeds; rather, their disbelief is based on their refusal to believe in him and the Father who sent him (see 5:36–37,45; 8:19). That leads into Jesus' remarks about his unity with the Father, and their at-one-ness (10:30), culminating in a charge of blasphemy for Jesus, a mere man, claiming to be God (10:33; cf. 5:18; 8:58–59).

John 10 is thus evidence for a Christian conception of messiahship. The works of the Messiah for salvation and judgement are executed in such a manner that he appropriates divine prerogatives and speaks with divine authority. That inevitably requires a redefinition of both the Messiah and the identity of God in his agency towards Israel through the Messiah.

The raising of Lazarus in John 11 brings further tension to the plot and contributes to the messianic theme. In terms of the narrative, it is the raising of Lazarus that results in a coalition of chief priests and Pharisees, with the Sanhedrin plotting to arrest Jesus (11:45–57; 12:9–10). In regards to messianism, Jesus' exchange with Martha climaxes in her messianic confession. Jesus promises her that her brother will rise again (11:23). Martha agrees, looking ahead to the resurrection 'at the last day' (11:24), but Jesus speaks of a present experience where those who believe in him 'will live' and 'will never die' because '[he is] the resurrection and the life' (11:25–26). Her concurrence is given in the confession: 'Yes, Lord . . . I believe that you are the Messiah, the Son of God, who was to come into the world' (11:27). The shift from 'resurrection' to 'Messiah' is based on her acknowledgement that Jesus is the life-giver. Earlier, Jesus declared that like the Father he has 'life in himself' (5:26) and he 'will raise them [i.e. believers] up at the last day' (6:39–40,44,54). Because 'in him [is] life' (1:4), Jesus is able to mediate 'eternal life' by laying down his own life (6:51; 10:11,15,17). A vivifying Messiah is not really an innovation. The Johannine conception of the Messiah as life-giver is really an extension of his work as healer since healings can include bringing the dead back to life (see Matt. 9:23–26/Mark 5:38–43/Luke 8:49–56; Luke 7:11–16; Luke 7:22/Matt. 11:5; 4Q521 2.9). The purpose of the messianic confession is, we are told at the end, '[so] that by believing you may have life in his name' (20:31).

The use of the perfect tense in Martha's words (πεπίστευκα) and of emphatic pronouns (σὺ εἶ) is highly reminiscent of Peter's confession on behalf of the disciples: 'We have come to believe (πεπιστεύκαμεν) and to know that you are the Holy One of God (σὺ εἶ ὁ ἅγιος τοῦ θεοῦ)' (6:69). Though Jesus has been heralded as 'the Messiah' (7:26–27,31,41–42; 9:22; 10:24) and 'the Son of God' (5:18–25; 10:36) earlier, only here and in the purpose statement in 20:31 are ὁ Χριστὸς and ὁ υἱὸς τοῦ θεοῦ linked together. Martha's confession also includes another significant element of Jesus as the 'coming one' (ὁ ἐρχόμενος) that is equally prominent (1:9,15,27,30; 3:31; 4:25; 6:14; 7:31,41–42; 12:13,15,46; 14:3,28; 16:28; 21:22–23). The only other important titles missing are 'king' and 'prophet', and they are overshadowed by 'the Messiah' and 'the Son of God'. This suggests that 11:27 is the penultimate christological confession of the Gospel ahead of 20:31.

As Jesus' confrontation with the Jerusalem authorities looms, the theme switches to kingship. Although Jesus' anointing by

Martha is for his burial (12:7), it is hard to avoid the connotations of kingship associated with anointing. This is all the more plausible since the anointing at Bethany is followed by the triumphal entry, which rehearses Jesus' kingship for the first time since 6:14–15, when the Galileans tried to make Jesus king by force.

The triumphal entry begins with the crowd gathering for the Passover festival and hearing that Jesus is coming to Jerusalem. In reaction to this 'they took palm branches and went out to meet him' (12:13). Since the Maccabean revolt, palm branches had been associated with national liberation, and functioned as a symbol for Israel (see 1 *Macc.* 13.51; 2 *Macc.* 10.7). That the crowd went out to 'meet him' is notable because ὑπάντησις was often used in Greco-Roman contexts for the occasion when a regent paid an official visit to a city and leading citizens would go out to 'meet' him and escort him on the final stages of his journey to the city (see 1 Thess. 4:17). Jesus' coming to Jerusalem is thus a royal visitation by the national deliverer. This is underscored by the acclamation of the crowd: 'Hosanna! Blessed is he who comes in the name of the Lord! Blessed is the king of Israel!' *Hosanna* is a transliteration of an underlying Hebrew or Aramaic equivalent for 'Save us'. The 'coming' figure who occasions this appeal for jubilant salvation is defined as 'the king of Israel'. That title has already been applied to Jesus by Nathanael (1:49), and the derogatory epithet 'king of the Jews' will reappear during the trials and crucifixion (18:33,39; 19:12,19). Jesus is most certainly king, though the character of his kingdom and the charter of his kingship is defined by a heavenly order.

John follows synoptic tradition by recounting the acquisition of a donkey to facilitate the entry. What was implicit in Mark (Mark 11:2–7) becomes explicit in John, namely, that Jesus fulfils Zech. 9:9 by entering Jerusalem on a donkey as the shepherd-king. The accompanying employment of Psalm 118 depicts Jesus as the *ideal* king, the Davidic king of messianic hopes, but also much more than that. Jesus' kingship is of a transcendent quality since he is also the ascending and descending Son of Man, the Son of God sent by the Father, and the eternal Word. It is divine kingship, his role as the Shepherd of Israel, and the reign of Yahweh that is expressed in Jesus' entry into Jerusalem. A point confirmed by the citation of Zech. 9:9:

> Do not be afraid, Daughter Zion;
>> see, your king is coming,
>> seated on a donkey's colt (John 12:15).

and by the allusion to Zeph. 3:14–15:

> Sing, Daughter Zion;
>> shout aloud, Israel!
> Be glad and rejoice with all your heart,
>> Daughter Jerusalem!
> The LORD has taken away your punishment,
>> he has turned back your enemy.
> The LORD, the King of Israel, is with you;
>> never again will you fear any harm.

Thus, messianic fulfilment and theophany are merged.[81]

As expected, the messianic question comes up again during Jesus' ministry in Jerusalem. There is a dramatic interaction with the crowd in what follows the triumphal entry. The scriptural script of Jesus' entry was only apparent to the disciples after Jesus was glorified (12:16). The crowd spreads the word of the raising of Lazarus, bringing further concern from the Pharisees (12:17–19). The request of Greeks to see Jesus becomes a tripwire indicating that the time of Jesus' glory has come (12:23). This glorification means the death (like wheat falling to the ground) and the lifting up (like the snake in the wilderness, see earlier 3:14; 8:28) of the Son of Man (12:24–33). The people in the crowd, despite hearing a voice from heaven (12:28–29), are perplexed when Jesus remarks, 'I, when I am lifted up from the earth, will draw all people to myself' (12:32), and they collectively ponder: 'We have heard from the Law that the Messiah will remain forever, so how can you say, "The Son of Man must be lifted up?" Who is this Son of Man?' (12:34). Jesus has referred to his lifting up earlier in relation to his approaching death (3:14; 8:28), and the question about the Son of Man was also raised earlier (9:36). The people figure out that the 'Son of Man' is a significant person equivalent to the Messiah, and they are thus puzzled at the notion of the Messiah being 'lifted up'. Though John tells his readers that this means Jesus' death (12:33), for the crowd it seems to mean a rapture of the Messiah from the earth. That is difficult to reconcile with their expectation for the Messiah to remain (i.e. rule) forever as several scriptural texts suggest (see 2 Sam. 7:12–13; Ps. 89:28–29,35–37; Isa. 9:7; *Pss. Sol.* 17.4; Justin, *Dial. Tryph.* 32.1). John's testimony, much like that of the other evangelists, is that Jesus' death is intrinsic to his messianic role rather than a disqualification for it. For the glory of God is revealed in the crucifixion, and the divine voice sanctions the destiny of a crucified and glorified Messiah. The testimony of the evangelist is that Jesus is the Son of Man who descends and who will be lifted up on the cross. The questions posed to Jesus about the origins of the Messiah and the Son of Man are resolved by the evangelist (8:48–59; 12:44–50), who emphasizes the continuity between the Father and the Son, which transcends all speculations and leaves them behind.[82] We find: 'Again ironically, it is precisely his being lifted up that secures the benefits of his victory, so that his followers may abide with him.'[83]

## The Glory of the Messiah

John 12 finishes with energized emphasis on the glory of Jesus, that is to say, his death (12:16,23,41). The words δόξα ('glory') and δοξάζω ('glorify') are used frequently in the Fourth Gospel (the noun nineteen times and the verb twenty-three times). Indeed, the Johannine confession 'We have seen his glory', in the prologue, summarizes the testimony to Jesus offered by the evangelist and his supporters (1:14). In light of Jewish expectations about the Messiah and the ignominious fate of crucifixion that Jesus actually suffered, it would be natural to ask: In what possible sense can Jesus be the Messiah when his demise was so inglorious? The other evangelists address that objection by locating Jesus' glory in his resurrection and exaltation (esp. Luke), by regarding his death as a first-order proof of his messiahship (esp. Mark), and by making Jesus' death the means for salvific blessings won by Israel's king (esp. Matthew). Put together, the Messiah must suffer and then enter his glory (see esp. Luke 24:46 and the various sayings about the suffering Son of Man [Mark 9:12 etc.]). However, for the Beloved Disciple, the glory was there all the way through Jesus' ministry. It was there in the signs that he performed and at the height of his humiliation on the cross. The evangelist knows of Jesus' future glory after his resurrection (7:39; 12:16; 16:14), but he primarily believes that Jesus' death testifies to the glory and honour of God revealed in Jesus' death. Jesus' death is the ultimate sign of his glory (12:23,41; 13:31–32; 17:4). The penultimate glory is the signs, and the ultimate glory is the cross.[84]

In counter-distinction to the Synoptics, the dominating question at Jesus' trial before the Sanhedrin is not his messiahship or temple actions (e.g. Mark 14:57–64). Rather, Jesus is questioned about 'his disciples and his teaching' (18:19). Nevertheless, messianic claims do form part of the complaint against Jesus as the Judean leaders seek warrant for his execution from Pilate on the grounds that he is a royal pretender. When Caiaphas hands Jesus over to Pilate, the immediate question Jesus is confronted with is whether he is indeed 'the king of the Jews' (18:33), which comports with synoptic tradition (Matt. 27:11 / Mark 15:2 / Luke 23:3). The kingship of Jesus dominates the entire Roman trial and the crucifixion scene of the Johannine passion story (18:28 – 19:42). The out-of-nowhere accusation seems to occur because the evangelist is following the tradition that the trial was about the issue of Jesus' royal claims about himself.

Jesus' response to Pilate contains the words: 'My kingdom [kingship] is not of this world. If it were, my servants would fight to prevent my arrest by the Jewish leaders. But now my kingdom [kingship] is from another place' (18:36). Jesus' kingship (ἡ βασιλεία) is affirmed in much the same way that Jesus accepted Nathanael's confession of him as king and the crowd's acclamation of him as the coming king of Israel (12:13). What is denied is a misconception of his kingly authority as driven by earthly ambitions and material pursuits as in 6:14–15. When Jesus denies that his kingship is of 'this world' and asserts that it comes 'from another place', he is not retreating to an interiorized, subjective, and spiritual notion of kingdom. The denials do not so much define the nature of Jesus' kingship as locate its origin in somewhere exterior to the world. Jesus' kingship is 'from above' and 'from heaven' where he is from (see 3:13,31; 6:51; 8:23). Jesus' kingship is not from Rome or Jerusalem, but from the heavenly

Father. Thus Jesus' kingship is not merely spiritual, but eschato-logical; like the Holy City in Revelation, it is coming down out of heaven from God (Rev. 3:12; 21:2,10). Though Pilate pronounces Jesus' kingship benign and harmless, he is seemingly unaware of how dangerous it actually is.[85] Pilate responds rightly by noting the substance of Jesus' answer: 'You are a king, then!' (18:37). Jesus' reply begins with the enigmatic 'You say [so]' (see Matt. 27:11/Mark 15:2/Luke 23:3), which is perhaps idiomatic for 'Bingo, you got it in one'. But then a further qualification is added: 'In fact, the reason I was born and came into the world is to testify to the truth. Everyone on the side of truth listens to me' (18:37). Jesus is the coming one, who comes to the world with a revelation to the truth (see 1:9; 3:19; 9:39; 11:27; 12:46–47; 18:20). Jesus' role as king cannot be separated from his role as revealer.

In the aftermath of the Pilate-Jesus exchange, the opposition calling for Jesus' execution increases. The soldiers mock Jesus as 'king of the Jews' (19:3; see Matt. 27:29/Mark 15:18). When Pilate tries to release Jesus, the Judeans clamour, warning Pilate that anyone who defends a royal pretender is not a friend of Caesar, and threatening him with treason for failing to do their bidding (19:12). Such is the opposition to Jesus that the crowd is even reduced to accepting Barabbas over Jesus (18:40) and to profession of Caesar's kingship over that of Jesus (19:15) – both lawless banditry and domination by a foreign power were preferable to Jesus' kingdom. The root of their objection is given in the words: 'We have a law, and according to that law he must die, because he claimed to be the Son of God' (19:7). This has been part of the charge all along, in that by claiming to be God's Son, Jesus is claiming to be equal with God (5:18; 10:33). The real reason for their animosity towards Jesus is exposed. It is not their loyalty to Caesar or affection for Roman peace, but their utter rejection of the testimony that Jesus is the Son of God.

Pilate gives in to their request and Jesus is crucified. A trilingual inscription is placed above Jesus' head at the cross: 'JESUS OF NAZARETH, THE KING OF THE JEWS' (19:19–20). The chief priests protest and want a disclaimer added to the inscription: 'Do not write "The King of the Jews", but that this man claimed to be king of the Jews' (19:21). The reader knows that Jesus had never said as much, even though the claim is true (1:14; 12:13,15; 18:33–36).

Pilate retorts, 'What I have written, I have written' (19:22). Such a reply is partly out of spite at the Judean aristocrats for pressing him into this action, and at another level the words are a confession. Scripture is what has been 'written' (γεγραμμένος), and Pilate's inscription becomes an inscripturated confession of Jesus' identity.

The resurrection material is not oozing with messianic statements, though it does assume them. The view that the Messiah will 'remain forever' (12:34) would imply that his death was the termination of his messianic reign. To the contrary, on John's perspective the Messiah remains forever not by avoiding death, but precisely by overcoming it. The abiding reign of the crucified Messiah comes through his resurrection.[86] Furthermore, at the Johannine Pentecost, Jesus breathes on the disciples and they receive the Holy Spirit (20:21–23). In this symbolic action, Jesus fulfils an outstanding task of his messianic role by dispensing the Spirit to his followers (1:33; 7:39), finally sending them the Paraclete whom he promised (14:26; 15:26; 16:7). In addition, we can note that the various post-Easter cameos about what the disciples would later remember show that the risen Jesus is the new temple of God (2:21–22) and that the whole of his ministry is to be understood as messianic (12:16). John's Easter narrative culminates in the assertion that Jesus is the divine Word who came into the world and is believed in as Israel's prophet, king, and God.

The purpose of the Fourth Gospel is given in 20:30–31 (possibly the ending to a first edition of the Gospel without the epilogue of John 21) where John asserts that 'Jesus performed many other signs in the presence of his disciples, which are not recorded in this book'; then the evangelist adds: 'But these are written that you may believe that Jesus is the Messiah, the Son of God, and that by believing you may have life in his name' (ταῦτα δὲ γέγραπται ἵνα πιστεύσητε ὅτι Ἰησοῦς ἐστιν ὁ Χριστὸς ὁ υἱὸς τοῦ θεοῦ, καὶ ἵνα πιστεύοντες ζωὴν ἔχητε ἐν τῷ ὀνόματι αὐτοῦ). This verse raises several issues for immediate decision.

First, there is a textual difficulty pertaining to 'you may believe' as to whether one should accept the aorist πιστεύσητε (attested by ℵ² A C D L N W Δ Ψ f¹ f¹³ 33 or the present πιστεύητε (attested by P⁶⁶ ℵ* B Θ 0250 157) tense-form. The material difference is based on the presence or absence of the letter 'sigma' in the verb to indicate either an aorist subjunctive or present sub-junctive verb. The actual difference is alleged to come down to whether one adopts an aorist subjunctive 'you might *come* to believe' (πιστεύσητε), or a present subjunctive 'you might *continue* to believe' (πιστεύητε).[87] The external evidence is evenly weighted, though perhaps marginally favours the aorist πιστεύσητε. What breaks the deadlock is the internal evidence because the conjunction ἵνα ('in order that') in the Fourth Gospel is normally followed by an aorist subjunctive, and the aorist is more likely here given the previous appearance of πιστεύσητε in 19:35, which uses the same verbal form for believing in a dramatic purpose clause (though again with some textual variants, but the aorist is even better attested there).

The problem is, however, that the tense of the verb alone will not tell you whether the type of belief is initial or continual.[88] The tense-form, either aorist or present, does not give us any grounds for supposing that John is talking about belief caused by evangelism (i.e. conversion) or belief reinforced through teaching (i.e. discipleship). The evangelist can use either tense-form of πιστεύω to signify coming to faith or continuing in the faith.[89] Furthermore, the difference between the aorist and present tense-forms is not temporal, but aspectival. The aorist is perfective and views an action from an exterior point of view, while the present is imperfective and provides an interiorized perspective. Concerning the aspect of subjunctive verbs, Constantine Campbell notes: 'Whereas the present subjunctive may be found giving expression to proverbial and general statements, due to its imperfective aspect, the aorist subjunctive typically portrays events that are particular.'[90] The present tense-form highlights the general state of believing, not the persistence of belief. That said, the aorist tense-form is arguably ingressive (i.e. it depicts the entrance or beginning of a new action) when the perfective aspect is combined with a stative lexeme (i.e. πιστεύω means the state of believing), so that πιστεύσητε in this case is more likely to mean 'coming to belief'.[91]

The fact remains that whether John was written to evoke faith or to reinforce faith, this must be determined by other contextual factors relating to the Fourth Gospel. On the one hand the Gospel of John seems to assume a certain degree of familiarity with the life story of Jesus by readers/auditors, which one would expect among a Christian audience (see esp. 1:32 [= Mark 1:9–10]; 3:24 [= Mark 6:17]; 6:70 [= Mark 3:13–15]).[92] It is difficult to imagine the rancorous polemic against 'the Jews' in 8:31–59 as inviting Jews to join a movement that denounces them as demonic.[93] Then again, one cannot help but notice that John is really pressing his case, through signs and witnesses, with apologetic ardour and evangelical ethos, that Jesus is the Messiah, the Son of God. People such as Andrew, Nathanael, the Samaritan woman, and Martha are paradigmatic examples of people who *come* to faith in Jesus as the Messiah, and the implied audience is urged to emulate them. In addition, the goal of believing in 20:31 is 'life' (ζωή), and life in the Fourth Gospel is what is received through believing in and coming to Jesus, which speaks to an evangelical purpose (3:15–16,36; 4:14; 5:24,39–40; 6:40,47; 17:3). Ultimately, it is difficult to restrict the Gospel to a single purpose for either evangelism or discipleship.[94] If the Gospel of John was written amidst a loose network of fellow Christ-believers who were still in contact with Jewish circles (though not necessarily an isolated and introspective 'Johannine community'),[95] then there is a high probability that at some level the Gospel was composed for an evangelical utility among the Jews and also to encourage believers in their faith despite Jewish objections to their beliefs. Similarly, the evangelist might have intended his account of Jesus to circulate widely among believers in other places and perhaps even among non-believers too—in which case, we do not have to choose between a believing or unbelieving audience. We can say, more confidently, that the Gospel of John can certainly function both to strengthen disciples in their faith and to invite people to faith in Jesus.

Second, it is grammatically possible to translate Ἰησοῦς ἐστιν ὁ Χριστὸς as 'the Messiah is Jesus' rather than 'Jesus is the Messiah'. Colwell's rule, though a grammatical generalization, determines that where two Greek substantive nouns stand in grammatical concord, the subject of the verb is normally the noun with the article.[96] Carson argues that an articular noun takes priority over a proper name as the subjective of a clause, so the phrase should be rendered, 'that you may believe that the Christ, the Son of God, is Jesus.'[97] Such a construct would carry weight primarily as an answer to the question, 'Who is the Messiah?' which Jews would ask, rather than Gentiles.[98] The way the purpose clause is put, then, might indicate a possible Jewish audience intended for the Fourth Gospel.[99] Dan Wallace objects, because in a clause with two substantive nouns either the first noun is the subject or else the proper name is the subject. He points to 1 John, where the same construction occurs with 'Jesus', 'Son of God', and 'Messiah' as the substantive nouns, but 'Jesus' is always the subject in these clauses (1 John 2:22; 4:15; 5:1,5).[100]

Third, the significance of the statement is that profession of Jesus as the Messiah stands as the summit of the Gospel and indicates its purpose. The belief that Jesus is the Son of God has been part of the Johannine testimony from the beginning (see 1:14,18,34,49). The designation *Messiah* is also implicit in the prologue and emerges at key points such as Andrew's confession (1:41), Jesus' acceptance of the title from a Samaritan woman (4:25–26), and in disputes with the Judeans over Jesus' origins (7:26–27,31,41–42; 9:29,33; 12:34). Much like Martha's confession in 11:27, it is belief in Jesus as the Messiah defined as the Son of God that is the key point in 20:31. 'Son of God' supplements and defines the nature of Jesus' messiahship.[101] Although Thomas's confession of Jesus – 'My Lord and my God!' – is certainly the more dramatic expression of devotion to Jesus (20:28), Martha's confession and the purpose statement of the evangelist are clearly the most paradigmatic for who Jesus is and what it means to believe in him (11:27; 20:31).[102] This means that however we understand John's Christology, messiahship must figure centrally. The titles Prophet, Son of God, Son of Man, and King of Israel are all glued together with reference to Jesus as the Messiah. The messianic concept also stands behind lesser designations such as Lamb of God and Good Shepherd. According to Brunson:

> John intends to show that *Jesus is the Messiah of Jewish expectation, but he is also much more than this*. Any approach that denies or treats as insignificant Jewish messianic expectations would make nonsense of the Gospel's stated purpose to persuade that Jesus is the Christ (20.31). Rather than using them simply as a foil, John takes up Jewish messianic criteria and shows Jesus fulfilling them, but also transcending and transforming them, for they are insufficient to account for his person and function.[103]

## Conclusion

John Pryor rightly concludes:

> More than any other New Testament document, John reiterates time and again the true Messianic status of Jesus. But again, it is a Messianic status which goes beyond Judaism's wildest expectation, for this title also finds its clarification in "the Son of God". Messiah, the longed for redeemer of Israel, turned out to be the eternal Logos, the pre-existent Son who shares the glory of the Father. Any other messianic confession is inadequate.[104]

I believe Pryor's claims have been vindicated further by this study.[105]

There is no superficiality to John's messianic testimony to Jesus. The Johannine Jesus is thoroughly Jewish in depiction, he is eminently messianic in portrayal, and he also breaks the mould of many expectations by exceeding them and redefining them around the signs of his glory, including his death and resurrection.[106] The messianism of the Fourth Gospel can be paralleled with depictions of eschatological figures in the Dead Sea Scrolls such as Melchizedek, and the Messiah in other Palestinian writings like *1 Enoch* and *4 Ezra*, analogous with Philo's description of the Logos and Moses as king, and coordinate with several remarks that Justin's Trypho makes about the Messiah. The Johannine Jesus is the Mosaic prophet and the Davidic Messiah who is all of Israel's hopes bound up in one person. He is the king of Israel who reigns on behalf of Yahweh. He is the special Son of God sent to save and to judge. He is the descending and ascending Son of Man who is the suffering and glorified human being. All these titles and roles are summed up in the confession of Jesus the Messiah. In this way the Johannine Jesus makes a distinct contribution among Jewish Christian groups as to exactly *how* Jesus is the Messiah and *what* it means to confess him as the Messiah. It is a confession that is clearly rooted in Jewish expectations, but it also demands a revision of who the Messiah is. As James McGrath puts it: 'Jesus as the Messiah and Son of Man fulfils the expectations that pointed to him, but is not limited to those traditional categories. Rather, traditional concepts of messiahship must be redefined in order to incorporate, and do justice to, who the Messiah turned out to be.'[107]

The Johannine Jesus, distinct as he is, remains relatable to the christological portraits of the Synoptic Gospels. John accents rather than invents a pre-existent Messiah. Like the Synoptics, the Messiah comes to Israel, dies for the sins of others and is raised to life, and this is for God's glory. What Jesus does is in accordance with Israel's Scriptures, and he acts on behalf of Israel's God, who sent him. The messianic office is described with a similar array of titles such as Son of God, Son of Man, and King of Israel. Among the other canonical Gospels, John is more like a variation on a Paganini theme than a reggae band playing at a blue-grass concert.

The messianic identity of Jesus is so acute in the Fourth Gospel because one of John's purposes is to persuade other Jews that Jesus is the Messiah, and to reinforce among his own network the conviction that Jesus is the messianic deliverer on whom they have rightly set their hope. The claim was controversial in John's post-70 AD context, though not because heralding someone as the Messiah was itself heretical. Let us remember that the great Rabbi Akiba acknowledged Simeon ben Kosiba as the Messiah, and though Akiba ended up with egg on his face for his profession of a failed messiah, the rabbinic tradition nowhere treats Akiba as a heretic. Rather, the messianism of Johannine Christianity had a controversial edge because messianism stood as the door to a mansion of christological claims that redefined the Jewish story and the very identity of God around Jesus.[108] The confession that Jesus is the Messiah, and the mode of sonship that it claimed for him, make it clear that Jesus is from, of, with, and even is God. Jesus fulfils the scriptural hopes in such a way as to eclipse the place of the law and Moses from the centre of Jewish belief, and Jesus stands in an unparalleled unity with the Father – that is what it means to call him the Messiah.

# Conclusion:

# Believing in the Messiah

The purpose of this volume has been to argue for the overarching significance of the messiahship of Jesus across all four Gospels. The evangelists clearly provide different appropriations of messianic traditions in their respective portrayal of Jesus, and the messiahship of Jesus functions differently in each Gospel. Yet there is a pervasive and shared conviction that Jesus is the *Christos*. The various titles assigned to Jesus (e.g. Son of God, Son of David, Son of Man) are expressions of the messianic role attributed to him. Also the citation, allusion, and echo of scriptural texts are built around the conviction that Jesus is the climax of Jewish scriptural expectations that point to the Messiah. For the evangelists, the Scriptures provided the interpretive grid in which Jesus was to be understood, or more precisely, to be understood as a messianic figure undertaking a messianic task. Furthermore, Jesus' birth, teachings, miraculous deeds, prophetic actions, death, and resurrection are put in service of a theologically embedded narrative that defines and defends the notion that Jesus is the Messiah.

Several disclaimers are now in order. No-one denies that the title 'Messiah' is a genuinely significant designation in the Gospels. However, in scholarship, messiahship is frequently relativized as a secondary gloss to the Jesus tradition and sometimes regarded as an inadequate tertiary title in the evangelists' overall Christology. In extreme cases, the title Χριστός is a just an unfortunate leftover from an earlier Jewish Christian phrase from which the evangelists have begun to extradite Jesus. I do not deny the significance of the complex elements of the Christology of the Gospels, such as the depiction of Jesus as teacher, allusions to scriptural figures such as Moses and Elijah, the importance of miraculous deeds, the bearing of Greco-Roman parallels, the widespread prophetic imagery that surrounds Jesus, or the big three titles Son of God-Son of Man-Son of David. My point is that when reduced to its most basic level, all Gospel Christology is a form of messianism and must be understood in that light.

The messianism of the Gospels paradoxically displays a creative stream of continuity and redefinition of extant Jewish messianic hopes. Absolute usage of 'the Messiah' is exceedingly rare in Judaism (only 1QSa 2:11–12 comes to my mind). Even so, the expectation of a coming one, a royal deliverer, a Davidic king was widely known, even if it was not a majority conviction among Jews of antiquity. The Jesus of the Gospels is both clearly like and radically unlike what we find attributed to messianic figures in extant Jewish literature around the time of the evangelists. Gathering followers, preaching about a kingdom, warning of judgement, condemning injustices, calling Israel to repentance, and performing mighty deeds could be lined up with messianic hopes if you put the pieces in a certain way and emphasize certain texts. Yet what sets Jesus apart from other Jewish messianic expectations, above all, is his death and resurrection. Yes, you do get peculiar exceptions like the anointed one of Daniel 9:26 put to death; in 4Q285 the reconstructed text might indicate that the Branch of David is slain by the *Kittim*; and the Messiah in *4 Ezra* 7:29 dies at the end of a 400-year interregnum. None of this changes what we already know: the evangelists' conviction that Jesus as the Messiah died and rose according to the Scriptures finds little support in contemporary Jewish interpretation of the Hebrew Scriptures.[1] What was a natural stumbling block to Jews about Jesus' role in God's plan, namely, the crucifixion, is ostentatiously transformed by the evangelists into a core conviction. For them the cross was, in fact, a key tenet of Jesus' messianic task and the goal of his messianic work. The salvation and glory of Israel's God is bound up with the narration of the Messiah who had to live, suffer, die, and be raised from the dead. For the evangelists, the scandal of the cross turns out to be the good news that Israel has been waiting to hear.

Evidently the evangelists go about this task in different ways, as I've tried to emphasize at length. The Gospel of Mark is an apology for a crucified Messiah where the death of Jesus is both royal and redemptive. It is the Marcan Jesus' self-giving service as the Son of Man that defines the meaning of the messianic office. The Gospel of Matthew builds on Mark, rather than repudiating his christological claims, by emphasizing that Jesus is the Son of David and Son of Abraham. He is the deliverer who effects the restoration of the lost sheep of the house of Israel; his messianic charism is both didactic and prophetic; he is the king who ushers in the kingdom of heaven, which climaxes in the reconstitution of a renewed Israel built on the Messiah. In the Gospel of Luke, Jesus is the prophetic Messiah who enacts the Isaianic New Exodus that brings salvation for Jews and Gentiles. For Luke, faithfulness to Jesus as Messiah and Lord is what secures the legitimate identity of the church and places them in a bond of unity with Israel all the way back to Abraham. Luke–Acts is a community-defining narrative that defines the community by its allegiance to Jesus the Messiah. Finally, in the Gospel of John, messiahship is the nexus in a constellation of christological convictions about Jesus as the incarnate Word, a prophet greater than Moses, the specially sent Son of God, the ascending-descending Son of Man, and even the warrior Lamb of God. John provides a forensic testimony through a stream of witnesses in signs, speeches, symbols, and Scripture that Jesus is the Messiah.

A Christology rooted in the Gospels, then, must take account of the messianism ascribed to Jesus. It is no good simply to see messianism as a blanket thrown over the Jesus tradition by the evangelists to underscore Jesus' significance. What scholarship has often regarded as peripheral to the development of Christology proves to be the bedrock and fulcrum for the most basic beliefs about Jesus in the early church. Affirmation of Jesus as Messiah was both the root of early Christology and something amplified in unique ways by the evangelists. The reconfiguration of Jewish beliefs by Jesus-believers was built around the conviction that Jesus is Israel's Messiah. Beliefs about God and the people of God were caught up with the notion that Jesus of Nazareth was the promised coming one whose identity is revealed as the Son of God and Son of Man. The Gospels then stand fully within the matrix of Jewish conceptions of God, intermediary figures, salvation, and messianism. However, there is also a radical rupture in many ways, since Jesus' identity is defined in such a way as to push the fixtures of monotheism, to question populist narratives of Israel's history, re-imagine hopes for the future, and even widen the boundaries of Israel's election.

The messiahship of Jesus was retained and affirmed in circles outside of Palestine and in ecclesial settings dominated by Gentiles, as Paul's letters clearly suggest. But the fact that Jesus' messiahship was a point of lasting division between Jews and Jesus-believers, combined with the fact that all the evangelists amplify the messianic theme in their own way, indicates that the Gospels were written in contexts where there was still a social-religious proximity to Jewish communities in either Palestine or the Diaspora. I am not sure if there is much to be gained about debates as to whether John's 'community' or Matthew's 'community' are still part of the synagogue. Apart from some agnosticism about speaking of such 'communities' in the first place, I'm not convinced that we can really excavate the Gospels for the socio-religious history of the author and audiences. What we can say is that the Gospels constitute Christian responses to intra-Jewish debates about God, the Messiah, Israel, and the future. It tells us that whatever we think of the social setting of each Gospel, somewhere along the line we have to identify it within a movement that is unswervingly Jewish by conviction, but is sporting many wounds from having its christological claims bitterly rejected by Jewish contemporaries. That results in a mixture of apologetics, polemics, and proclamation about the story of Israel in relation to the story of Jesus. What we find in the Gospels, then, is the attempt by some to plot the identity, mission, and future hope of the people of God, by those who believe that they have received a new revelation of God in Messiah Jesus.

I want to add that the messianism of the Gospels is crucial to Christian theology for a few reasons too. First, the messiahship of Jesus means that the church will always be umbilically linked to Israel. The church is never called the 'true Israel' or the 'new Israel' in the New Testament. Though such sentiments have a genuine grain of truth, it is more accurate to say that the church continues the story of Israel through the story of the Messiah. The messiahship of Jesus is according to the Scriptures of Israel and thus the church can only ever understand its identity within the aegis of a renewed Israel. The church is not *adversus Iudaeos*, but is made up of the representatives of Israel in the messianic age who wait, hope, and pray (as Luke certainly does) for the rest of national Israel to catch up. In other words, the messiahship of Jesus drives us to develop a messianic ecclesiology that reinforces the Israelite heritage of Jews and Christians. The point of contention will no doubt be eschatology, specifically the Christian claim that the kingdom has come in Messiah Jesus, but the enormity of the claim can perhaps be defended by a witness that shows visible signs of new creation in the community of the Messiah, and in the message of reconciliation to the world through Israel's Messiah. The Gospels are exercises in exactly that task: explaining and celebrating the belief that the hope of Israel and the world has come in Jesus the Christ.

Second, messiahship was quickly marginalized in developing Christian Christologies of the second to fourth centuries, where the focus rested mainly on ontological and metaphysical questions raised by the intellectual currents of the day. Let's remember that the Nicene and Chalcedonian statements represent clarifications of Christian belief rooted in the Scriptures, rather than speculative pontifications by Platonic philosophers in a Christian garb. The developing Christologies of the church fathers were responses to the biblical pressures to move in a Trinitarian direction and to answer questions about the nature(s) of Jesus that the New Testament itself creates. However, what must partner with a Christology that engages with ontology is a redemptive-historical framework that places the identity of the Messiah in a singular narrative stretching from creation to new creation. The orthodox claim that only the nature that is assumed by Jesus can be redeemed by Jesus presupposes a certain narrative of creation, incarnation, and consummation. Moreover, seeing Jesus as the messianic climax to Israel's history immediately draws us into discussions about author and agent, since Jesus is both sent by God and also represents God from an interior point of view. His unmediated divine authority, from which he speaks in the Gospels about his mission, suggests that he is more than a man chosen by God to liberate the nation from oppression. In other words, if the Messiah is the Son of God, then he begins to reveal what it means for God to be God-in-the-flesh. The most complex christological questions are raised by the evangelists, who are firmly of the conviction that an encounter with the Messiah is also an encounter with Israel's God. Therefore, the nature of God is understood in light of the Messiah's person.

Third, the messiahship of Jesus can also serve as a benchmark for establishing boundaries of authentic Christian belief. The Jesus received in the church, the Jesus of apostolic tradition, is that Jesus is the Messiah according to the Scriptures. Where messiahship is denied, so is Scripture; where Scripture is denied, then it is not the God of Abraham, Isaac, or Jacob about whom we are talking. Certain developing Christologies in the second century – both proto-orthodox and Gnostic varieties – had a proclivity to marginalize the messianic office of Jesus, albeit for different reasons. For instance, the proto-orthodox *Epistle of Barnabas* appears to reject the category of 'Son of David' as an inadequate Jewish title for one who is more properly the 'Son of God' (*Ep. Barn.* 12.10–11). In the *Gospel of Philip* we read:

> 'Jesus' is a hidden name, 'Christ' is a revealed name. For this reason 'Jesus' is not particular to any language; rather he is always called by the name 'Jesus'. While as for 'Christ', in Syriac it is 'Messiah', in Greek it is 'Christ'. Certainly all the others have it according to their own language. 'The Nazarene' is he who reveals what is hidden. Christ has everything in himself, whether man, or angel, or mystery, and the Father (*Gos. Phil.* 19; cf. 47).

Here the etymology and background of Jesus as Χριστός is rightly remembered and then resoundingly rejected in favour of a depiction of him as an esoteric revealer. As Longenecker writes:

> In a Greek milieu the title Messiah-Christ very soon became unintelligible, and under Gnostic influence Jesus as the revealer of truth received exclusive emphasis. But the *Gospel of Philip*, rooted as it is in a Jewish subsoil and probably independent of the canonical Gospels, still preserves the memory of what Χριστός originally meant – even though it does it in very garbled fashion and even though it prefers to use it as a name and present for it a decidedly secondary etymology.[2]

The witness of the church has always insisted that Jesus' messianic office – traditionally expounded through the roles of prophet, priest, and king – cannot be reduced to an ontology of sonship or rejected in favour of making Jesus a dispenser of Neoplatonic advice. Where the claims of messiahship are denied or threatened, there emerges a Christology, a Jesus, different from the one received in the gospel and in the four Gospels!

The Matthean Jesus asks his audience the question, 'What do you think about the Messiah?' (Matt. 22:42). In many ways that is the quintessential question that the Jesus of canonical testimony raises for all readers, be they Jewish or Gentile, ancient or modern. In effect, people are asked, 'Do you believe that Jesus is the Messiah?' The answer to that question is answered affirmatively by people from Peter, to Nathanael, to Martha. Readers of all types are then invited to follow their example and to believe the scripture that 'the Messiah will suffer and rise from the dead' (Luke 24:46) and to experience the promise that 'by believing [in the Messiah] you may have life in his name' (John 20:31).

# Bibliography

Abbot, E., A.P. Peabody and J.B. Lightfoot. *The Fourth Gospel: Evidences External and Internal of Its Johannean Authorship* (London: Hodder & Stoughton, 1892).

Achtemeier, Paul. *Mark*. Proclamation (Philadelphia: Fortress Press, 1976).

Allison, Dale C. *The New Moses: A Matthean Typology* (Minneapolis: Fortress Press, 1993).

— *Studies in Matthew: Interpretation Past and Present* (Grand Rapids, MI: Baker, 2005).

— *The Historical Christ and the Theological Jesus* (Grand Rapids, MI: Eerdmans, 2009).

— *Constructing Jesus: Memory, Imagination, and History* (Grand Rapids, MI: Baker, 2010).

Aune, D.E. 'Christian Prophecy and the Messianic Status of Jesus.' Pages 404–22 in *The Messiah: Developments in Earliest Judaism and Christianity* (ed. J.H. Charlesworth; Minneapolis: Fortress Press, 1992).

— 'Eschatology (Early Christian).' In *Anchor Bible Dictionary*, ABRL (6 vols; ed. D.N. Freedman; New York: Doubleday, 1992), 2:594–609.

Barnett, Paul. 'Mark: Story and History.' Pages 29–44 in *In the Fullness of Time: Biblical Studies in Honour of Archbishop Donald Robinson* (ed. D. Peterson and J. Pryor; Sydney: Lancer, 1992).

— *The Servant King* (Sydney: AIO, 2000).

Barrett, C.K. *The Gospel according to St John: An Introduction with Commentary and Notes on the Greek Text* (London: SPCK, 2nd edn, 1978).

Barton, Stephen C. 'The Gospel according to Matthew.' Pages 121–38 in *The Cambridge Companion to the Gospels* (ed. Stephen C. Barton; Cambridge: Cambridge University Press, 2006).

Bateman, Herbert W. 'Defining the Titles "Christ" and "Son of God" in Mark's Narrative Presentation of Jesus'. *Journal of the Evangelical Theological Society* 50 (2007): pp. 546–57.

Bauckham, Richard. 'Jesus' Demonstration in the Temple.' Pages 72–89 in *Law and Religion: Essays on the Place of the Law in Israel and Early Christianity* (ed. B. Lindars; Cambridge: James Clarke, 1988).

— 'John for Readers of Mark.' Pages 147–71 in *The Gospels for All Christians* (ed. R. Bauckham; Grand Rapids, MI: Eerdmans, 1998).

— 'Monotheism and Christology in the Gospel of John.' Pages 148–66 in *Contours of Christology in the New Testament* (ed. R.N. Longenecker; Grand Rapids, MI: Eerdmans, 2005).

— 'Messianism according to the Gospel of John.' Pages 34–68 in *Challenging Perspectives on the Gospel of John*. WUNT 2.219 (ed. J. Lierman; Tübingen: Mohr Siebeck, 2006).

Beasley-Murray, G.R. *John*. WBC (Waco, TX: Word, 1987).

Beaton, Richard. *Isaiah's Christ in Matthew's Gospel*. SNTSMS 123 (Cambridge: Cambridge University Press, 2002).

Bird, Michael F. 'The Crucifixion of Jesus as the Fulfillment of Mark 9:1'. *Trinity Journal* 24 (2003): pp. 23–36.

— 'Bauckham's The Gospels for All Christians Revisited'. *European Journal of Theology* 15 (2006): pp. 5–13.

— *Jesus and the Origins of the Gentile Mission*. LNTS 331 (London: T&T Clark, 2006).

— *A Bird's-Eye View of Paul* (Nottingham: Apollos, 2008).

— 'Birth of Jesus.' Pages 71–5 in *Encyclopedia of the Historical Jesus* (ed. C.A. Evans; New York: Routledge, 2008).

— 'Passion Predictions.' Pages 442–6 in *Encyclopedia of the Historical Jesus* (ed. Craig A. Evans; New York: Routledge, 2008).

— *Are You the One Who Is to Come? The Historical Jesus and the Messianic Question* (Grand Rapids, MI: Baker, 2009).

— *Colossians and Philemon*. NCCS (Eugene, OR: Cascade, 2009).

— 'The Historical Jesus and the "Parting of the Ways".' In *The Handbook of the Study of the Historical Jesus* (4 vols; ed. T. Holmén and S.E. Porter; Leiden: Brill, 2010), 2:1183–215.

— 'Mark: Interpreter of Peter and Disciple of Paul.' Pages 30–61 in *Paul and the Gospels: Christologies, Conflicts, and Convergences.* LNTS 411 (ed. M.F. Bird and J. Willitts; London: T&T Clark, 2011).

— 'Jesus and the Continuing Exile of Israel in the Writings of N.T. Wright.' In *Jesus as Israel's Messiah: Engaging the Work of N. Thomas Wright.* LNTS (ed. R.L. Webb and M.A. Powell; London: T&T Clark, forthcoming 2012).

Blomberg, Craig. 'Messiah in the New Testament.' Pages 125–32 in *Israel's Messiah in the Bible and the Dead Sea Scrolls* (ed. R.S. Hess and M. Daniel Carroll; Grand Rapids, MI: Eerdmans, 2003).

Bock, Darrell L. *Proclamation from Prophecy and Pattern: Lucan Old Testament Christology.* JSNTSup 12 (Sheffield: JSOT Press, 1987).

Bockmuehl, Markus. *This Jesus: Martyr, Lord, Messiah* (Edinburgh: T&T Clark, 1994).

— 'A "Slain Messiah" in 4Q Serekh Milhûamah (4Q285)?' *Tyndale Bulletin* 43 (1992): pp. 155–70.

— and James Carleton Paget, eds. *Redemption and Resistance: The Messianic Hopes of Jews and Christians in Antiquity* (London: T&T Clark, 2007).

Bolt, Peter. 'Feeling the Cross: Mark's Message of Atonement'. *Reformed Theological Review* 60 (2001): pp. 1–17.

— *Jesus' Defeat of Death: Persuading Mark's Early Readers.* SNTSMS 125 (Cambridge: Cambridge University Press, 2003.

— *The Cross from a Distance: Atonement in Mark's Gospel.* NSBT (Downers Grove, IL: IVP, 2004).

Boring, M. Eugene. 'The Kingdom of God in Mark.' Pages 131–45 in *The Kingdom of God in 20th Century Interpretation* (ed. Wendell Willis; Peabody, MA: Hendrickson, 1975).

— 'Markan Christology: God-Language for Jesus?' *New Testament Studies* 45 (1999): pp. 451–71.

— *Mark: A Commentary.* NTL (Louisville, KY: Westminster John Knox Press, 2006).

Bousset, Wilhelm. *Kyrios Christos* (trans. J.E. Steely; Nashville: Abingdon, 1970).

Brandon, S.G.F. *Jesus and the Zealots* (Manchester: Manchester University Press, 1967).

Brawley, R.L. *Luke–Acts and the Jews: Conflict, Apology, and Conciliation* (Atlanta, GA: Scholars Press, 1987).

Briggs, Charles A. *The Messiah of the Gospels* (New York: Charles Scribner's Sons, 1894).

Brower, Kent. 'Mark 9:1 – Seeing the Kingdom in Power'. *Journal for the Study of the New Testament* 6 (1980): pp. 17–41.

Brown, R.E. *The Gospel according to John.* AB (2 vols; New York: Doubleday, 1966–70).

Bruce, F.F. 'The Speeches in Acts: Thirty Years After.' Pages 53–68 in *Reconciliation and Hope: New Testament Essays on Atonement and Eschatology Presented to L.L. Morris on His 60th Birthday* (ed. R. Banks; Carlisle: Paternoster Press, 1974).

— *The Gospel and Epistles of John* (Grand Rapids, MI: Eerdmans, 1983).

Brunson, Andrew C. *Psalm 118 in the Gospel of John: An Intertextual Study of the New Exodus Pattern in the Theology of John.* WUNT 2.158 (Tübingen: Mohr Siebeck, 2003).

Bryan, Steven M. *Jesus and Israel's Traditions of Judgement and Restoration.* SNTSMS 117 (Cambridge: Cambridge University Press, 2002).

Bultmann, Rudolf. 'Die Frage nach dem messianischen Bewusstein Jesu und das Petrus-Bekenntnis'. *Zeitschrift für die Neutestamentliche Wissenschaft* 19 (1919-20): pp. 165–74.

— *A Theology of the New Testament* (2 vols; trans. K. Grobel; London: SCM Press, 1952).

Byrne, Brendan. 'Jesus as Messiah in the Gospel of Luke: Discerning a Pattern of Correction'. *Catholic Bible Quarterly* 65 (2003): pp. 80–95.

Campbell, Constantine R. *Basics of Verbal Aspect in Biblical Greek* (Grand Rapids, MI: Zondervan, 2008).

— *Verbal Aspect and Non-Indicative Verbs* (New York: Peter Lang, 2008).

Carson, D.A. 'Matthew.' *EBC* (12 vols; ed. Frank E. Gaeblein; Grand Rapids, MI: Eerdmans, 1984), 8:1–599.

— 'The Purpose of the Fourth Gospel: John 20:30–31 Reconsidered'. *Journal of Biblical Literature* 108 (1987): pp. 639–51.

— *The Gospel according to John.* PNTC (Grand Rapids, MI: Eerdmans, 1991).

— 'Syntactical and Text-Critical Observations on John 20:30–31: One More Round on the Purpose of the Fourth Gospel'. *Journal of Biblical Literature* 124 (2005): pp. 693–714.

Casey, P.M. *From Jewish Prophet to Gentile God: The Origins and Development of New Testament Christology* (Cambridge: James Clarke, 1991).

Chae, Young S. *Jesus as the Eschatological Davidic Shepherd: Studies in the Old Testament, Second Temple Judaism, and in the Gospel of Matthew*. WUNT 2.216 (Tübingen: Mohr Siebeck, 2006).

Chapman, David. *Ancient Jewish and Christian Perceptions of Crucifixion* (Grand Rapids, MI: Baker, 2008).

Chester, Andrew. 'The Christ in Paul.' Pages 109–21 in *Redemption and Resistance* (ed. M. Bockmuehl and J.C. Paget; London: T&T Clark, 2007).

— *Messiah and Exaltation: Jewish Messianic and Visionary Traditions in New Testament Christology*. WUNT 207 (Tübingen: Mohr Siebeck, 2007).

Chilton, Bruce. 'Jesus ben David: Reflections on the Davidssohnfrage'. *Journal for the Study of the New Testament* 4 (1982): pp. 88-112.

Collins, Adela Yarbro. 'Establishing the Text: Mark 1:1.' Pages 111–27 in *Texts and Contexts: The Function of Biblical Texts in Their Textual and Situational Contexts* (ed. T. Fornberg and D. Hellholm; Oslo: Scandinavian University Press, 1995).

Collins, A.Y., and J.C. Collins. *King and Messiah as Son of God: Divine, Human, and Angelic Messianic Figures in Biblical and Related Literature* (Grand Rapids, MI: Eerdmans, 2008).

Collins, John C. *The Scepter and the Star: The Messiahs of the Dead Sea Scrolls and Other Ancient Literature*. ABRL (New York: Doubleday, 1995).

Crawford, Barry S. 'Christos as Nickname.' Pages 337–48 in *Redescribing Christian Origins* (ed. R. Cameron and M.P. Miller; Leiden: Brill, 2004).

Cullmann, Oscar. *Christology of the New Testament* (trans. S.C. Guthrie and C.A.M. Hall; London: SCM Press, 2nd edn, 1963).

Cummins, S.A. 'Divine Life and Corporate Christology: God, Messiah Jesus, and the Covenant Community in Paul.' Pages 190–209 in *The Messiah in the Old and New Testaments* (ed. S.E. Porter; Grand Rapids, MI: Eerdmans, 2007).

Davies, Philip R. 'Mark's Christological Paradox.' Pages 163–77 in *The Synoptic Gospels: A Sheffield Reader*. BS 31 (ed. C.A. Evans and S.E. Porter; Sheffield: Sheffield Academic Press, 1995).

Dahl, N.A. *Jesus the Christ: The Historical Origins of Christological Doctrine* (ed. D.H. Juel; Minneapolis: Fortress Press, 1991).

— 'The Passion Narrative in Matthew.' Pages 63–7 in *The Interpretation of Matthew* (ed. G.N. Stanton; London: SPCK, 2nd edn, 1995).

Davies, W.D., and Dale C. Allison. *The Gospel according to Saint Matthew*. ICC (3 vols; Edinburgh: T&T Clark, 1988-97).

Dennis, John A. *Jesus' Death and the Gathering of True Israel*. WUNT 2.217 (Tübingen: Mohr Siebeck, 2006).

— 'Jesus' Death in John's Gospel: A Survey of Research from Bultmann to the Present with Specific Reference to the Johannine Hyper-Texts'. *Currents in Biblical Research* 4 (2006): pp. 331–6.

Denova, Rebecca I. *The Things Accomplished among Us: Prophetic Tradition in the Structural Pattern of Luke-Acts* (Sheffield: Sheffield Academic Press, 1997).

deSilva, David A. *An Introduction to the New Testament: Context, Methods and Ministry Formation* (Downers Grove, IL: IVP, 2004).

Dodd, C.H. *The Interpretation of the Fourth Gospel* (Cambridge: Cambridge University Press, 1968).

Donahue, John R. *The Gospel of Mark*. SP (Collegeville, MN: Liturgical Press, 2002).

Donaldson, Terence L. 'The Vindicated Son: A Narrative Approach to Matthean Christology.' Pages 100–21 in *Contours of Christology in the New Testament* (ed. R.N. Longenecker; Grand Rapids, MI: Eerdmans, 2005).

Dowd, Sharyn. *Reading Mark: A Literary and Theological Commentary on the Second Gospel* (Macon, GA: Smyth & Helwys, 2000).

Duling, Dennis C. 'Solomon, Exorcism, and the Son of David'. *Harvard Theological Review* 68 (1975): pp. 235–52.

Dunn, James D.G. 'Let John Be John – a Gospel for Its Time.' Pages 309–39 in *Das Evangelium und die Evangelien*. WUNT 28 (ed. P. Stuhlmacher; Tübingen: Mohr Siebeck, 1983).

— *Romans 1 – 8*. WBC (Dallas, TX: Word, 1988).

— *Unity and Diversity in the New Testament* (London: SCM Press, 2nd edn, 1990).

— *Theology of Paul the Apostle* (Edinburgh: T&T Clark, 1998).

— *Christology in the Making* (London: SCM Press, 2nd edn, 2003).

— *Jesus Remembered*. CITM 1 (Grand Rapids, MI: Eerdmans, 2003).

— *Beginning from Jerusalem*. CITM 2 (Grand Rapids, MI: Eerdmans, 2009).

Ellis, E. Earle. *The Gospel of Luke*. NCBC (Greenwood, SC: Attic, 1974).

Esler, Philip. *Community and Gospel in Luke–Acts*. SNTSMS 57 (Cambridge: Cambridge University Press, 1987).

Evans, Craig A. *Jesus and His Contemporaries* (Leiden: Brill, 1995).

— 'Root Causes of the Jewish-Christian Rift: From Jesus to Justin.' Pages 20–35 in *Christian-Jewish Relations through the Centuries* (ed. S.E. Porter and B.W.R. Pearson; Sheffield: Sheffield Academic Press, 2000).

— *Mark 8:27 – 16:20*. WBC (Waco, TX: Thomas Nelson, 2001).

— 'Defeating Satan and Liberating Israel: Jesus and Daniel's Visions'. *Journal for the Study of the Historical Jesus* 1 (2003): pp. 161–70.

— 'Messianic Hopes and Messianic Figures in Late Antiquity'. *Journal of Greco-Roman Christianity and Judaism* 3 (2006): pp. 9–40.

Farmer, William R., ed. *Anti-Judaism and the Gospels* (Harrisburg, PA: Trinity Press, 1999).

Fee, Gordon D. *Pauline Christology: An Exegetical-Theological Study* (Peabody, MA: Hendrickson, 2007).

Ferguson, Everett. *Backgrounds of Early Christianity* (Grand Rapids, MI: Eerdmans, 2nd edn, 1993).

Fitzmyer, Joseph A. *The Gospel according to Luke*. AB (2 vols; New York: Doubleday, 1981–5).

— *The One Who Is to Come* (Grand Rapids, MI: Eerdmans, 2007).

Foster, Paul. *Community, Law, and Mission in Matthew's Gospel*. WUNT 2.177 (Tübingen: Mohr Siebeck, 2004).

Fowler, Robert. *Loaves and Fishes: The Function of the Feeding Stories in the Gospel of Mark* (Chico, CA: Scholars Press, 1981).

France, R.T. *The Gospel of Mark*. NIGTC (Grand Rapids, MI: Eerdmans, 2002).

— *The Gospel of Matthew*. NICNT (Grand Rapids, MI: Eerdmans, 2007).

Fuller, Reginald H. *The Foundations of New Testament Christology* (New York: Charles Scribner's Sons, 1965).

Gadenz, Pablo T. *Called from the Jews and from the Gentiles: Pauline Ecclesiology in Romans 9 – 11.* WUNT 2.267 (Tübingen: Mohr Siebeck, 2009).

Gaston, Lloyd. 'The Messiah of Israel as Teacher of the Gentiles'. *Interpretation* 29 (1975): pp. 24–40.

— 'Anti-Judaism and the Passion Narrative in Luke and Acts.' Pages 127–153 in *Anti-Judaism in Early Christianity, vol. 1: Paul and the Gospels* (ed. P. Richardson and D. Granskou, SCJ; Waterloo, ONT: Wilfrid Laurier University Press, 1986).

— *Paul and the Torah* (Vancouver: University of British Columbia Press, 1987).

Gathercole, Simon. 'The Son of Man in Mark's Gospel'. *Expository Times* 115 (2004): pp. 366–72.

Green, Joel B. *The Gospel of Luke*. NICNT (Grand Rapids, MI: Eerdmans, 1997).

Gundry, Robert H. *Mark: A Commentary on His Apology for the Cross* (Grand Rapids, MI: Eerdmans, 1993).

— *Matthew: A Commentary on His Handbook for a Mixed Church under Persecution* (Grand Rapids, MI: Baker, 2nd edn, 1994).

— 'A Rejoinder to Joel F. Williams's "Is Mark's Gospel an Apology for the Cross?"' *Bulletin for Biblical Research* 12 (2002): pp. 123–40.

Hafemann, S.J. 'Roman Triumph.' Pages 1004–8 in *Dictionary of New Testament Background* (ed. C.A. Evans and S.E. Porter; Downers Grove, IL: IVP, 2000).

Hagner, D.A. *Matthew*. WBC (2 vols; Dallas, TX: Word, 1993–5).

Hahn, Ferdinand. *The Titles of Jesus in Christology: Their History in Early Christianity* (trans. H. Knight and G. Ogg; London: Lutterworth Press, 1969).

Hare, Douglas R.A. 'The Rejection of the Jews in the Synoptic Gospels and Acts.' Pages 27–47 in *Antisemitism and the Foundations of Christianity* (ed. Alan Davies; New York: Paulist Press, 1979).

Harvey, John D. 'Mission in Matthew.' Pages 119–36 in *Mission in the New Testament: An Evangelical Approach* (ed. W. Larkin and J.F. Williams; Maryknoll, NY: Doubleday, 1998).

Hays, Richard. 'The Gospel of Matthew: Reconfigured Torah'. *Harvard Theological Studies* 61 (2001): pp. 165–90.

— *The Conversion of the Imagination: Essays on Paul as Interpreter of Israel's Scripture* (Grand Rapids, MI: Eerdmans, 2005).

Head, Peter. 'A Text-Critical Study of Mark 1.1: "The Beginning of the Gospel of Jesus Christ."' *New Testament Studies* 37 (1993): pp. 621–9.

Hengel, Martin. *Judaism and Hellenism* (2 vols; trans. J. Bowden; London: SCM Press, 1974).

— *Crucifixion in the Ancient World and the Folly of the Message of the Cross* (trans. John Bowden; London: SCM Press, 1977).

— *Between Jesus and Paul: Studies in the Earliest History of Christianity* (trans. J. Bowden; London: SCM Press, 1983).

— *Studies in Early Christology* (London: SCM Press, 1995).

— 'Eye-witness Memory and the Writing of the Gospels: Form Criticism, Community Tradition and the Authority of the Authors.' Pages 70–96 in *The Written Gospel* (ed. M.A. Bockmuehl and D.A. Hagner; FS Graham Stanton; Cambridge: Cambridge University Press, 2005).

Hood, Jason. *The Messiah, His Brothers, and the Nations*. LNTS 441 (London: T&T Clark, 2011).

Hooker, Morna D. 'The Johannine Prologue and the Messianic Secret'. *New Testament Studies* 21 (1974): pp. 40–58.

— *Not Ashamed of the Gospel: New Testament Interpretations of the Death of Christ* (Carlisle: Paternoster Press, 1994).

— '"Who Can This Be?" The Christology of Mark's Gospel.' Pages 79–99 in *Contours of Christology in the New Testament* (ed. R.N. Longenecker; Grand Rapids, MI: Eerdmans, 2005).

Horbury, William. *Jewish Messianism and the Cult of Christ* (London: SCM Press, 1998).

— *Messianism among Jews and Christians* (London: T&T Clark, 2003).

— 'Jewish Messianism and Early Christology.' Pages 17–23 in *Contours of Christology in the New Testament* (ed. R.N. Longenecker; Grand Rapids, MI: Eerdmans, 2005).

Hurtado, Larry. 'Christ.' Pages 106–17 in *Dictionary of Jesus and the Gospels* (ed. J.B. Green, S. McKnight, and I.H. Marshall; Downers Grove, IL: IVP, 1992).

— *Lord Jesus Christ: Devotion to Jesus in Earliest Christianity* (Grand Rapids, MI: Eerdmans, 2003).

Janse, Sam. *"You are My Son": The Reception History of Psalm 2 in Early Judaism and the Early Church*. CBET 51 (Leuven: Peeters, 2009).

Jeremias, Joachim. *New Testament Theology* (trans. J. Bowden; London: SCM Press, 1971).

Jervell, Jacob. *Luke and the People of God: A New Look at Luke–Acts* (Minneapolis: Augsburg, 1972).

— 'The Lucan Interpretation of Jesus as Biblical Theology,' in *New Directions in Biblical Theology*, ed. S. Pedersen (Leiden: Brill, 1994), 86, pp. 77–92.

— *The Theology of the Acts of the Apostles* (Cambridge: Cambridge University Press, 1996).

Johansson, Daniel. 'Kyrios in the Gospel of Mark'. *Journal for the Study of the New Testament* 22 (2010): pp. 101–24.

Johnson, Luke Timothy. 'The Christology of Luke–Acts.' Pages 49–65 in *Who Do You Say That I Am? Essays on Christology* (ed. M.A. Powell and D.R. Bauer; FS J.D. Kingsbury; Louisville, KY: Westminster John Knox Press, 1999).

— *The Writings of the New Testament: An Interpretation* (London: SCM Press, 3rd edn, 2003).

Jonge, Marinus de. 'The Use of the Word "Anointed" in the Time of Jesus'. *Novum Testamentum* 8 (1966): pp. 132–48.

— 'Jewish Expectations about the "Messiah" according to the Fourth Gospel'. *New Testament Studies* 19 (1972–3): pp. 246–70.

Juel, Donald. *Messianic Exegesis: Christological Interpretation of the Old Testament in Early Christianity* (Philadelphia: Fortress Press, 1988).

— 'The Origins of Mark's Christology.' Pages 449–60 in *The Messiah: Developments in Earliest Judaism and Christianity* (ed. J.H. Charlesworth; Minneapolis: Fortress Press, 1992).

Kähler, Martin. *The So-Called Historical Jesus and the Historic Biblical Christ* (Philadelphia: Fortress Press, 1964).

Keener, Craig. *Gospel of John: A Commentary* (2 vols; Peabody, MA: Hendrickson, 2003).

— *Matthew: A Socio-Rhetorical Commentary* (Grand Rapids, MI: Eerdmans, 2nd edn, 2009).

Kennard, Douglas. *Messiah Jesus: Christology in His Day and Ours* (New York: Peter Lang, 2008).

Kennedy, R. Joel. *The Recapitulation of Israel.* WUNT 2.257 (Tübingen: Mohr Siebeck, 2008).

Kim, Jintae. 'The Concept of Atonement in the Gospel of John'. *Journal for the Study of Greco-Roman Christianity and Judaism* 6 (2009): pp. 9–27.

Kingsbury, J.D. *The Christology of Mark's Gospel* (Philadelphia: Fortress Press, 1983).

— 'Jesus as the "Prophetic Messiah" in Luke's Gospel.' Pages 29–42 in *The Future of Christology* (ed. A.J. Malherbe and W.A. Meeks; FS L.E. Keck; Minneapolis: Fortress Press, 1993).

— 'The Significance of the Cross within Mark's Story.' Pages 95–105 in *Gospel Interpretation: Narrative Critical and Social-Scientific Approaches* (ed. J.D. Kingsbury; Harrisburg, PA: Trinity Press, 1997).

Kirk, David. 'The Heavens Opened: Intertextuality and Meaning in John 1:51.' Unpublished dissertation (Highland Theological College, University of the Highlands and Islands, 2010).

Klink, Edward. 'The Gospel Community Debate: The State of the Question'. *Currents in Biblical Research* 3 (2004): pp. 60–85.

— *The Sheep of the Fold: The Audience and Origin of the Gospel of John*. SNTSMS 141 (Cambridge: Cambridge University Press, 2007).

— 'Expulsion from the Synagogue? Rethinking a Johannine Anachronism'. *Tyndale Bulletin* 59 (2008): pp. 99–118.

Koester, Craig R. 'Messianic Exegesis and the Call of Nathanael (John 1:45-51)'. *Journal for the Study of the New Testament* 39 (1990): pp. 23–34.

— *The Word of Life: A Theology of John's Gospel* (Grand Rapids, MI: Eerdmans, 2008).

Koester, Helmut. *Paul and His World: Interpreting the New Testament in Its Context* (Minneapolis: Fortress Press, 2007).

Köhler, W.-D. *Die Rezeption des Matthäusevangeliums in der Zeit vor Irenäus* (Tübingen: Mohr Siebeck, 1987).

Köstenberger, Andreas. *A Theology of John's Gospel and Letters*. BTNT (Grand Rapids, MI: Zondervan, 2009).

— and Peter T. O'Brien. *Salvation to the Ends of the Earth: A Biblical Theology of Missions*. NSBT (Downers Grove, IL: IVP, 2001).

Kramer, Werner. *Christ, Lord, Son of God*. SBT 50 (trans. B. Hardy; London: SCM Press, 1966).

LaGrand, James. *The Earliest Christian Mission to 'All Nations' in the Light of Matthew's Gospel* (Grand Rapids, MI: Eerdmans, 1999).

Lee, Aquila H.I. *From Messiah to Preexistent Son: Jesus' Self-Consciousness and Early Christian Exegesis of Messianic Psalms*. WUNT 2.192 (Tübingen: Mohr Siebeck, 2005).

Levine, Amy-Jill. 'Matthew, Mark, and Luke: Good News or Bad?' Pages 92–7 in *Jesus, Judaism and Christian Anti-Judaism: Reading the New Testament after the Holocaust* (ed. P. Fredriksen and A. Reinhartz; Louisville, KY: Westminster John Knox Press, 2002).

Lindars, Barnabas. *The Gospel of John*. NCBC (London: Marshall, Morgan & Scott, 1972).

Loader, William. *The Christology of the Fourth Gospel: Structure and Issues* (Frankfurt am Main: Peter Lang, 1989).

Longenecker, Richard N. *The Christology of Early Jewish Christianity* (Grand Rapids, MI: Baker, 1970).

Lührmann, Dieter. *Das Markusevangelium*. HNTC (Tübingen: Mohr Siebeck, 1987).

Macaskill, Grant. *Revealed Wisdom and Inaugurated Eschatology in Ancient Judaism and Early Christianity* (Leiden: Brill, 2007).

MacRae, George. 'Messiah and Gospel.' Pages 169–85 in *Judaisms and Their Messiahs at the Turn of the Christian Era* (ed. J. Neusner, W.S. Green, and E.S. Frerichs; Cambridge: Cambridge University Press, 1987).

Maddox, Robert. *The Purpose of Luke–Acts* (Edinburgh: T&T Clark, 1982).

Malina, Bruce. *The New Testament World: Insights from Cultural Anthropology* (Atlanta: John Knox Press, 1981).

Manson, William. *Jesus the Messiah* (London: Hodder & Stoughton, 1943).

Marcus, Joel. 'Mark 14:61: "Are You the Messiah-Son-of-God?"' *Novum Testamentum* 31 (1989): pp. 125–41.

— *The Way of the Lord: Christological Exegesis of the Old Testament in the Gospel of Mark* (Edinburgh: T&T Clark, 1993).

— 'Mark – Interpreter of Paul'. *New Testament Studies* 46 (2000): pp. 473–87.

Marshall, I. Howard. 'Palestinian and Hellenistic Christianity: Some Critical Comments'. *New Testament Studies* 19 (1972–3): pp. 271–87.

— *The Origins of New Testament Christology* (Downers Grove, IL: IVP, 1977).

— '"Israel" and the Story of Salvation: One Theme in Two Parts.' Pages 340–57 in *Jesus and the Heritage of Israel: Luke's Narrative Claim upon Israel's Legacy* (ed. D.P. Moessner; Harrisburg, PA: Trinity Press, 1999).

— 'The Christology of Luke's Gospel and Acts.' Pages 122–47 in *Contours of Christology in the New Testament* (ed. R.N. Longenecker; Grand Rapids, MI: Eerdmans, 2005).

— 'Jesus as Messiah in Mark and Matthew.' Pages 117–43 in *The Messiah in the Old and New Testaments* (ed. S.E. Porter; Grand Rapids, MI: Eerdmans, 2007).

Martyn, J.L. *History and Theology in the Fourth Gospel* (Nashville: Abingdon, 2nd edn, 1979).

Massoux, Edouard. *The Influence of the Gospel of Saint Matthew on Christian Literature before Saint Irenaeus* (2 vols; ed. Arthur J. Bellinzoni; trans. Norman J. Belval and Suzanne Hect; Macon, GA: Mercer University Press, 1990–93).

Matera, Frank. *The Kingship of Jesus: Composition and Theology in Mark 15.* SBLDS 66 (Chico, CA: Scholars Press, 1982).

— *New Testament Christology* (Louisville, KY: Westminster John Knox Press, 1999).

McCasland, S. Vernon. 'Christ Jesus.' *Journal of Biblical Literature* 65 (1946): pp. 377–83.

McDonald, Lee Martin, and Stanley E. Porter. *Early Christianity and Its Sacred Literature* (Peabody, MA: Hendrickson, 2001).

McKnight, Scot. *Jesus and His Death* (Baylor, TX: Baylor University Press, 2005).

McWhirter, Jocelyn. *The Bridegroom Messiah and the People of God: Marriage in the Fourth Gospel.* SNTSMS 138 (Cambridge: Cambridge University Press, 2006).

— 'Messianic Exegesis in Mark's Passion Narrative.' Pages 69–97 in *The Trial and Death of Jesus: Essays on the Passion Narrative in Mark* (ed. Geert van Oyen and Tom Shepherd; Leuven: Peeters, 2006).

Meeks, Wayne A. *The Prophet-King: Moses Traditions and Johannine Christology* (Leiden: Brill, 1967).

— 'The Man from Heaven in Johannine Sectarianism.' Pages 141–73 in *The Interpretation of John* (ed. J. Ashton; London: SPCK, 1986).

Meier, John P. 'From Elijah-Like Prophet to Royal Davidic Messiah.' Pages 45–83 in *Jesus: A Colloquium in the Holy Land* (ed. Doris Donnelly; London: Continuum, 2001).

Metzger, Bruce. *A Textual Commentary on the Greek New Testament* (Stuttgart: Deutsche Bibelgesellschaft, 2nd edn, 1994).

Miller, Merrill. 'The Problem of the Origins of a Messianic Conception of Jesus.' Pages 303–36 in *Redescribing Christian Origins* (ed. R. Cameron and M.P. Miller; Leiden: Brill, 2004).

Miura, Yuzuru. *David in Luke–Acts: His Portrayal in the Light of Early Judaism*. WUNT 2.232 (Tübingen: Mohr Siebeck, 2007).

Moloney, Francis J. *Mark: Storyteller, Interpreter, Evangelist* (Peabody, MA: Hendrickson, 2004).

Moo, Douglas J. *The Epistle to the Romans*. NICNT (Grand Rapids, MI: Eerdmans, 1996).

Morris, Leon. 'The Atonement in John's Gospel'. *Criswell Theological Review* 3 (1988): pp. 49–64.

— *The Gospel According to John*. NICNT (Grand Rapids, MI: Eerdmans, rev. edn, 1995).

Moule, C.F.D. 'The Christology of Acts.' Pages 159–85 in *Studies in Luke–Acts* (ed. L.E. Keck and J.L. Martyn; FS Paul Schubert; London: SPCK, 1966).

Moxnes, Halvor. 'Honor and Shame.' *Biblical Theology Bulletin* 23 (1993): pp. 167–76.

Neusner, Jacob. 'Varieties of Judaism in the Formative Age.' Pages 171–97 in *Jewish Spirituality* (ed. A. Green; London: SCM Press, 1989).

Nicklesburg, G.W.E. 'The Genre and Function of the Markan Passion Narrative'. *Harvard Theological Review* 73 (1980): pp. 153–84.

Nolland, John. *Luke*. WBC (3 vols; Dallas, TX: Word, 1989–93).

— *The Gospel of Matthew*. NIGTC (Grand Rapids, MI: Eerdmans, 2005).

Novakovic, Lidija. *Messiah, the Healer of the Sick: A Study of Jesus as the Son of David in the Gospel of Matthew*. WUNT 2.170 (Tübingen: Mohr Siebeck, 2003).

O'Toole, R.F. 'Reflections on Luke's Treatment of Jews in Luke–Acts'. *Biblica* 75 (1994): pp. 124–46.

Pao, David W., and Eckhard J. Schnabel. 'Luke.' Pages 251–414 in *CNTUOT* (ed. D.A. Carson and G.K. Beale; Grand Rapids, MI: Baker, 2007).

Paget, James Carleton. 'The Four among Jews.' Pages 205–21 in *The Written Gospel* (ed. M. Bockmuehl and D.A. Hagner; Cambridge: Cambridge University Press, 2005).

Painter, John. *The Quest for the Messiah: The History, Literature and Theology of the Johannine Community* (Edinburgh: T&T Clark, 1991).

Parker, David. *An Introduction to the New Testament Manuscripts and Their Texts* (Cambridge: Cambridge University Press, 2008).

Perrin, Nicholas. *Jesus the Temple* (London: SPCK, 2010).

— 'From One Stone to the Next: Messiahship and Temple in N.T. Wright's Jesus and the Victory of God.' In *Jesus as Israel's Messiah: Engaging the Work of N.T. Wright*. LHJS (ed. R.L. Webb and M.A. Powell.; London: T&T Clark, forthcoming).

Pokorný, Petr. *The Genesis of Christology: Foundations for a Theology of the New Testament* (trans. M. Lefébure; Edinburgh: T&T Clark, 1987).

Porter, Stanley E. *Idioms of the Greek New Testament* (Sheffield: Sheffield Academic Press, 2nd edn, 1999).

— 'The Messiah in Luke and Acts: Forgiveness for Captives.' Pages 152–4 in *The Messiah in the Old and New Testaments* (ed. S.E. Porter; Grand Rapids, MI: Eerdmans, 2007).

Pryor, John W. *John: Evangelist of the Covenant People: The Narrative and Themes of the Fourth Gospel* (London: Darton, Longman & Todd, 1992).

Reynolds, Benjamin E. *The Apocalyptic Son of Man in the Gospel of John*. WUNT 2.249 (Tübingen: Mohr Siebeck, 2008).

Robinson, J.A.T. 'The Most Primitive Christology of All?' *Journal of Theological Studies* 7 (1956): pp. 177–89.

— *Twelve More New Testament Studies* (London: SCM Press, 1984).

Rowe, C. Kavin. *Early Narrative Christology: The Lord in the Gospel of Luke*. BZNW 139 (Berlin: Walter de Gruyter, 2006).

Sanders, Jack T. *The Jews in Luke–Acts* (London: SCM Press, 1987).

Sanders, James. 'From Isaiah 61 to Luke 4.' Pages 46–69 in *Luke and Scripture: The Function of Sacred Traditions in Luke–Acts* (ed. J.A. Sanders and C.A. Evans; Minneapolis: Fortress Press, 1993).

Schmidt, T.E. 'Mark 15:16–32: The Crucifixion Narrative and the Roman Triumphal Procession'. *New Testament Studies* 41 (1995): pp. 1–18.

Schnackenburg, Rudolf. 'Die Messias Frage im Johannesevangelium.' Pages 240–64 in *Neutestamentliche Aufsätze* (ed. J. Blinzler, O. Kuss, and F. Mussner; FS Joseph Schmid; Regensburg: Friedrich Pustet, 1963).

— *The Gospel according to St John* (3 vols; trans. K. Smyth; New York: Herder & Herder, 1968–82).

Schneiders, Sandra M. *Written That You May Believe: Encountering Jesus in the Fourth Gospel* (New York: Crossroads, 1999).

Schreiner, Thomas R. *Paul: Apostle of God's Glory in Christ* (Downers Grove, IL: IVP, 2001).

Schwemer, Anna Maria. 'Jesus Christus als Prophet, König und Priester. Das munus triplex und die frühe Christologie.' Pages 165–230 in *Der messianische Anspruch Jesu und die Anfänge der Christologie: Vier Studien.* WUNT 138 (ed. M. Hengel and A.M. Schwemer; Tübingen: Mohr Siebeck, 2001).

Seeley, David. 'Rulership and Service in Mark 10:41–45.' *Novum Testamentum* 35 (1993): pp. 234–50.

Senior, Donald. *The Passion of Jesus in the Gospel of Mark* (Wilmington, DE: Michael Glazier, 1984).

Smalley, Stephen. *John: Evangelist and Interpreter* (Carlisle: Paternoster Press, 2nd edn, 1998).

Smith, Stephen H. 'The Function of the Son of David Tradition in Mark's Gospel'. *New Testament Studies* 42 (1996): pp. 523–39.

Stanton, Graham. 'Messianism and Christology: Mark, Matthew, Luke and Acts.' Pages 78–96 in *Redemption and Resistance* (ed. M. Bockmuehl and J.C. Paget; London: T&T Clark, 2007).

Stendahl, Krister. 'Quis et Unde? An Analysis of Matthew 1 – 2.' Pages 69–80 in *The Interpretation of Matthew* (ed. G.N. Stanton; Edinburgh: T&T Clark, 2nd edn, 1995).

Sterling, G.E. *Historiography and Self-Definition: Josephus, Luke–Acts and Apologetic Historiography.* NovTSup 64 (Leiden: Brill, 1992).

Stibbe, Mark W.G. 'The Elusive Christ: A New Reading of the Fourth Gospel'. *Journal for the Study of the New Testament* 44 (1991): pp. 19–38.

— *John* (Sheffield: JSOT Press, 1993).

Stonehouse, Ned B. *The Witness of Luke to Christ* (London: Tyndale Press, 1951).

Strauss, Mark L. *The Davidic Messiah in Luke-Acts: The Promise and Fulfilment in Luke's Christology.* JSNTSup 110 (Sheffield: Sheffield Academic Press, 1995).

Svartvik, Jesper. 'Matthew and Mark.' Pages 27–49 in *Matthew and His Christian Contemporaries.* LNTS 333 (ed. D.C. Sim and B. Repschinski; London: T&T Clark, 2008).

Tannehill, Robert C. 'The Story of Israel within the Lukan Narrative.' Pages 325–39 in *Jesus and the Heritage of Israel: Luke's Narrative Claim upon Israel's Legacy* (ed. D.P. Moessner; Harrisburg, PA: Trinity Press, 1999).

Tuckett, Christopher M. 'The Christology of Luke–Acts.' Pages 133–64 in *The Unity of Luke–Acts* (ed. J. Verheyden; Leuven: Leuven University Press, 1999).

— *Christology and the New Testament: Jesus and His Earliest Followers* (Louisville, KY: Westminster John Knox Press, 2001).

Tyson J.B., ed. *Images of Judaism in Luke–Acts* (Columbia: University of South Carolina Press, 1992).

Wallace, Daniel B. *Greek Grammar beyond the Basics* (Grand Rapids, MI: Zondervan, 1996).

Wasserman, Tommy. 'The "Son of God" Was in the Beginning (Mark 1:1)'. *Journal of Theological Studies* 62 (2011): pp. 1–31.

Watts, Rikki E. *Isaiah's New Exodus and Mark*. WUNT 2.88 (Tübingen: Mohr Siebeck, 1997).

— 'Mark.' Pages 111–249 in *CNTUOT* (ed. D.A. Carson and G.K. Beale; Grand Rapids, MI: Baker, 2007).

Weiss, Johannes. 'Das Problem der Entstehung des Christentums'. *Archiv für Religionswissenschaft* 16 (1913): pp. 423–515.

Wilk, Florian. *Jesus und die Völker in der Sicht der Synoptiker*. BZNW 109 (Berlin: Walter de Gruyter, 2002).

Williams, Joel F. 'Is Mark's Gospel an Apology for the Cross?' *Bulletin for Biblical Research* 12 (2002): pp. 97–122.

Willitts, Joel. *Matthew's Messianic Shepherd-King*. BZNW 147 (Berlin: Walter de Gruyter, 2007).

Winn, Adam. *The Purpose of Mark's Gospel: An Early Christian Response to Roman Imperial Propaganda*. WUNT 2.245 (Tübingen: Mohr Siebeck, 2008).

Witherington, Ben. *Paul's Narrative Thought World: The Tapestry of Tragedy and Triumph* (Louisville, KY: Westminster John Knox Press, 1994).

— *The Many Faces of the Christ* (New York: Crossroads, 1998).

— *John's Wisdom: A Commentary on the Fourth Gospel* (Louisville, KY: Westminster John Knox Press, 1995).

— *The Gospel of Mark: A Socio-Rhetorical Commentary* (Grand Rapids, MI: Eerdmans, 2001).

Wolter, Michael. 'Israel's Future and the Delay of the Parousia.' Pages 307–24 in *Jesus and the Heritage of Israel: Luke's Narrative Claim upon Israel's Legacy* (ed. D.P. Moessner; Harrisburg, PA: Trinity Press, 1999).

Wrede, William. *The Messianic Secret* (trans. J.C.G. Greig; Cambridge: James Clarke, 1971).

Wright, N.T. 'The Paul of History and the Apostle of Faith'. *Tyndale Bulletin* 29 (1978): pp. 61–88.

— *Climax of the Covenant* (Edinburgh: T&T Clark, 1991).

— *The New Testament and the People of God*. COQG (London: SPCK, 1992).

— *Jesus and the Victory of God*. COQG 2 (London: SPCK, 1996).

— *Resurrection of the Son of God*. COQG 3 (London: SPCK, 2003).

Yieh, John Yueh-Han. *One Teacher: Jesus' Teaching Role in Matthew's Gospel Report*. BZNW 124 (New York: Walter de Gruyter, 2004).

Zetterholm, Magnus, ed. *The Messiah: In Early Judaism and Christianity* (Minneapolis: Fortress Press, 2007).

— 'Paul and the Missing Messiah.' Pages 33–56 in *The Messiah in Early Judaism and Christianity* (ed. M. Zetterholm; Minneapolis: Fortress Press, 2007).

# Endnotes

## Introduction: When Did Jesus Become the Messiah?

[1] My translations. Scripture quotations are drawn from TNIV unless otherwise indicated.

[2] James D.G. Dunn (*Unity and Diversity in the New Testament* [London: SCM, 2nd edn, 1990], pp. 44–5) comments: 'In short, we may say that *where the confrontation between Judaism remained a factor of importance in the development of confessional Christianity, the confession "Jesus is the Christ" retained its significance and importance . . . but almost nowhere else'* (italics original). I can grant that the contention over Jesus as Messiah was acute and acidic in Jewish Christian circles that were still within the aegis of Jewish communities. However, Paul's letters, the Gospels, and Revelation all touch upon Palestinian, Diasporan, and Gentile contexts, literary and geographical, as the context in which their messianism is worked out. Thus, the 'almost' that Dunn employs here needs to be stretched to breaking point. Messianism was significant even outside Jewish Christian confrontation with non-Christ-believing Jews.

[3] Rudolf Bultmann, *A Theology of the New Testament* (2 vols; trans. K. Grobel; London: SCM, 1952), 1:27 (italics original).

[4] Lidija Novakovic, *Messiah, the Healer of the Sick: A Study of Jesus as the Son of David in the Gospel of Matthew*, WUNT 2.170 (Tübingen: Mohr Siebeck, 2003), p. 5. Novakovic is repeating the thought of Donald Juel, *Messianic Exegesis: Christological Interpretation of the Old Testament in Early Christianity* (Philadelphia: Fortress, 1988), pp. 175, 177.

[5] Helmut Koester, *Paul and His World: Interpreting the New Testament in Its Context* (Minneapolis: Fortress, 2007), p. 99.

[6] Cf. Craig A. Evans, 'Messianic Hopes and Messianic Figures in Late Antiquity', *JGRChJ* 3 (2006): pp. 9–40.

[7] See further Michael F. Bird, *Are You the One Who Is to Come? The Historical Jesus and the Messianic Question* (Grand Rapids, MI: Baker, 2009), pp. 31–62. For recent and thorough studies of Jewish messianic hopes and figures, consult Joseph A. Fitzmyer, *The One Who Is to Come* (Grand Rapids, MI: Eerdmans, 2007); *Redemption and Resistance: The Messianic Hopes of Jews and Christians in Antiquity* (ed. Markus Bockmuehl and James Carleton Paget; London: T&T Clark, 2007); *The Messiah: In Early Judaism and Christianity* (ed. Magnus Zetterholm; Minneapolis: Fortress, 2007); A.Y. Collins and J.C. Collin, *King and Messiah as Son of God: Divine, Human, and Angelic Messianic Figures in Biblical and Related Literature* (Grand Rapids, MI: Eerdmans, 2008).

[8] Cf. William Horbury, *Jewish Messianism and the Cult of Christ* (London: SCM, 1998), pp. 83–108; idem, 'Jewish Messianism and Early Christology', in *Contours of Christology in the New Testament* (ed. R.N. Longenecker; Grand Rapids, MI: Eerdmans, 2005), pp. 17–23.

[9] John C. Collins, *The Scepter and the Star: The Messiahs of the Dead Sea Scrolls and Other Ancient Literature*, ABRL (New York: Doubleday, 1995), pp. 11–12.

[10] On this subject see Bird, *One Who Is to Come*, passim. See also Markus Bockmuehl, *This Jesus: Martyr, Lord, Messiah* (Edinburgh: T&T Clark, 1994), pp. 51–8; Craig A. Evans, *Jesus and His Contemporaries* (Leiden: Brill, 1995), pp. 437–56; Martin Hengel, 'Jesus, the Messiah of Israel', in *Studies in Early Christology* (London: SCM, 1995): pp. 1–70; N.T. Wright, *Jesus and the Victory of God*, COQG 2 (London: SPCK, 1996), pp. 477–539; Andrew Chester, *Messiah and Exaltation: Jewish Messianic and Visionary Traditions in New Testament Christology*, WUNT 207 (Tübingen: Mohr Siebeck, 2007), pp. 307–24.

[11] Johannes Weiss, 'Das Problem der Entstehung des Christentums', *Archiv für Religionswissenschaft* 16 (1913): p. 470.

[12] William Wrede, *The Messianic Secret* (trans. J.C.G. Greig; Cambridge: James Clarke, 1971).

[13] Ps. 110 appears to have informed two streams of speculation: (1) the combination of priestly and royal roles as in the Hasmonean usurpation of kingship and priesthood and in 11Q13 from Qumran; and (2) the expectation of the exaltation of a supreme eschatological figure as found in Isa. 52, Dan. 7, and *1 Enoch*.

[14] Dale C. Allison, *Constructing Jesus: Memory, Imagination, and History* (Grand Rapids, MI: Baker, 2010), p. 240.

[15] Oscar Cullmann, *Christology of the New Testament* (trans. S.C. Guthrie and C.A.M. Hall; London: SCM, 2nd edn, 1963), p. 8.

[16] Cf. Michael F. Bird, *Jesus and the Origins of the Gentile Mission*, LNTS 331 (London: T&T Clark, 2006).

[17] Part of the charge that Trypho brings against Christians is: "You Christians . . . have remolded for yourselves a Messiah (χριστὸν ἑαυτοῖς τινὰ ἀναπλάσσετε) for whom you are blindly giving up your lives' (*Dial. Tryph.* 8.4). It was the continuity and discontinuity of Christian messianic beliefs with Jewish messianic hopes that formed a point of contention in Jewish-Christian relationships.

[18] Though the speeches in Acts do have a certain homogeneity attributable to Luke's rhetorical and theological designs, I still think it clear that Luke is working from some traditional material in his précis of early Christian preaching. See further F.F. Bruce, 'The Speeches in Acts: Thirty Years After', in *Reconciliation and Hope: New Testament Essays on Atonement and Eschatology Presented to L.L. Morris on His 60th Birthday* (ed. R. Banks; Carlisle: Paternoster, 1974), pp. 53–68.

[19] Larry Hurtado, *Lord Jesus Christ: Devotion to Jesus in Earliest Christianity* (Grand Rapids, MI: Eerdmans, 2003), pp. 75, 178, 196.

[20] Cf. similarly, Ferdinand Hahn, *The Titles of Jesus in Christology: Their History in Early Christianity* (trans. H. Knight and G. Ogg; London: Lutterworth, 1969), p. 192. For 1 Cor. 3:11 the Textus Receptus reads Ἰησοῦς ὁ Χριστός ('Jesus the Messiah'). Wonderful as it would be for a lucidly titular understanding of Χριστός in Paul's letters, the variant is clearly secondary, though it does suggest that the name Ἰησοῦς Χριστός was understood to mean in effect Ἰησοῦς ὁ Χριστός. See also witnesses related to Acts 8:37, 1 John 4:3, and Rev. 12:17 that use the article with Χριστός.

[21] Personally, I rather enjoy writing on Christmas cards to friends that I wish them a joyous holiday celebrating the birth of 'Jesus the Christ'. It has led to many interesting conversations.

[22] Reginald H. Fuller (*The Foundations of New Testament Christology* [New York: Charles Scribner's Sons, 1965], p. 163) writes, contra J.A.T. Robinson, 'First the anarthrous Χριστός in 1 Peter is not to be interpreted as a proper name, but is a survival of the titular anarthrous use in the Palestinian tradition enshrined in 1 Cor. 15:3b. Second, and consequently, the Lucan usage also is not a Lucan invention but a continuation of early Palestinian usage.'

[23] Cf. for example on Col. 1:1–3, Michael F. Bird, *Colossians and Philemon,* NCCS (Eugene, OR; Cascade, 2009), pp. 33–4.

[24] Cf. Lee Martin McDonald and Stanley E. Porter, *Early Christianity and Its Sacred Literature* (Peabody, MA: Hendrickson, 2001), pp. 233–4.

[25] Bird, *One Who Is to Come,* pp. 154–8; Dunn, *Beginning from Jerusalem,* p. 215.

[26] For example, Bultmann (*Theology of the New Testament,* 1:27) wrote, 'Paul, like others, also did not understand it [Jesus' life] as messianic'. Bultmann's student, Helmut Koester (*Paul and His World,* p. 7) offers the same thought: 'Jesus is for Paul not the Messiah of Israel but the Servant of God, who gives his life for the establishment of justice for all . . . Jesus is for Paul and his churches the Servant of God, not the Messiah'. According to Lloyd Gaston (*Paul and the Torah* [Vancouver: University of British Columbia Press, 1987], p. 7): 'Jesus is then for Paul not the Messiah. He is neither the climax of the history of Israel nor the fulfilment of the covenant'. Merrill Miller ('The Problem of the Origins of a Messianic Conception of Jesus', in *Redescribing Christian Origins* [ed. R. Cameron and M.P. Miller; Leiden: Brill, 2004], p. 313) contends: 'I would argue that the Pauline usage does not presuppose the messianic status of Jesus as a figure of expectation or the use of *christos* as an absolute and titular designation as we find in a range of contexts in the Gospels and Acts.' For David Aune ('Eschatology [Early Christian],' in *ABD, ABRL* [6 vols; ed. D.N. Freedman; New York: Doubleday, 1992], 2:601): 'Paul had no particular concerns about the messianic status of Jesus'. According to Magnus Zetterholm ('Paul and the Missing Messiah', in *The Messiah in Early Judaism and Christianity* [ed. M. Zetterholm; Minneapolis: Fortress, 2007], p. 37), 'In Paul's letters . . . any tendency to stress the messiahship of Jesus has vanished into thin air'. For a final example, Andrew Chester ('The Christ in Paul', in *Redemption and Resistance* [ed. M. Bockmuehl and J.C. Paget; London: T&T Clark, 2007], pp. 109, 112) declares, 'his main focus is not on Jesus as messiah; nor do messianic categories play a prominent part in his theology . . . the number of specifically messianic references in Paul is very limited, and so is also their significance . . . he lays no real emphasis either on Christ being the messiah, or on the specifically messianic implications of his use of χριστός'.

[27] See the banal study of Werner Kramer (*Christ, Lord, Son of God,* SBT 50 [trans. B. Hardy; London: SCM, 1966]), pp. 203–14) who focuses on

noun cases, prepositions, and articles in search of a criterion as to when χριστός means 'Messiah' in Paul.

[28] On this incorporative aspect see N.T. Wright, *Climax of the Covenant* (Edinburgh: T&T Clark, 1991), pp. 41–56; S.A. Cummins, 'Divine Life and Corporate Christology: God, Messiah Jesus, and the Covenant Community in Paul,' in *The Messiah in the Old and New Testaments* (ed. S.E. Porter; Grand Rapids, MI: Eerdmans, 2007), pp. 190–209.

[29] Martin Hengel, 'Christos in Paul', in *Between Jesus and Paul: Studies in the Earliest History of Christianity* (trans. J. Bowden; London: SCM, 1983), p. 66.

[30] Cf. Wright, *Climax of the Covenant*, pp. 44–5.

[31] Wright (*Climax of the Covenant*, p. 46) avers: 'The distinction between Χριστός and Ἰησοῦς in these various phrases, and indeed where they occur by themselves in Paul, is quite straightforward. Though both words *denote* the same human being, Paul uses Ἰησοῦς to refer to that man as Jesus, the man from Nazareth, who died on the cross and rose again as a human being, and through whose human work, Paul believed Israel's God had achieved his long purposes; and he uses Χριστός to refer to that same man, but this time precisely as Israel's Messiah in whom the true people of God are summed up and find their identity.' I suspect that Wright has perhaps over-cooked the texts a bit since a nominal meaning seems fairly straightforward especially when there is explicit reference to Jesus' 'name'. However, there is something intuitively correct about his observation that Χριστός never lost its titular significance in Pauline usage.

[32] Cf. similarly Miller, 'Origins of a Messianic Conception of Jesus', p. 326.

[33] Cf. S. Vernon McCasland, 'Christ Jesus', *JBL* 65 (1946): pp. 377–83; Cullmann, *Christology*, pp. 133–4; N.A. Dahl, *Jesus the Christ: The Historical Origins of Christological Doctrine* (ed. D.H. Juel; Minneapolis: Fortress, 1991), p. 16.

[34] Hahn (*Christology*, p. 186): 'Christos plays a decisive role in Paul'; Wright (*Climax of the Covenant*, p. 41): 'I want now to suggest that this consensus is wrong; that Χριστός in Paul should regularly be read as "Messiah".' Thomas R. Schreiner (*Paul: Apostle of God's Glory in Christ* [Downers Grove, IL: IVP, 2001], p. 85): 'As a Jew, Paul would continue to recognize the titular associations of the term. He speaks of "Jesus Christ" and "Christ Jesus" so often because one of the

foundations of Paul's worldview is that Jesus is the promised Messiah. No extended defense of such a view was needed since the messianic status of Jesus was apparently well accepted in all his churches.' Richard B. Hays (*The Conversion of the Imagination: Essays on Paul as Interpreter of Israel's Scripture* [Grand Rapids, MI: Eerdmans, 2005], p. 117): 'The Davidic messiahship of Jesus is a significant aspect of Pauline Christology, at least at the presuppositional level. This is most clearly evident in Romans. Critical Studies of Pauline Christology have seriously underestimated the importance of this element of Paul's thought about Jesus . . . The conventional wisdom that *Christos* in Paul is a name, not a title, is seriously misleading'. Hurtado (*Lord Jesus Christ*, pp. 98–101): '[T]he varying position of the term in the fuller expressions is one of several indications that for Paul and others who use these terms, *Christos* had not simply been reduced to a name (e.g., Jesus' cognomen) but instead retained something of its function as a title . . . the prevalence of *Christos* in Paul's christological expressions can be accounted for only by positing the messianic claim as a feature of Christian proclamation for a considerable period earlier than his letters'; Collins (*The Scepter and the Star*): 'Jesus is called *Christos*, anointed, the Greek equivalent of messiah, 270 times in the Pauline corpus. If this is not ample testimony that Paul regarded Jesus as messiah, then words have no meaning'. See further Hengel, '*Christos in Paul*', pp. 65–77; James D.G. Dunn, *Theology of Paul the Apostle* (Edinburgh: T&T Clark, 1998), pp. 195–7; Wright, *Climax of the Covenant*, pp. 41–56; idem, *Resurrection of the Son of God*, COQG 3 (London: SPCK, 2003), pp. 393–8, 553–83; Ben Witherington, *Paul's Narrative Thought World: The Tapestry of Tragedy and Triumph* (Louisville: Westminster John Knox, 1994), pp. 131–7; Craig Blomberg, 'Messiah in the New Testament', in *Israel's Messiah in the Bible and the Dead Sea Scrolls* (ed. R.S. Hess and M. Daniel Carroll (Grand Rapids, MI: Eerdmans, 2003), pp. 125–32; Pablo T. Gadenz, *Called from the Jews and from the Gentiles: Pauline Ecclesiology in Romans 9 – 11*, WUNT 2.267 (Tübingen: Mohr Siebeck, 2009), pp. 53–6.

[35] Kramer, *Christ, Lord, Son of God*, p. 210.

[36] Dahl, *Jesus the Christ*, p. 24 n. 11; Dunn, *Theology of Paul the Apostle*, p. 198; Blomberg, 'Messiah in the New Testament', p. 127.

[37] Luke Timothy Johnson, *The Writings of the New Testament: An Interpretation* (London: SCM, 3rd edn, 2003), p. 263.

[38] In fact the Pauline phrase 'the Gospel of Christ' has remarkable parity with the preaching of 'Jesus is the Messiah' by the Lucan Paul in Acts.

[39] Irenaeus (*Adv. Haer.* 3.18.3) takes 'anointed' in a Trinitarian direction when he writes, 'For in the name of Christ is implied, He that anoints, He that is anointed, and the unction itself with which He is anointed. And it is the Father who anoints, but the Son who is anointed by the Spirit, who is the unction, as the Word declares by Isaiah, "The Spirit of the Lord is upon me, because He hath anointed me", – pointing out both the anointing Father, the anointed Son, and the unction, which is the Spirit.'

[40] Cf. Allison, *Constructing Jesus*, p. 290 n. 290.

[41] James D.G. Dunn, *Romans 1 – 8*, WBC; (Dallas, TX: Word, 1988), p. 14; Douglas J. Moo, *The Epistle to the Romans*, NICNT (Grand Rapids, MI: Eerdmans, 1996), p. 48; Hengel, 'Messiah of Israel', p. 11. Against some scholars (George MacRae, 'Messiah and Gospel', in *Judaism and Their Messiahs at the Turn of the Christian Era* [ed. J. Neusner, W.S. Green, and E.S. Frerichs; Cambridge: CUP, 1987], pp. 171–2; Chester, 'Christ of Paul', p. 111) I contend that Rom. 1:2–4 does not depict Paul moving messianic expectations to a transcendent level away from earthly conceptions of messiahship. This is because: (1) Eschatological saviours such as those found in *4 Ezra* and *1 Enoch* are very much transcendent in their qualities and equally messianic by title and vocation; and (2) Focus on Jesus' exaltation is not a removal from an earthly role as Messiah, but accentuates the royal status of Jesus as an exalted Messiah. (3) Granted that 'Son' is not exclusively a messianic title, still the reception-history of Ps. 2 and 2 Sam. 7:12–16 (in e.g. 4Q246; 4Q174) makes it hard to avoid the messianic significance especially when the Davidic ancestry of Jesus is explicitly noted. There could be a removal from a militaristic conception of Messiah by Paul and other Jews (if that is what one means by 'earthly'), but not a disengagement from any messianic vocation by calling Jesus 'Son' and 'Lord'.

[42] Gordon D. Fee, *Pauline Christology: An Exegetical-Theological Study* (Peabody, MA: Hendrickson, 2007), p. 253 (see further pp. 272–7).

[43] Hays, *Conversion of the Imagination*, pp. 101–18 (esp. pp. 110–15).

[44] Greco-Roman authors knew about Jewish messianic predictions about a world ruler. See Tacitus, *Hist.* 5.13; Suetonius, *Vesp.* 4.5; Josephus, *War* 6.312–13; Philo, *Life of Moses* 1.290.

[45] Cf. e.g. 1QSb 5.22,25,26; 4Q161 8,9,10,15–29; 4Q285 5.1–6; *1 Enoch* 62.2; *Pss. Sol.* 17.24,29,36–37; *T.Jud.* 24.6; *T.Levi* 18.7; *Tg. Isa.*; Justin; *1 Apol.* 32; *Dial. Tryph.* 87.

[46] Cf. also MacRae, 'Messiah and Gospel', pp. 171–3.

[47] Douglas Kennard, *Messiah Jesus: Christology in His Day and Ours* (New York: Peter Lang, 2008), pp. 415–38.

[48] Cf. Michael F. Bird, *A Bird's-Eye View of Paul* (Nottingham: Apollos, 2008), p. 121.

[49] David E. Aune, 'Christian Prophecy and the Messianic Status of Jesus', in *The Messiah: Developments in Earliest Judaism and Christianity* (ed. J.H. Charlesworth; Minneapolis: Fortress, 1992), p. 406.

[50] Several reasons against this reconstruction are often put forward: (1) It is claimed that Jesus' career was non-messianic because the title Χριστός does not appear in the sayings material common to Matthew and Luke known as 'Q'. In response: First, Q is a hypothetical document and hardly a solid bedrock of data for theories of Christian origins. Second, absence of data in Q, whether it is the title 'Messiah' or reference to Jesus' death and resurrection, does not mean ignorance or denial of a subject by a given group. It only means that a document's function and repertoire of ideas points elsewhere (see Hurtado, *Lord Jesus Christ*, p. 244; Allison, *Constructing Jesus*, p. 279). Third, when it comes to messianism, roles are more important than titles, and there is good evidence that there is a healthy amount of material in Q that can be characterized as messianic, not least of which is Matt. 11:2–5 / Luke 7:18–22 especially when compared with 4Q521 2.1–10 (see Bird, *One Who Is to Come*, pp. 102–4, 145–8). (2) It is often objected that to postulate Jesus as a messianic claimant requires the existence of a well-known and monolithic messianic concept that was then redefined by Jesus and/or the early church. First, no-one can deny that messianic expectations were diverse, but that does not mean that there were no common themes or shared narratives between them. The fact that Jewish groups from Philo to Qumran could appeal to the same texts like Gen. 49:10 or Num. 24:19 meant that similarities were inevitable. In addition, our ability to define messianism itself depends on some degree of shared consistency among the diverse notions of a messianic agent, hence general descriptions of a Messiah as an eschatological and royal agent who brings deliverance. Second, redefinition is essential in all forms of messianism as each group/author defines what they expect a

Messiah to do. Messianism is redefined in *1 Enoch, 4 Ezra, Pss. Sol.,* the Qumran scrolls, Philo, and Jesus/early church in order to accommodate it to a matrix of additional expectations related to socio-political circumstances and ideological tenets. All forms of messianism involve a reshaping of the messianic epic.

[51] Hurtado, *Lord Jesus Christ*, p. 178; James D.G. Dunn, *Beginning from Jerusalem*, CITM 2 (Grand Rapids, MI: Eerdmans, 2009), p. 214. See Richard N. Longenecker (*The Christology of Early Jewish Christianity* [Grand Rapids, MI: Baker, 1970], p. 63): 'Basic to the christology of the earliest Jewish Christians was the conviction of Jesus as the Messiah. Subject as it was to political and nationalistic connotations, and requiring definition in order to be serviceable, it was the application of this title to Jesus which laid the foundation for the church's continuing thought about, and further acclamation of, the Man from Nazareth. So basic and central, in fact, was the messiahship of Jesus in the consciousness of early believers that it was the Greek word for Messiah, χριστός, and not another, which became uniquely associated with the person of Jesus, first as an appellative and then as a proper name, and which became the basis for their own cognomen in the ancient world as well.' N.A. Dahl (*Jesus the Christ*, pp. 37–8.) 'Thus from the beginnings of Greek-speaking Christianity (within a few years of the crucifixion), the name "Christ" as applied to Jesus must have been firmly established. But this presupposes that Jesus was already designated "the Messiah" and "Jesus the Messiah" in Aramaic-speaking regions. To this extent the Christology of the primitive community from the very first must have been a Messiah Christology.' John P. Meier ('From Elijah-Like Prophet to Royal Davidic Messiah', in *Jesus: A Colloquium in the Holy Land* [ed. Doris Donnelly; London: Continuum, 2001], p. 61) says that belief in Jesus' Davidic descent 'reaches back in many forms to the earliest days of the church and continues to be referred to throughout the first and second generations down to the relatively late books of Acts and Revelation'.

[52] Rudolf Bultmann, 'Die Frage nach dem messianischen Bewusstsein Jesu und das Petrus-Bekenntnis', *ZNW* 19 (1919–20): pp. 165–74.

[53] Bultmann, *Theology of New Testament*, 1:43.

[54] Bultmann, *Theology of New Testament*, 1:32.

[55] Bultmann, *Theology of New Testament*, 1:26.

[56] Allison, *Constructing Jesus*, pp. 243–4.

[57] Cf. Martin Hengel, *Judaism and Hellenism* (2 vols; trans. J. Bowden; London: SCM, 1974), esp. 1:103–6; I. Howard Marshall, 'Palestinian and Hellenistic Christianity: Some Critical Comments', *NTS* 19 (1972–3): pp. 271–87. To give an example, John Mark and Barnabas seem to represent figures who moved quite freely and easily between Aramaic-speaking and Greek-speaking Christian circles. To posit entirely different theologies between the two groups does not seem possible when the distinctions between them were often faint and fluid.

[58] Hahn, *Titles*, pp. 136–222.

[59] Hahn, *Titles*, pp. 148–61.

[60] Hahn, *Titles*, p. 161.

[61] Cf. earlier J.A.T. Robinson, 'The Most Primitive Christology of All?' *JTS* 7 (1956): pp. 177–89.

[62] I. Howard Marshall, '"Israel" and the Story of Salvation: One Theme in Two Parts', in *Jesus and the Heritage of Israel: Luke's Narrative Claim upon Israel's Legacy* (ed. David P. Moessner; Harrisburg, PA: Trinity), p. 355.

[63] Hahn, *Titles*, pp. 162–8.

[64] Hahn, *Titles*, p. 168.

[65] Hahn, *Titles*, pp. 168–72.

[66] Hahn, *Titles*, pp. 172–89.

[67] Hahn, *Titles*, pp. 189–93.

[68] Fuller (*New Testament Christology*, pp. 109–11, 158–64, 184–92) follows a scheme similar to that of Hahn. Fuller thinks that the early church spiritualized the term *Christos*, albeit under influence from Jesus (p. 111). He regards the Son of Man and Messiah titles as equivalents, with the latter introduced to designate Jesus as the end-time ruler (p. 159). In his view the title *Christos* entered the Jesus tradition in divergent ways through different strata of the church. He writes: 'In the Palestinian tradition *Christos* covers first the parousia, then the passion. In the earliest Jewish Hellenistic stratum *Christos* was extended to cover the exaltation, and only much later and sparingly to cover the earthly life' (p. 200 n. 28).

[69] Longenecker, *Christology*, p. 78.

[70] I. Howard Marshall, *The Origins of New Testament Christology* (Leicester: IVP, 1977), pp. 92–3.

[71] Especially in Mark, Matthew, Luke–Acts, the Johannine corpus, Paul's letters, and Revelation.

[72] Cf. Kramer, *Christ, Lord, Son of God*, pp. 38–44.

73 Petr Pokorný, *The Genesis of Christology: Foundations for a Theology of the New Testament* (trans. M. Lefébure; Edinburgh: T&T Clark, 1987), pp. 83–6.

74 Pokorný, *Genesis of Christology*, p. 84.

75 Pokorný, *Genesis of Christology*, pp. 85–6.

76 Cf. Fuller, *New Testament Christology*, pp. 160–61.

77 On the authenticity of the passion predictions see Michael F. Bird, 'Passion Predictions', in *Encyclopedia of the Historical Jesus* (ed. Craig A. Evans; New York: Routledge, 2008), pp. 442–6.

78 P.M. Casey, *From Jewish Prophet to Gentile God: The Origins and Development of New Testament Christology* (Cambridge: James Clarke, 1991), pp. 149–50.

79 Miller, 'Origins of a Messianic Conception of Jesus', pp. 301–36.

80 Miller, 'Origins of a Messianic Conception of Jesus', p. 326.

81 On the influence of Ps. 2 on messianic expectations, see 4Q174 3.10–13; 3.18–19; *Pss. Sol.* 17.23; *1 Enoch* 48.10; *4 Ezra* 13.32,37,52. See on the reception history of Ps. 2, Sam Janse, *"You are My Son": The Reception History of Psalm 2 in Early Judaism and the Early Church*, CBET 51 (Leuven: Peeters, 2009).

82 Cf. Marinus de Jonge, 'The Use of the Word "Anointed" in the Time of Jesus', *NovT* 8 (1966): pp. 133–4; Longenecker, *Christology*, pp. 64–5.

83 1 Sam. 10:1; 12:3; 16:1,13; 24:6,10; 2 Sam. 2:4,7; 5:3,17; 19:21; 1 Kgs 1:39; 19:15–16; Pss. 2:2; 18:50; 84:9; 89:20,38,51; 132:10; Dan. 9:25–26.

84 Exod. 28:41; 30:30; Lev. 4:3,5,16; 6:22; 8:12; 21:10; cf. *2 Macc.* 1.10; *Sir* 45.15; *T. Levi* 17.2–3.

85 1 Kgs 19:16; 1 Chron. 16:22; Ps. 105:15; Isa. 61:1–3.

86 Cf. Andrew Chester, *Messiah and Exaltation: Jewish Messianic and Visionary Traditions and New Testament Christology*, WUNT 207 (Tübingen: Mohr Siebeck, 2007), p. 383.

87 An essay in the same volume by Miller, Barry S. Crawford, 'Christos as Nickname', in *Redescribing Christian Origins* (ed. R. Cameron and M.P. Miller; Leiden: Brill, 2004), pp. 337–48, investigates the application of nicknames to philosophers as a test case for Miller's thesis. Crawford notes that philosophers got their nicknames because of some trait or quality that they possessed, whereas Miller thinks that the nickname *Christos* was applied to Jesus because of forces at work in the social formation of the group. Also, the nicknames were always applied to philosophers while they were still alive, whereas Miller sees the nickname *Christos* applied to Jesus after his death (pp.

347–8). I think this shows that the purported analogy between Jesus nicknamed as *Christos* and nicknames given to Greek philosophers is imprecise.

[88] Cf. Dahl (*Jesus the Christ*, pp. 39–40): 'The messiahship of the crucified Jesus is rather the presupposition that lies at the root of all the scriptural evidence *de Christo*'; James D.G. Dunn (*Jesus Remembered*, CITM 1 [Grand Rapids, MI: Eerdmans, 2003], p. 627): 'The messiahship of the crucified Jesus is the *presupposition* of the scriptural apologetic mounted by the first Christians, not its achievement'.

[89] Cf. Michael F. Bird, 'The Historical Jesus and the "Parting of the Ways"', in *The Handbook of the Study of the Historical Jesus* (ed. T. Holmén and S.E. Porter; 4 vols; Leiden: Brill, 2010), 2:1183–1215.

[90] Jacob Neusner, 'Varieties of Judaism in the Formative Age', in *Jewish Spirituality* (ed. A. Green; London: SCM, 1989), p. 190.

[91] Joachim Jeremias, *New Testament Theology* (trans. J. Bowden; London: SCM, 1971), p. 255.

[92] In regards to development of the messianic idea in early Christianity, according to MacRae ('Messiah and Gospel', p. 174), the Gospels of Mark and John represent a development away from traditional Jewish understanding of the Messiah, while the Gospels of Matthew and Luke represent emphases of continuity through biblical prophecies and their fulfilment. Yet this is a gross over-simplification. First, Luke and Matthew (and perhaps even John) take over Mark's messianic redefinition and intensify his redefinition in some regards, pressing for greater continuity with Judaism on the other hand. Second, Mark and John are both credibly Jewish messianic writings that are equally imbibed with a promise-fulfilment motif. Third, though Matthew and Luke are thoroughly Jewish documents, they also contributed in their own way to an ideological parting between 'Christianity' and 'Judaism'. I do not wish to flatten out the distinctions of the Gospels and the diverse ways that they construct their messianic picture of Jesus in relationship to Jewish hopes. However, all four Gospels clearly constitute an *interpretatio christiana* of the messianic story while simultaneously representing a thoroughly Jewish narrative built on the sacred texts, hermeneutics, community life, and socio-politics of Jews in the Greco-Roman world.

# 1. The Gospel of Mark: The Crucified Messiah

[1] *b.Sanh.* 43a, 107b; Mark 3:22/Matt. 12:24/Luke 11:15; Matt. 27:64; Mark 14:62–64; Luke 23:2; John 7:12,20,47; 8:48–49,52; 10:19–21; Justin, *Dial. Tryph.* 69; 108.

[2] Note the comment by Trypho in Justin's dialogue: 'For you utter many blasphemies, in that you seek to persuade us that this crucified man was with Moses and Aaron, and spoke to them in the pillar of the cloud; then that he became man, was crucified, and ascended up to heaven, and comes again to earth, and ought to be worshipped' (*Dial. Tryph.* 38).

[3] Matt. 21:42; Mark 12:10–11; Luke 20:17; Acts 4:11; 1 Pet. 2:6–8; *Ep. Barn.* 6.24; Justin, *Dial. Tryph.* 36.

[4] Luke 11:29–32/Matt. 12:38–42; Luke 10:12–15/Matt. 10:15; 11:20–24; cf. Luke 4:25–27.

[5] Cf. Craig A. Evans, 'Root Causes of the Jewish-Christian Rift: From Jesus to Justin', in *Christian–Jewish Relations through the Centuries* (ed. Stanley E. Porter and Brook W.R. Pearson; Sheffield: Sheffield Academic Press, 2000), pp. 20–35.

[6] Martin Kähler, *The So-Called Historical Jesus and the Historic Biblical Christ* (Philadelphia: Fortress, 1964 [1892]), p. 80 n. 11. Martin Hengel ('Eye-witness Memory and the Writing of the Gospels: Form Criticism, Community Tradition and the Authority of the Authors', in *The Written Gospel* [ed. M.A. Bockmuehl and D.A. Hagner; FS Graham Stanton; Cambridge: CUP, 2005], p. 72 and n. 11) points out that Plutarch also has two biographies that could be described as passion narratives with extended introductions: *Cato the Younger* and *Eumenes*. Thus Mark's climaxing of Jesus' story in death is not unique in ancient literature.

[7] J.D. Kingsbury, 'The Significance of the Cross within Mark's Story', in *Gospel Interpretation: Narrative Critical and Social-Scientific Approaches* (ed. J.D. Kingsbury; Harrisburg: Trinity, 1997), p. 95.

[8] Acts 5:30; 10:39; 13:29; Gal. 3:13; 4Q169 frags. 3–4; 1.6–9; 11QT 64.7–13; Philo, *Poster. C.* 26; *Spec. Leg.* 3.152.

[9] N.T. Wright, 'The Paul of History and the Apostle of Faith', *TynBul* 29 (1978): p. 68.

[10] Cited from Martin Hengel, *Crucifixion in the Ancient World and the Folly of the Message of the Cross* (trans. John Bowden; London: SCM, 1977), pp. 30–31.

11 Everett Ferguson, *Backgrounds of Early Christianity* (Grand Rapids, MI: Eerdmans, 2nd edn, 1993), p. 560.

12 In addition to Hengel, *Crucifixion*, see recently David Chapman, *Ancient Jewish and Christian Perceptions of Crucifixion* (Grand Rapids, MI: Baker, 2008).

13 Tacitus, *Hist.* 5.13; Suetonius, *Vesp.* 4.5.

14 Josephus, *War* 2.433–34; 4.503–4; 7.25–36.

15 Acts 11:26; 26:28–29; 1 Pet. 4:16; Tacitus, *Ann.* 15.44; Suetonius, *Nero* 16; Pliny the Younger, *Ep.* 10.96.1–5; Josephus, *Ant.* 18.64; Ignatius, *Rom.* 3.2.

16 Tacitus, *Ann.* 15.44; Josephus, *Ant.* 18.64.

17 On the secondary nature of 'Son of God' in Mark 1:1, see Peter Head, 'A Text-Critical Study of Mark 1.1: "The Beginning of the Gospel of Jesus Christ"', *NTS* 37 (1993): pp. 621–9; Adela Yarbro Collins, 'Establishing the Text: Mark 1:1', in *Texts and Contexts: The Function of Biblical Texts in Their Textual and Situational Contexts* (ed. T. Fornberg and D. Hellholm; Oslo: Scandinavian University Press, 1995), pp. 111–27. Yet see in counter-point Tommy Wasserman, 'The "Son of God" Was in the Beginning (Mark 1:1)', *JTS* 62 (2011): pp. 1–31.

18 All emphasis in Scripture quotations is my own.

19 Collins and Collins, *King and Messiah as Son of God*, p. 126. See too Collins, *Mark*, pp. 131–2.

20 John R. Donahue, *The Gospel of Mark*, SP (Collegeville, MN: Liturgical, 2002), p. 60.

21 Francis J. Moloney, *Mark: Storyteller, Interpreter, Evangelist* (Peabody, MA: Hendrickson, 2004), p. 132; I. Howard Marshall, 'Jesus as Messiah in Mark and Matthew', in *The Messiah in the Old and New Testaments* (ed. S.E. Porter; Grand Rapids, MI: Eerdmans, 2007), p. 121.

22 See now Peter Bolt, *The Cross from a Distance: Atonement in Mark's Gospel*, NSBT (Downers Grove, IL: IVP, 2004).

23 *Ant.* 14.172–76; *War* 1.208–15; *Ant.* 15.369–71; 17.41–45; *War* 1.571–73; *Ant.* 17.149–67; *War* 1.648–655.

24 Robert Fowler, *Loaves and Fishes: The Function of the Feeding Stories in the Gospel of Mark* (Chico, CA: Scholars, 1981), p. 159 (italics original).

25 On this peculiar pericope see Steven M. Bryan, *Jesus and Israel's Traditions of Judgement and Restoration*, SNTS 117 (Cambridge: CUP, 2002), pp. 89–129.

26 G.W.E. Nicklesburg, 'The Genre and Function of the Markan Passion Narrative', *HTR* 73 (1980): p. 172.

[27] Cf. Collins and Collins (*King and Messiah as Son of God*, pp. 132–3): 'The anonymous woman of 14:3–9 is a culturally unlikely choice for the role of choosing and anointing Jesus as king, but her action suggests that such is what she is doing: she pours a bottle of aromatic oil upon his head [see 1 Sam. 10:1; 1 Kgs 19:15–16]. Yet the gesture is reinterpreted by Jesus as anointment for burial; this reinterpretation contributes to the author's redefinition of messiahship to include suffering and death'. Similarly Collins, *Mark*, p. 71. See also Craig A. Evans (*Mark 8:27 – 16:20*, WBC [Waco, TX: Thomas Nelson, 2001], p. 360): 'Her action was spontaneous and impromptu and would not have been interpreted in any official sense, to be sure, but anointing the head of one whom she and the disciples regarded as Israel's Messiah would in all probability have been perceived in a messianic sense.'

[28] D.H. Juel, 'The Origins of Mark's Christology', in *The Messiah: Developments in Earliest Judaism and Christianity* (ed. J.H. Charlesworth; Fortress: Minneapolis: 1992), p. 458.

[29] Kent Brower, 'Mark 9:1 – Seeing the Kingdom in Power', *JSNT* 6 (1980): pp. 17–41; Paul Barnett, *The Servant King* (Sydney: AIO, 2000), pp. 171-4; Wright, *Jesus and the Victory of God*, p. 470; Michael Bird, 'The Crucifixion of Jesus as the Fulfillment of Mark 9:1', *TrinJ* 24 (2003): pp. 23–36.

[30] Cf. Joachim Jeremias, *New Testament Theology* (trans. John Bowden; London: SCM, 1971), pp. 292–3; Rikki E. Watts, *Isaiah's New Exodus and Mark*, WUNT 2.88 (Tübingen: Mohr Siebeck, 1997), pp. 258–87; Craig A. Evans, *Mark 8:27 – 16:20*, WBC 34b (Nashville: Thomas Nelson, 2001), pp. 121–2; Ben Witherington, *The Gospel of Mark: A Socio-Rhetorical Commentary* (Grand Rapids, MI: Eerdmans, 2001), pp. 288–90; R.T. France, *The Gospel of Mark*, NIGTC (Grand Rapids, MI: Eerdmans, 2002), pp. 420–1.

[31] Rom. 3:24; 8.23; 1 Cor. 1:30; Gal. 1:4; 4:5; Eph. 1:7,14; 4.30; Col. 1:14; 1 Tim. 2:6; Titus 2:14. On Pauline influence on Mark see Joel Marcus, 'Mark – Interpreter of Paul', *NTS* 46 (2000): pp. 473–87; Michael F. Bird, 'Mark: Interpreter of Peter and Disciple of Paul', in *Paul and the Gospels: Christologies, Conflicts, and Convergences*, LNTS 411 (ed. M.F. Bird and J. Willitts; London: T&T Clark, 2011), pp. 30–61.

[32] Morna D. Hooker, *Not Ashamed of the Gospel: New Testament Interpretations of the Death of Christ* (Carlisle: Paternoster, 1994), p. 67.

[33] Juel, 'The Origins of Mark's Christology', p. 456.

[34] Christopher M. Tuckett, *Christology and the New Testament: Jesus and His Earliest Followers* (Louisville: Westminster John Knox, 2001), p. 116.

[35] Larry Hurtado, 'Christ', in *DJG* (ed. J.B. Green, S. McKnight, I.H. Marshall; Downers Grove, IL: IVP, 1992), p. 111.

[36] Although many scholars still regard Mark 14:62 as a reference to Jesus' *parousia* (e.g. Gundry, *Mark*, pp. 886–7; M. Eugene Boring, *Mark: A Commentary*, NTL [Louisville: KY: Westminster John Knox, 2006], p. 250), the tide has very much turned and most see it as a reference to Jesus' enthronement (e.g. France, *Mark*, pp. 612–3).

[37] Paul Barnett, 'Mark: Story and History', *In the Fullness of Time: Biblical Studies in Honour of Archbishop Donald Robinson* (ed. D. Peterson and J. Pryor; Sydney: Lancer, 1992), p. 34.

[38] My translation.

[39] My translation.

[40] Suetonius, *Caligula* 32.2; *Domitian* 10.1; Dio Cassius 54.3.6–7; Juvenal, *Sat.* 6.230; Pliny, *Ep.* 6.10.3; 9.19.3; Eusebius, *Hist. Eccl.* 5.1.44.

[41] M. Eugene Boring, 'The Kingdom of God in Mark', in *The Kingdom of God in 20th Century Interpretation* (ed. Wendell Willis; Peabody, MA: Hendrickson, 1975), p. 144.

[42] Bird, 'Crucifixion of Jesus', pp. 31–2.

[43] Juel, 'Origins of Mark's Christology', p. 452.

[44] Juel ('Origins of Mark's Christology', p. 453) states: 'The irony in the story is pronounced, but it only works if Jesus is the Christ.'

[45] Cf. Frank Matera (*The Kingship of Jesus: Composition and Theology in Mark 15*, SBLDS 66 (Chico, CA: Scholars, 1982], p. 150): 'Jesus is the King of the Jews and the King of Israel because, as the centurion correctly confessed, he is the royal Son of the Baptism, the Transfiguration, and the parable of the vineyard. Thus, the royal theme may be the thread which runs through the titles of Mark's Gospel.'

[46] Wilhelm Bousset, *Kyrios Christos* (trans. J.E. Steely; Nashville: Abingdon, 1970), p. 71.

[47] On Jews as a subset of Greco-Roman readers, see Peter Bolt, *Jesus' Defeat of Death: Persuading Mark's Early Readers*, SNTS 125 (Cambridge: CUP, 2003), p. 10.

[48] T.E. Schmidt, 'Mark 15.16–32: The Crucifixion Narrative and the Roman Triumphal Procession', *NTS* 41 (1995): pp. 1–18; cf. S.J. Hafemann, 'Roman Triumph', in *DNTB* (ed. Craig A. Evans and Stanley E. Porter; Downers Grove, IL: IVP, 2000), pp. 1004–8; Evans, *Mark 8:27 – 16:20*, pp. lxxv–lxxxix.

[49] Schmidt, 'The Crucifixion Narrative', p. 16.

[50] Schmidt, 'The Crucifixion Narrative', p. 1.

[51] Isa. 40:11; 49:9–10; Jer. 23:1–6; Ezek. 34; Philo, *Agric.* 41; *Leg. Gai.* 44; Homer, *Il.* 2.75–109; *Odys.* 3.156; Dio Chrysostom, *Disc.* 1.13–28; 2.6; 3.41; 4.43–44. See Sharyn Dowd, *Reading Mark: A Literary and Theological Commentary on the Second Gospel* (Macon, GA: Smyth & Helwys, 2000), p. 68 and Bolt, *Jesus' Defeat of Death*, pp. 193–4 for discussion of this image.

[52] David Seeley, 'Rulership and Service in Mark 10:41–45', *NovT* 35 (1993): pp. 236, 238.

[53] Cf. Bruce Malina, *The New Testament World: Insights from Cultural Anthropology* (Atlanta: John Knox, 1981), pp. 29–46; Halvor Moxnes, 'Honor and Shame', *BTB* 23 (1993): pp. 167–76; David A. deSilva, *An Introduction to the New Testament: Context, Methods and Ministry Formation* (Downers Grove, IL: IVP, 2004), pp. 125–30.

[54] Mark 2:1–11,14–17,18–22,23–28; 3:1–6,22–30; 12:13–17,18–27.

[55] Dowd, *Reading Mark*, pp. 88, 113.

[56] Plato, *Gorg.* 526d–527a; Sir. 2.15–17; 23.18-19; Wis 2.12 – 3.5; 4.16 – 5.8; *4 Macc.* 13.3,17; 17.5. deSilva, *Introduction*, p. 128.

[57] Paul Achtemeier, *Mark*, Proclamation (Philadelphia: Fortress), p. 102; see too Peter Bolt, 'Feeling the Cross: Mark's Message of Atonement', *RTR* 60 (2001): p. 6.

[58] According to Helmut Koester (*Paul and His World*, p. 107): 'Mark's Gospel confronted the challenge to reconcile the christology of Jesus as the miracle-working Messiah with the Christology of the Suffering Servant/Son of Man.'

[59] Bird, 'Crucifixion of Jesus', p. 30. W. Grundmann (*TDNT* 9.528–29) wrote: 'These expound one another. Jesus is the Messiah as the Son of God, and as such He is the Son of Man. New precision is thus given to the meaning of the Messiah by the history of Jesus.' See too Collins and Collins, *King and Messiah as Son of God*, pp. 130, 133; Collins, *Mark*, p. 704; Marshall, *'Jesus as Messiah'*, pp. 129–31; Blomberg, 'Messiah', p. 115; Dieter Lührmann, *Das Markusevangelium*, HNT (Tübingen: Mohr Siebeck, 1987), pp. 149, 250.

[60] There is a variant in Mark 1:34 (attested by B L W Θ $f^1$ 28 33$^{vid}$ et al.) that reads αὐτον χριστόν εἰναι ('him to be Messiah').

[61] Cf. Hurtado, 'Christ', p. 110.

[62] Cf. Bird, *One to Come*, pp. 130–2.

[63] Hurtado, 'Christ', p. 111.

[64] Dale C. Allison, *The Historical Christ and the Theological Jesus* (Grand Rapids, MI: Eerdmans, 2009), p. 27; Bolt, *Cross at a Distance*, pp. 97–9.

[65] Contrast the views of Jack Kingsbury (*The Christology of Mark's Gospel* [Philadelphia: Fortress, 1983], pp. 47–156) who takes 'Son of God' as central in Mark, and Paul Achtemeier (*Mark*, pp. 58–60) who takes 'Son of Man' as the most central.

[66] On the Son of Man and messianism, see Bird, *One to Come*, pp. 78–98.

[67] Cf. Rudolf Bultmann, *Theology of the New Testament* (2 vols; trans. Kendrick Grobel; London: SCM, 1952), 1:30.

[68] Cf. Craig A. Evans, 'Defeating Satan and Liberating Israel: Jesus and Daniel's Visions', *JSHJ* 1 (2003): pp. 161–70; Simon Gathercole, 'The Son of Man in Mark's Gospel', *ExpT* 115 (2004): pp. 366–72.

[69] MacRae, 'Messiah and Gospel', p. 175.

[70] Hurtado, 'Christ', p. 111. R.E. Watts ('Mark', in *CNTUOT* (ed. D.A. Carson and G.K. Beale [Grand Rapids, MI: Baker, 2007], p. 235) sees in Mark 14:62: 'Here, in another climactic moment, he is faithful Israel's representative messianic Son of Man sharing God's authority. By the same token, ecclesiologically, those who follow him constitute the authentic remnant Israel, and the temple authorities, in opposing him, have ironically put themselves in the same category as Daniel's fourth beast and little horn.'

[71] William Horbury, 'The Messianic Associations of the Son of Man', in *Messianism among Jews and Christians* (London: T&T Clark, 2003), pp. 125-5; Wright, *Jesus and the Victory of God*, pp. 512–19; Bird, *One to Come*, pp. 78–98.

[72] Reference to son(s) of God in the Old Testament can also describe angels (Job 1:6; 2:1; 38:7), Israel (Exod. 4:22; Hos. 1:10), special leaders (Num. 16:30; Isa. 8:21), and the righteous (Wis 2.18; 5.5).

[73] Herbert W. Bateman, 'Defining the Titles "Christ" and "Son of God" in Mark's Narrative Presentation of Jesus', *JETS* 50 (2007): pp. 546–57.

[74] Cf. Collins (*Mark*, p. 65): 'In the Gospel of Mark, therefore, the divine voice suggests to an audience familiar with the messianic reading of Psalm 2, that Jesus is the royal Messiah or the Messiah of Israel'. The claim of Aquila H.I. Lee (*From Messiah to Preexistent Son: Jesus' Self-Consciousness and Early Christian Exegesis of Messianic Psalms*, WUNT 2.192 [Tübingen: Mohr Siebeck, 2005], p. 318) that Jesus was the Messiah because he was the Son of God is certainly possible, but I find no reason to make Jesus' messianic identity subservient to his sense of divine sonship, or vice versa.

[75] Bateman, 'Defining the Titles', p. 549.

[76] Cf. Juel, *Messianic Exegesis*, pp. 93–9; Jocelyn McWhirter, 'Messianic Exegesis in Mark's Passion Narrative', in *The Trial and Death of Jesus: Essays on the Passion Narrative in Mark* (ed. Geert van Oyen and Tom Shepherd; Leuven: Peeters, 2006), pp. 69–97.

[77] Cf. Robert H. Gundry (*Mark: A Commentary on His Apology for the Cross* [Grand Rapids, MI: Eerdmans, 1993], p. 886): 'Jesus' affirmation, "I am" (cf. 1 Tim. 6:13), feeds into Mark's writing this gospel to argue for Jesus' christhood and divine sonship despite the scandal of the Cross.'

[78] Collins (*Mark*, p. 72) claims that 'this passage shows clearly that the suffering and rejection of Jesus belong to the period in which he is the hidden Son of Man (cf. Mark 8:30–31) and that the exercise of the messianic office will commence after his resurrection and exaltation.' Yet this fails to reckon with the messianic ministry of Jesus from his exorcisms to his triumphal entry. Also, Mark 14:62 may refer to Jesus' death upon the cross as the beginning of his messianic enthronement! Joel Marcus ('Mark 14:61: "Are You the Messiah-Son-of-God?"', *NovT* 31 [1989]: pp. 125–41) wonders whether the two titles ὁ Χριστὸς ὁ υἱὸς τοῦ εὐλογητοῦ ('the Messiah, the son of the Blessed One') are in non-restrictive apposition (i.e. synonymous) or in 'restrictive apposition' (i.e. one qualifies the other). If the latter, then Jesus is not simply asked if he is the Messiah-Son-of-David (i.e. a national Messiah), but if he is the Messiah-Son-of-God (i.e. a quasi-divine Messiah). Though I think that Mark does at places indicate Jesus' 'intrinsic divinity' (Philip R. Davies, 'Mark's Christological Paradox', in *The Synoptic Gospels: A Sheffield Reader*, BS 31 [ed. C.A. Evans and S.E. Porter; Sheffield: Sheffield Academic Press, 1995], p. 175; cf. Eugene M. Boring, 'Markan Christology: God-Language for Jesus?' *NTS* 45 [1999]: pp. 451–71), the title 'Son of God' when used of messianic figures does not necessarily imply divinity (see e.g. 4Q246).

[79] Boring, *Mark*, p. 414.

[80] Collins, *Mark*, p. 75.

[81] Hurtado, 'Christ', p. 111.

[82] Stephen H. Smith, 'The Function of the Son of David Tradition in Mark's Gospel', *NTS* 42 (1996): p. 523.

[83] Cf. similarly Kingsbury, *The Christology of Mark's Gospel*, p. 111; Hooker, '"Who Can This Be?"' p. 93.

[84] Daniel Johansson, 'Kyrios in the Gospel of Mark', *JSNT* 22 (2010): pp. 116–19.

85 Smith, 'Son of David', p. 535.

86 Hurtado, *Lord Jesus Christ*, p. 289.

87 Cf. Joel Marcus (*The Way of the Lord: Christological Exegesis of the Old Testament in the Gospel of Mark* [Edinburgh: T&T Clark, 1993], p. 202) who writes: 'there seems to be no Jewish parallel for Mark's thought that the Messiah's kingship and the kingdom of God are manifested already and in a definitive way in his [Jesus'] suffering and death'.

88 Donald Senior, *The Passion of Jesus in the Gospel of Mark* (Wilmington, DE: Michael Glazier, 1984), p. 121.

89 Moloney, *Mark*, p. 136 (italics added).

90 Cf. Juel, 'The Origins of Mark's Christology', p. 450.

91 Contra S.G.F. Brandon, *Jesus and the Zealots* (Manchester: Manchester University Press, 1967), pp. 221–82.

92 Gundry, *Mark*, pp. 1022–6; Evans, *Mark 8:27 – 16:20*, p. xciii; Joel F. Williams, 'Is Mark's Gospel an Apology for the Cross?' *BBR* 12 (2002): pp. 97–122; Robert H. Gundry, 'A Rejoinder to Joel F. Williams's "Is Mark's Gospel an Apology for the Cross?"' *BBR* 12 (2002): pp. 123–40; Adam Winn, *The Purpose of Mark's Gospel: An Early Christian Response to Roman Imperial*, WUNT 2.245 (Tübingen: Mohr Siebeck, 2008), pp. 28–31.

93 Cf. W. Manson (*Jesus the Messiah* [London: Hodder & Stoughton, 1943], p. 169): 'From saying that Jesus was the Messiah despite the event of the cross they came to say that he was the Messiah in virtue of that event'; Dowd (*Reading Mark*, p. 155): 'According to the author of Mark, of course, it was precisely Jesus' crucifixion that qualified him as Messiah.' Morna D. Hooker ('"Who Can This Be?" The Christology of Mark's Gospel', in *Contours of Christology in the New Testament* [ed. R.N. Longenecker; Grand Rapids, MI: Eerdmans, 2005], p. 94): 'It is not that Jesus is the Messiah and Son of God *in spite of suffering*. Rather, it is (1) *because* he is the Messiah that he will not come down from the cross (15:32) and (2) *because* he is God's Son that he dies in obedience to what he believes to be his Father's will (15:39; cf. 14:36)' (italics original).

## 2. The Gospel of Matthew: The Davidic Messiah

1 Cf. Jesper Svartvik, 'Matthew and Mark', in *Matthew and His Christian Contemporaries*, LNTS 333 (ed. D.C. Sim and B. Repschinski; London: T&T Clark, 2008), pp. 36–41.

[2] Stephen C. Barton, 'The Gospel according to Matthew', in *The Cambridge Companion to the Gospels* (ed. Stephen C. Barton; Cambridge: CUP, 2006), pp. 121–4.

[3] According to James Carleton Paget ('The Four among Jews', in *The Written Gospel* [ed. Markus Bockmuehl and Donald A. Hagner; Cambridge: CUP, 2005], p. 207): 'The best case for something approximating to a Jewish audience can be made for the Gospel of Matthew. In making such a case we might combine the external testimony of Origen that the Gospel was written for Jews who had come to believe (*tois apo Ioudaismou pisteusasin*: Eusebius, *Hist. Eccl.* 6.25.4), which may itself reflect an old tradition, emerging from the view that Matthew was originally written in Hebrew or Aramaic . . . the fact that, in whatever form, groups described as Jewish Christian possessed copies of Matthew, and certain internal indicators (Matthew's apparently more conservative attitude to the Jewish law, for instance). Such a case assumes Jewish Christian rather than non-Christian Jewish readers, but we should not hold to such a clear division between the two in the first century. If Jewish Christians were the intended audience of some Gospels, then we should assume that they would have spoken to unconverted Jews about them.'

[4] Edouard Massoux (*The Influence of the Gospel of Saint Matthew on Christian Literature before Saint Irenaeus* [2 vols; ed. Arthur J. Bellinzoni; trans. Norman J. Belval and Suzanne Hect; Macon, GA: Mercer University Press, 1990–93], 2:187) writes: 'Until the end of the second century, the first gospel remained the gospel par excellence. People looked to Mt. for teaching which conditioned Christian behavior so that the Gospel of Mt. became the norm for Christian life.' See also W.-D. Köhler, *Die Rezeption des Matthäusevangeliums in der Zeit vor Irenäus* (Tübingen: Mohr Siebeck, 1987).

[5] Cf. David Parker, *An Introduction to the New Testament Manuscripts and Their Texts* (Cambridge: CUP, 2008), pp. 317–19.

[6] Dunn, *Unity and Diversity*, p. 384.

[7] R.T. France, *The Gospel of Matthew*, NICNT (Grand Rapids, MI: Eerdmans, 2007), p. 25.

[8] Cf. Dale C. Allison, 'Matthew's First Two Words (Matt I.I)', in *Studies in Matthew: Interpretation Past and Present* (Grand Rapids, MI: Baker, 2005), pp. 157–62.

[9] Keener (*Matthew: A Socio-Rhetorical Commentary* [Grand Rapids, MI: Eerdmans, 2nd edn, 2009], p. 77) writes: 'By evoking great heroes

of the past like David and Josiah, Matthew points his readers to the ultimate hero to whom all those stories pointed. For Matthew and his circle of Jewish Christians, Jesus was not an afterthought to Judaism, a distinct and unexpected addition to God's plan in the Old Testament. Jesus was the goal to which Israel's lovingly remembered history had pointed.'

10   Cf. e.g. D.A. Hagner, *Matthew 1 – 14*, WBC (Dallas, TX: Word, 1993), p. 9.

11   Cf. Joseph, *Ant.* 20.200: Ἰησοῦ τοῦ λεγόμενου Χριστοῦ. See also Justin Martyr (*Dial. Tryph.* 32) where Trypho refers to 'this so-called Christ of yours' (οὗτος δὲ ὁ ὑμέτερος λεγόμενος Χριστός).

12   Jack Dean Kingsbury, *Matthew: Structure, Christology, Kingdom* (Minneapolis: Fortress, 1975), p. 97.

13   Cf. 'Behold, O Lord, and raise up to them their king, the son of David, at the time, in the which you choose, O God, that he may reign over Israel your servant' (*Pss. Sol.* 17.21); 'He is the Branch of David who shall arise with the Interpreter of the Law [to rule] in Zion [at the end] of time. As it is written, I will raise up the tent of David that is fallen [Amos 9:11]. That is to say, the fallen tent of David is he who shall arise to save Israel' (4Q174 1.10–14); 'this is the Messiah whom the Most High has kept until the end of days, who will arise from the offspring of David' (*4 Ezra* 12.32); 'the kingship of the house of David, thy righteous Messiah' (*Shemoneh 'Esreh* 14).

14   Cf. 'It has been found in writing concerning the Spartans and the Jews that they are brothers and are of the family of Abraham' (*1 Macc.* 12.21); 'For these things I leave you instead of inheritance. Therefore, give them to your children for an everlasting possession; for so did both Abraham, Isaac, and Jacob. All these things they gave us for an inheritance, saying: Keep the commandments of God, until the Lord will reveal His salvation to all nations' (*T. Benj.* 10.4–5); 'You know, Sedrach, that there are nations that have not the law and that do the works of the law: for [if] they are unbaptized and my divine spirit come to them and they turn to my baptism, I also receive them with my righteous ones into the bosom of Abraham' (*Apoc. Sed.* 14.5); 'I will make Adam first . . . and if he goes astray I will send Abraham to sort it out' (*Gen. Rab.* 14.6). See further Bird, *Jesus and the Origins of the Gentile Mission*, pp. 126–7.

15   N.T. Wright, *The New Testament and the People of God*, COQG (London: SPCK, 1992), pp. 385–6.

16 Cited in Karl Barth, *Church Dogmatics* I/1.176.

17 Jason Hood, *The Messiah, His Brothers, and the Nations*, LNTS 441 (London: T&T Clark, 2011).

18 Richard Hays, 'The Gospel of Matthew: Reconfigured Torah', *HTS* 61 (2001): p. 187.

19 4QpIsaᵃ frags. 7–10.iii.25; 4Q252 5.1–7; *T.Jud.* 22.1–3; 24.1; *Sib. Or.* 5.415; Justin, *1 Apol.* 32; 54; *Dial. Tryph.* 52; 120; Clement of Alexandria, *Paed.* 1.5–6; Irenaeus, *Adv. Haer.* 4.10.2.

20 Hood, *Messiah*, pp. 67–87.

21 Hood, *Messiah*, pp. 88–138.

22 On mission in Matthew's Gospel see John D. Harvey, 'Mission in Matthew', in *Mission in the New Testament: An Evangelical Approach* (ed. W. Larkin and J.F. Williams; Maryknoll, NY: Doubleday, 1998), pp. 119–36; James LaGrand, *The Earliest Christian Mission to 'All Nations' in the Light of Matthew's Gospel* (Grand Rapids, MI: Eerdmans, 1999); Andreas Köstenberger and Peter T. O'Brien, *Salvation to the Ends of the Earth: A Biblical Theology of Missions* (Downers Grove, IL: IVP, 2001), pp. 87–109; Florian Wilk, *Jesus und die Völker in der Sicht der Synoptiker*, BZNW 109 (Berlin: Walter de Gruyter, 2002); Paul Foster, *Community, Law, and Mission in Matthew's Gospel*, WUNT 2.177 (Tübingen: Mohr Siebeck, 2004), pp. 218–52.

23 The exilic theme reappears in Matthew. The citation of Hos. 11:1 ('Out of Egypt I called my son') in Matt. 2:15 is peculiar not because of the typology that it employs, but because of its literary location. Whereas one might naturally expect the Hosea passage to be cited after Joseph's dream to return to Israel in Matt. 2:20–21, whereby Jesus then recapitulates the story of Israel in his person by also coming out of Egypt, the Hosea text is actually cited earlier while the child Jesus is still in Israel and under the jurisdiction of Herod. This unexpected intertextual device perhaps indicates that it is Israel and not Egypt that is regarded as the land of exile and bondage (R. Joel Kennedy, *The Recapitulation of Israel*, WUNT 2.257 [Tübingen: Mohr Siebeck, 2008], pp. 125–43). Later, the reference to Rachel weeping for her children from Jer. 31:15 cited in Matt. 2:18 relates the theme of exilic suffering to the tribulations being experienced in Judea at the time of Jesus' birth. As D.A. Carson ('Matthew', in *EBC* [12 vols; ed. Frank E. Gaeblein; Grand Rapids, MI: Eerdmans, 1984], 8:50) writes: 'The tears of exile are now being "fulfilled" – i.e., the tears begun in Jeremiah's day are climaxed and ended by the tears of the mothers of

Bethlehem. The heir to David's throne has come, the Exile is over, the true Son of God has arrived, and he will introduce the new covenant (26:28) promised by Jeremiah'. The Matthean combination of Jesus' encounter with a centurion (Matt. 8:5–10) with a logion about many coming from the 'east and the west' to join the patriarchal banquet (Matt. 8:11–13) is designed to show that Christian communities and the Christian mission are the mode in which the prophetic promises of Israel's return from exile and the eschatological pilgrimage of the Gentiles are fulfilled (see Ps. 107:3; Isa. 43:5; Zech. 8:7,23; *Bar* 5.5; *Tob.* 14.5–6). See further Michael F. Bird, 'Jesus and the Continuing Exile of Israel in the Writings of N.T. Wright', in *Jesus as Israel's Messiah: Engaging the Work of N. Thomas Wright*, LNTS (eds. Robert L. Webb and Mark Allan Powell; London: T&T Clark, forthcoming 2012).

[24] So Wright, *New Testament and the People of God*, pp. 299–338.

[25] Kennedy, *Recapitulation of Israel*, pp. 100–01.

[26] Several Latin and Syriac texts omit Ἰησοῦς, resulting in 'The Messiah's origin'. Several scholars (e.g. France, *Gospel of Matthew*, p. 46 n. 13; Metzger, *Textual Commentary*, pp. 6–7) regard the minority reading as more probably since Ἰησοῦς Χριστὸς is generally never used in the New Testament with the article. Yet the wider attestation of the majority reading in the earliest Greek texts and the parallel double name Ἰησοῦς Χριστὸς in 1:1 makes the reading τοῦ δὲ Ἰησοῦς Χριστὸς slightly more probable in my mind.

[27] On critical issues relating to the virgin conception, see Michael F. Bird, 'Birth of Jesus', *Encyclopedia of the Historical Jesus* (ed. Craig A. Evans; New York: Routledge, 2008), pp. 71–5.

[28] Novakovic, *Messiah, the Healer of the Sick*, pp. 43–5.

[29] Krister Stendahl, '*Quis et Unde? An Analysis of Matthew 1 – 2*', in *The Interpretation of Matthew* (ed. G.N. Stanton; Edinburgh: T&T Clark, 2nd edn, 1995), p. 76.

[30] Bird, *Jesus and the Origins of the Gentile Mission*, pp. 90–92.

[31] Kennedy, *Recapitulation of Israel*, pp. 128–53.

[32] Cf. Keener, *Matthew*, p. 112.

[33] Nolland, *Gospel of Matthew*, p. 125; similar is Terence Donaldson ('The Vindicated Son: A Narrative Approach to Matthean Christology', in *Contours of Christology in the New Testament* [ed. Richard N. Longenecker; Grand Rapids, MI: Eerdmans, 2005] p. 116): 'Matthew, therefore, presents Jesus as one who in his experience recapitulates the story of Israel. Like Israel of old, Jesus has been called by God out

of Egypt to a life of humble obedience; like Israel, this calling was put to the test in the wilderness. The hope of the story is that, unlike Israel, Jesus will remain faithful where Israel was disobedient.'

[34] Stendahl, *'Quis et Unde?'* pp. 69–80.

[35] Kingsbury, *Matthew*, p. 98.

[36] Joel Willitts, *Matthew's Messianic Shepherd-King*, BZNW 147 (Berlin: Walter de Gruyter, 2007), p. 115.

[37] Matera, *Christology*, p. 40.

[38] Kingsbury, *Matthew*, p. 103.

[39] Dennis C. Duling, 'Solomon, Exorcism, and the Son of David', *HTR* 68 (1975): pp. 235–52; Bruce Chilton, 'Jesus ben David: Reflections on the Davidssohnfrage', *JSNT* 4 (1982): pp. 88–112; Stephen H. Smith, 'The Function of the Son of David Tradition in Mark's Gospel', *NTS* 42 (1996): pp. 523–39; but see criticism in Marcus, *Way of the Lord*, pp. 151–2; Gundry, *Matthew*, p. 231.

[40] Richard Beaton (*Isaiah's Christ in Matthew's Gospel*, SNTSMS 123 [Cambridge: CUP, 2002], p. 192) examines the usage of Isa. 42:1–4 in Matt. 11 – 12, particularly concerning the theme of justice for the nations, and he concludes: 'With regard to Isa. 42.1–4, it seems that the quotation was employed by Matthew to validate a particular view of Jesus as royal messiah, namely that he was the Spirit-endowed compassionate servant of the Lord whose words and deeds evinced the justice anticipated with the advent of the messiah and the inauguration of the Kingdom of God.'

[41] The pictures of Jesus as the eschatological shepherd and the therapeutic Davidic king in addition to being a divinely appointed judge do not have to be played off against each other as Jesus exercises both roles sequentially (see Young S. Chae, *Jesus as the Eschatological Davidic Shepherd: Studies in the Old Testament, Second Temple Judaism, and in the Gospel of Matthew*, WUNT 2.216 (Tübingen: Mohr Siebeck, 2006], p. 285).

[42] Marshall, 'Jesus as Messiah', pp. 135–6.

[43] See exploration of this theme in Jewish literature and in Willitts, *Matthew's Messianic Shepherd-King*, pp. 49–92.

[44] Novakovic (*Messiah*, pp. 153–7) suggests that 'coming one' reflects the LXX of Hab. 2:3 so that John, like Habakkuk, is concerned with the problem of the apparent delay of God's deliverance.

[45] Cf. Grant Macaskill, *Revealed Wisdom and Inaugurated Eschatology in Ancient Judaism and Early Christianity* (Leiden: Brill, 2007), pp. 137–8.

46 Novakovic, *Messiah*, p. 90.

47 France, *Gospel of Matthew*, p. 425.

48 D.A. Hagner, *Matthew 14 – 28*, WBC (Waco, TX: Word, 1995), p. 463.

49 Nolland, *Gospel of Matthew*, p. 665.

50 Robert H. Gundry (*Matthew: A Commentary on His Handbook for a Mixed Church under Persecution* [Grand Rapids, MI: Baker, 2nd edn, 1994], p. 330) sees the confession combined with the birth narrative as indicating a 'connotation of essential deity'. W.D. Davies and Dale C. Allison (*The Gospel according to Saint Matthew*, ICC [3 vols; Edinburgh: T&T Clark, 1988–97], 1:217) believe that Jesus is a human being 'in whom God's active presence, that is, the divine favor and blessing and aid, have manifested themselves'.

51 Cf. Davies and Allison, *Saint Matthew*, 2:609–15; Hagner, *Matthew 14 – 28*, pp. 465–6.

52 Bird, *Jesus and the Origins of the Gentile Mission*, pp. 159–60.

53 But see John 4:25: '"I know that Messiah" (called Christ) "is coming. When he comes, he will *explain everything to us.*"'

54 N.A. Dahl, 'The Passion Narrative in Matthew', in *The Interpretation of Matthew* (ed. G.N. Stanton; London: SPCK, 2nd edn, 1995), p. 64.

55 John Yueh-Han Yieh, *One Teacher: Jesus' Teaching Role in Matthew's Gospel Report*, BZNW 124 (New York: Walter de Gruyter, 2004), p. 243.

56 Dale C. Allison, *The New Moses: A Matthean Typology* (Minneapolis: Fortress, 1993), p. 277.

57 Cf. discussion in Lloyd Gaston, 'The Messiah of Israel as Teacher of the Gentiles', *Int* 29 (1975): pp. 24–40.

58 Nolland, *Gospel of Matthew*, p. 929.

59 France, *Gospel of Matthew*, p. 1027.

60 Gundry, *Matthew*, p. 413.

61 Cf. Wis 2.17–18 about God rescuing the righteous sufferer.

62 Nolland, *Gospel of Matthew*, p. 1197; cf. Keener, *Matthew*, p. 682.

63 Kingsbury, *Matthew*, p. 98.

64 Frank Matera, *New Testament Christology* (Louisville, KY: Westminster John Knox, 1999), p. 27.

65 Donaldson, 'The Vindicated Son', p. 120.

66 Marshall ('Jesus as Messiah', p. 138) rightly comments: 'There has been some discussion as to whether the concept of Messiah or that of Son of God has priority in Matthew's Christology. The debate is probably futile, and we should recognize that both lines of thought are essential for a full understanding of the role and status of Jesus.'

[67] MacRae, 'Messiah and Gospel', p. 180.

[68] Willitts, *Matthew's Messianic Shepherd–King*, pp. 224–32.

## 3. The Gospel of Luke (and Acts): The Prophetic Messiah

[1] E. Earle Ellis, *The Gospel of Luke*, NCBC (Greenwood, SC: Attic, 1974), p. 11.

[2] Walter Grundmann, *TDNT* 9.533.

[3] Brendan Byrne, 'Jesus as Messiah in the Gospel of Luke: Discerning a Pattern of Correction', *CBQ* 65 (2003): p. 85.

[4] Mark L. Strauss, *The Davidic Messiah in Luke–Acts: The Promise and Fulfilment in Luke's Christology*, JSNTSup 110 (Sheffield: Sheffield Academic Press, 1995), p. 340. See also Yuzuru Miura, *David in Luke–Acts: His Portrayal in the Light of Early Judaism*, WUNT 2.232 (Tübingen: Mohr Siebeck, 2007).

[5] Strauss, *Davidic Messiah in Luke–Acts*, p. 89.

[6] C. Kavin Rowe, *Early Narrative Christology: The Lord in the Gospel of Luke*, BZNW 139 (Berlin: Walter de Gruyter, 2006), pp. 203–4.

[7] Notably the closest parallel to 'horn of my salvation' occurs in 2 Sam. 22:3 and Ps. 18:2 (LXX), both in relation to David. David W. Pao and Eckhard J. Schnabel, 'Luke', in *CNTUOT* (ed. D.A. Carson and G.K. Beale; Grand Rapids, MI: Baker, 2007), p. 263 (pp. 251–414).

[8] In Zech. 6:12 and Jer. 23:5 (LXX) there is a deliberate play on words with ἀνατολή ('rising dawn') and ἀνατέλλω ('rise up') and ἀνίστημι ('stand up'). See also the reference to 'light' (φῶς) in relation to the messianic star in Num. 24:17 and also Isa. 60:1, Mal. 3:20, and 2 Sam. 23:4 (LXX). Mention should also be made of Ezek. 43:2, which refers to 'God', 'glory', 'Israel', 'light', and 'east'.

[9] Graham Stanton, 'Messianism and Christology: Mark, Matthew, Luke and Acts', in *Redemption and Resistance* (ed. M. Bockmuehl and J.C. Paget; London: T&T Clark, 2007), p. 88.

[10] Gathercole, *Preexistent Son*, pp. 240–42.

[11] John Nolland, *Luke 1 – 9:20*, WBC (Dallas, TX: Word, 1989), p. 90.

[12] Strauss, *Davidic Messiah in Luke–Acts*, p. 107.

[13] Strauss, *Davidic Messiah in Luke–Acts*, p. 124; italics original (see pp. 76–125).

[14] Joel B. Green, *The Gospel of Luke*, NICNT (Grand Rapids, MI: Eerdmans, 1997), p. 207. According to Ned B. Stonehouse (*The*

*Witness of Luke to Christ* [London: Tyndale, 1951], p. 153), Luke 4:16–21 is not programmatic or summative of Jesus' teaching; rather it introduces Jesus' teaching and indicates the pattern of the kingdom as it relates to Jesus' deeds.

[15] Jack Dean Kingsbury, 'Jesus as the "Prophetic Messiah" in Luke's Gospel', in *The Future of Christology* (ed. A.J. Malherbe and W.A. Meeks; FS L.E. Keck; Minneapolis: Fortress, 1993), p. 34.

[16] Stanley E. Porter, 'The Messiah in Luke and Acts: Forgiveness for Captives', in *The Messiah in the Old and New Testaments* (ed. S.E. Porter; Grand Rapids, MI: Eerdmans, 2007), pp. 152–4.

[17] Cf. e.g. J.A. Fitzmyer, *The Gospel according to Luke*, AB (2 vols; New York: Doubleday, 1981–5), 1:529–30.

[18] Strauss, *Davidic Messiah in Luke–Acts*, pp. 244–9.

[19] Pao and Schnabel, 'Luke', p. 290.

[20] James Sanders, 'From Isaiah 61 to Luke 4', in *Luke and Scripture: The Function of Sacred Traditions in Luke–Acts* (ed. James A. Sanders and Craig A. Evans; Minneapolis: Fortress, 1993), p. 62.

[21] Fitzmyer, *Gospel according to Luke*, 1:774.

[22] There is considerable debate about the title and function of Jesus as 'prophet' in Luke–Acts. Including: whether or not the designation of Jesus as prophet is an adequate way to describe the Lucan Jesus; whether the title functions as a proper title for Jesus; its connection to 'the prophet' of Deut. 18:15 (cf. Acts 3:22–23; 7:37); and whether there is a difference between use of 'prophet' in the two volumes, since the Gospel depicts Jesus as 'a prophet', and Acts as 'the prophet'. See further Darrell L. Bock, *Proclamation from Prophecy and Pattern: Lucan Old Testament Christology*, JSNTSup 12 (Sheffield: JSOT Press, 1987), pp. 115, 191–4; Kingsbury, 'Prophetic Messiah', pp. 29–42; C.F.D. Moule, 'The Christology of Acts', in *Studies in Luke–Acts* (ed. L.E. Keck and J.L. Martyn; FS Paul Schubert; London: SPCK, 1966), pp. 161–2; Christopher M. Tuckett, 'The Christology of Luke-Acts', in *The Unity of Luke–Acts* (ed. J. Verheyden; Leuven: Leuven University Press, 1999), pp. 145–7.

[23] Frank J. Matera, *New Testament Christology* (Louisville, KY: Westminster John Knox, 1999), p. 59.

[24] Josephus, *Ant.* 14.403.

[25] Josephus, *War* 2.80–97, 111–13.

[26] Rowe, *Early Narrative Christology*, p. 204.

[27] Miura, *David in Luke–Acts*, p. 237.

[28] Matera, *New Testament Christology*, p. 61.

[29] Matera, *New Testament Christology*, p. 62.

[30] Strauss, *Davidic Messiah in Luke–Acts*, p. 342.

[31] Walter Grundmann, *TDNT* 9:534.

[32] Green, *Gospel of Luke*, p. 849; cf. Strauss, *Davidic Messiah in Luke–Acts*, p. 257.

[33] Hurtado, *Lord Jesus Christ*, pp. 343–4.

[34] J. Jervell, *The Theology of the Acts of the Apostles* (Cambridge: CUP, 1996), p. 26. Alternatively, Matera (*New Testament Christology*, p. 64) thinks that Acts provides further access into Luke's narrative Christology.

[35] Jacob Jervell, *Luke and the People of God: A New Look at Luke–Acts* (Minneapolis: Augsburg, 1972); Douglas R.A. Hare, 'The Rejection of the Jews in the Synoptic Gospels and Acts', in *Antisemitism and the Foundations of Christianity* (ed. Alan Davies; New York: Paulist, 1979), pp. 27–47; Lloyd Gaston, 'Anti-Judaism and the Passion Narrative in Luke and Acts', in *Anti-Judaism in Early Christianity, vol. 1: Paul and the Gospels* (ed. Peter Richardson and David Granskou, SCJ; Waterloo, ONT: Wilfrid Laurier University Press, 1986), pp. 127–53; R.L. Brawley, *Luke–Acts and the Jews: Conflict, Apology, and Conciliation* (Atlanta, GA: Scholars, 1987); Jack T. Sanders, *The Jews in Luke–Acts* (London: SCM, 1987); J.B. Tyson, ed., *Images of Judaism in Luke–Acts* (Columbia: University of South Carolina Press, 1992); R.F. O'Toole, 'Reflections on Luke's Treatment of Jews in Luke–Acts', *Bib* 75 (1994): pp. 124–46; William R. Farmer, ed., *Anti-Judaism and the Gospels* (Harrisburg, PA: Trinity, 1999); Amy-Jill Levine, 'Matthew, Mark, and Luke: Good News or Bad?' in *Jesus, Judaism and Christian Anti-Judaism: Reading the New Testament after the Holocaust* (ed. P. Fredriksen and A. Reinhartz; Louisville, KY: Westminster John Knox, 2002), pp. 92–7.

[36] Gaston, 'Anti-Judaism and the Passion Narrative in Luke and Acts', p. 153.

[37] Cf. I. Howard Marshall, 'The Christology of Luke's Gospel and Acts', in *Contours of Christology in the New Testament* (ed. Richard N. Longenecker; Grand Rapids, MI: Eerdmans, 2005), p. 143.

[38] Acts 2:23, my translation.

[39] Strauss, *Davidic Messiah in Luke–Acts*, p. 147.

[40] Jervell, *Theology of the Acts of the Apostles*, p. 28; 'The Lucan Interpretation of Jesus as Biblical Theology,' in *New Directions in Biblical Theology*, ed. S. Pedefsen (Leiden: Brill, 1994), 86, pp. 77–92.

41 Michael Wolter, 'Israel's Future and the Delay of the Parousia', in *Jesus and the Heritage of Israel: Luke's Narrative Claim upon Israel's Legacy* (ed. David P. Moessner; Harrisburg, PA: Trinity), p. 319.

42 Robert C. Tannehill ('The Story of Israel within the Lukan Narrative', in *Jesus and the Heritage of Israel* [ed. Moessner], p. 339) thinks that Luke was just plain wrong when it comes to the matter of whether the Jews need to be converted to faith in Jesus.

43 Matera, *New Testament Christology*, pp. 68, 89 (italics original).

44 Jervell, *Theology*, p. 27. See also Tuckett, 'Christology of Luke–Acts', p. 161; Strauss, *Davidic Messiah*, p. 343.

45 Stanton, 'Messianism and Christology', p. 95.

46 Against Luke Timothy Johnson ('The Christology of Luke–Acts', in *Who Do You Say That I Am? Essays on Christology* [ed. M.A. Powell and D.R. Bauer; FS J.D. Kingsbury; Louisville, KY: Westminster John Knox, 1999], pp. 49–65) who thinks that Jesus' role as prophet is central in Luke–Acts, I am more inclined to follow Marshall ('*Christology of Luke's Gospel and Acts*', p. 144) who sees Luke's Christology built around the two foci of 'Christship' and 'Lordship'. See also Strauss, *Davidic Messiah in Luke–Acts*, pp. 340–41.

47 Rebecca I. Denova, *The Things Accomplished among Us: Prophetic Tradition in the Structural Pattern of Luke–Acts* (Sheffield: Sheffield Academic Press, 1997), pp. 230–31, though I remain unsure of Denova's claim that the author of Luke–Acts was a Jew. Ben Witherington ('Lord and Saviour: The Christology of Luke–Acts', in *The Many Faces of the Christ* [New York: Crossroads, 1998], p. 160) is similar: 'It is in the witness to the synagogue that this issue [i.e. Jesus as the Christ] is pressed'. Contrast with the view of Tuckett ('Christology of Luke–Acts', p. 163) who thinks it 'impossible to conceive of Luke addressing any real non-Christian Jews in any meaningful way' since Luke's redefinition of messiahship would make 'any meaningful dialogue all but impossible right from the outset'. Tannehill ('Narrative Unity', 2:3) admits that Luke believes that Christians should try to persuade Jews to become followers of Jesus, but he himself thinks that Luke is wrong.

48 Cf. Tuckett, 'Christology of Luke–Acts', pp. 162–3; Marshall, 'Christology', p. 131.

49 Tuckett, 'Christology of Luke–Acts', p. 163.

50 Cf. G.E. Sterling, *Historiography and Self-Definition: Josephus, Luke–Acts and Apologetic Historiography*, NovTSup 64 (Leiden: Brill, 1992), pp.

374–76; Robert Maddox, *The Purpose of Luke–Acts* (Edinburgh: T&T Clark, 1982), pp. 183–5; Philip Esler, *Community and Gospel in Luke–Acts*, SNTSMS 57; Cambridge: CUP, 1987), pp. 69–70; Jervell, *Theology of the Acts of the Apostles*, p. 1.

## 4. The Gospel of John: The Elusive Messiah

1. Mark W.G. Stibbe, 'The Elusive Christ: A New Reading of the Fourth Gospel', *JSNT* 44 (1991): p. 20.
2. Charles A. Briggs, *The Messiah of the Gospels* (New York: C. Scribner's Sons, 1894), p. 257.
3. Wayne A. Meeks, 'The Man from Heaven in Johannine Sectarianism', in *The Interpretation of John* (ed. J. Ashton; London: SPCK, 1986), p. 141.
4. E. Abbot, A.P. Peabody, and J.B. Lightfoot, *The Fourth Gospel: Evidences External and Internal of Its Johannean Authorship* (London: Hodder & Stoughton, 1892), p. 152.
5. C.H. Dodd, *The Interpretation of the Fourth Gospel* (Cambridge: CUP, 1968), p. 229.
6. Rudolf Schnackenburg, 'Die Messias Frage im Johannesevangelium', in *Neutestamentliche Aufsätze* (ed. J. Blinzler, O. Kuss and F. Mussner; FS Joseph Schmid; Regensburg: Friedrich Pustet, 1963), p. 240.
7. C.K. Barrett, *The Gospel according to St John: An Introduction with Commentary and Notes on the Greek Text* (London: SPCK, 2nd edn, 1978), p. 70.
8. John Painter, *The Quest for the Messiah: The History, Literature and Theology of the Johannine Community* (Edinburgh: T&T Clark, 1991).
9. MacRae, 'Messiah and Gospel', p. 178.
10. Justin Martyr, *Dial. Tryph.* 8.4.
11. Dodd, *Interpretation of the Fourth Gospel*, p. 228.
12. Mark W.G. Stibbe, *John* (Sheffield: JSOT Press, 1993), p. 24.
13. J.A.T. Robinson, *Twelve More New Testament Studies* (London: SCM, 1984), p. 69 (pp. 65–76).
14. James D.G. Dunn's (*Christology in the Making*, pp. 71–2) denial that there was a concept of a pre-existent Messiah in pre-Christian Judaism before the *Similitudes of Enoch* breaks down on the bedrock of evidence in the sources. William Horbury (*Jewish Messianism and the Cult of Christ* [London: SCM, 1998], pp. 86–106) points to several texts (1.

LXX texts: Num. 24:17; Pss 72(71):5,17; 110(109):3; Isa. 9:1–2,5–6; 11:1–2; Lam. 4:20; Amos 4:12; Zech. 6:12; 2. Other texts: *Psalms of Solomon*; apocalypses from the Herodian period; fifth book of the Sibylline Oracles; and rabbinic materials) which show that 'the messianic king, a human figure endued with heavenly virtue and might, can be regarded as the manifestation and embodiment of a spirit sent by God' (p. 90). Texts that I would specifically point to for consideration include Dan. 7:13–14; Mic. 5:2; *1 Enoch* 39.6–7; 46.1–4; 48.3,6; 62.7; *4 Ezra* 7.28; 13.25–26; *2 Bar.* 30.1; *Odes Sol.* 41.15; Justin, *Dial. Tryph.* 49; *b.Pesah.* 54a; *b.Ned.* 39b; *Pesiq. Rab.* 33.6; 36.1. Whereas the notion of a pre-existent Messiah certainly developed in Christian circles, Emil Schürer (*History of the Jewish People*, 2:522) wrote: 'At the same time, such ideas are fully comprehensible from Old Testament premises'. See further discussion in Gathercole, *Preexistent Son*, pp. 234–8 and Lee, *Messiah to Preexistent Son*, pp. 99–114.

15  Hippolytus, *Ref. Omn. Haer.* 9.25.

16  Gathercole, *Preexistent Son*, pp. 111–12.

17  Andreas Köstenberger, *A Theology of John's Gospel and Letters*, BTNT (Grand Rapids, MI: Zondervan, 2009), pp. 381–82.

18  For a good introduction to the 'signs' materials, see Craig Keener, *Gospel of John: A Commentary* (2 vols; Peabody, MA: Hendrickson, 2003), 1:251–79.

19  Cf. Painter, *Quest*, pp. 138–54.

20  *Tg. Ps.-Jon.* Exod. 4:13; 6:18; 40:10; Deut. 30:4.

21  Justin, *Dial. Tryph.* 8.4; 49.1.

22  Richard Bauckham, 'Messianism according to the Gospel of John', in *Challenging Perspectives on the Gospel of John*, WUNT 2.219 (ed. J. Lierman; Tübingen: Mohr Siebeck, 2006), p. 38 (see pp. 36–9 on Elijah as priest).

23  Cf. Anna Maria Schwemer, 'Jesus Christus als Prophet, König und Priester. Das munus triplex und die frühe Christologie', in *Der messianische Anspruch Jesu und die Anfänge der Christologie: Vier Studien*, WUNT 138 (ed. M. Hengel and A.M. Schwemer; Tübingen: Mohr Siebeck, 2001), pp. 165–230.

24  D.A. Carson, *The Gospel according to John*, PNTC (Grand Rapids, MI: Eerdmans, 1991), p. 146.

25  Carson, *Gospel according to John*, p. 151.

26  Cf. Leon Morris, 'The Atonement in John's Gospel', *CTR* 3 (1988): pp. 49–64. McKnight, *Jesus and His Death*, pp. 367–71; John Dennis, 'Jesus'

Death in John's Gospel: A Survey of Research from Bultmann to the Present with Specific Reference to the Johannine Hyper-Texts', CBR 4.3 (2006): pp. 331–6; Jintae Kim, 'The Concept of Atonement in the Gospel of John', *JGRChJ* 6 (2009): pp. 9–27.

[27] Dodd, *Interpretation of the Fourth Gospel*, p. 237; Keener, *Gospel of John*, 1:475.

[28] Dodd, *Interpretation of the Fourth Gospel*, pp. 230–38; Carson, *Gospel according to John*, p. 150.

[29] Several witnesses read instead 'the Son of God' (ὁ υἱὸς τοῦ θεοῦ), e.g. ℵ[2] A B Θ Ψ 083 0233[vid] (see Tischendorf; Westcott-Hort; UBS[4]; NA27; NRSV; NIV; ESV; NASB); while others contain 'the chosen one of God' (ὁ ἐκλεκτὸς τοῦ θεοῦ) i.e. p[5vid] ℵ* it[b, e, ff2*] syr[c, s] Ambrose (see SBLGNT; TNIV; NJB; NLT); and a few even read 'the chosen Son of God' (*filius electus dei*), i.e. it[a, ff2c] syr[palmss] cop[sa]. Metzger (*Textual Commentary*, p. 172) writes: 'On the basis of age and diversity of witnesses a majority of the Committee preferred the reading ὁ υἱὸς, which is also in harmony with the theological terminology of the Fourth Evangelist.' Yet 'elect one' has a good representation of witnesses and arguably constitutes the more difficult reading. It is more likely that a copyist would change 'elect one' to 'son' than vice versa since 'son' was a more profound christological title for Jesus.

[30] *1 Enoch* 39.6; 40.5; 45.3; 48.6; 49.2,4; 51.3, 5; 52.6,9, 53.6; 55.4; 61.5,8,10; 62.1; *Apoc. Abr.* 31.1. See also among the Qumran scrolls, 4Q534.

[31] Carson, *Gospel according to John*, p. 152.

[32] J.L. Martyn (*History and Theology in the Fourth Gospel* [Nashville: Abingdon, 2nd edn, 1979], p. 45) thinks that this is perhaps the message of the first missionaries to the Jewish synagogues.

[33] Craig R. Koester ('Messianic Exegesis and the Call of Nathanael (John 1:45–51)', *JSNT* 39 [1990]: pp. 23–34) believes that in the background is Zech. 3:8–10, a passage that regards being called by a neighbour to sit under his vine and fig tree as a sign of the advent of the 'Branch' (i.e. Davidic Messiah).

[34] Barnabas Lindars, *The Gospel of John*, NCBC (London: Marshall, Morgan & Scott, 1972), p. 119.

[35] Whether 'king' was a messianic title in Judaism is disputed. The Qumran scrolls, following Ezekiel and Daniel, prefer to call the Davidic Messiah 'prince' (נשיא) rather than king. However 'king' is used in several messianic texts (*Pss. Sol.* 17.21,32,42; *Sib. Or.* 5.108) and there is ample evidence that several scriptural passages

about the king (e.g. Ps. 2:6; 72:1; Jer. 23:5; Zech. 9:9) were inter-preted messianically by Jewish and Christian interpreters. See Bauckham, 'Messianism', pp. 59–60 against Meeks, *Prophet-King*, p. 79 n. 1.

[36] David Kirk, 'The Heavens Opened: Intertextuality and Meaning in John 1:51', unpublished dissertation, Highland Theological College, University of the Highlands and Islands (2010).

[37] Andreas J. Köstenberger and Michael J. Kruger, *The Heresy of Orthodoxy: How Contemporary Culture's Fascination with Diversity Has Reshaped Our Understanding of Early Christianity* (Wheaton, IL: Crossway, 2010), p. 80.

[38] Benjamin E. Reynolds, *The Apocalyptic Son of Man in the Gospel of John*, WUNT 2.249 (Tübingen: Mohr Siebeck, 2008), p. 228.

[39] Cf. Lincoln, *Gospel according to Saint John*, p. 124.

[40] Cf. Morna D. Hooker, 'The Johannine Prologue and the Messianic Secret', *NTS* 21 (1974): pp. 40–58.

[41] Hurtado, *Lord Jesus Christ*, p. 358.

[42] Stephen Smalley, *John: Evangelist and Interpreter* (Carlisle: Paternoster, 2nd edn, 1998), p. 246.

[43] Joachim Jeremias, *TDNT* 4:1101–2.

[44] Rudolf Schnackenburg, *The Gospel according to St John* (3 vols; trans. K. Smyth; New York: Herder & Herder, 1968–82), 1:416–17.

[45] Sandra M. Schneiders, *Written That You May Believe: Encountering Jesus in the Fourth Gospel* (New York: Crossroads, 1999), pp. 35, 135.

[46] Jocelyn McWhirter, *The Bridegroom Messiah and the People of God: Marriage in the Fourth Gospel*, SNTSMS 138 (Cambridge: CUP, 2006).

[47] See discussion in Bird, *Jesus and the Origins of the Gentile Mission*, pp. 148–55.

[48] Josephus, *War* 2.247.

[49] Josephus, *Ant.* 20.206.

[50] See discussion of the literature in Richard Bauckham, 'Jesus' Demonstration in the Temple', in *Law and Religion: Essays on the Place of the Law in Israel and Early Christianity* (ed. B. Lindars; Cambridge: James Clarke, 1988), pp. 72–89.

[51] Cf. Bird, *Jesus and the Origins of the Gentile Mission*, pp. 156–7.

[52] Nicholas Perrin, *Jesus the Temple* (London: SPCK, 2010), p. 99.

[53] Sir 5.1–2,5–6; 50.1–2; *T.Dan.* 5.10–12; *1 Enoch* 53.6; 90.29; *Pss. Sol.* 17.21–23; *Sib. Or.* 5.414–27,432–33; *Tg. Isa.* 53.5; *Tg. Zech.* 4.7; 6.12. See further Nick Perrin, 'From One Stone to the Next: Messiahship and

Temple in N.T. Wright's *Jesus and the Victory of God'*, in *Jesus as Israel's Messiah: Engaging the Work of N.T. Wright*, LHJS (ed. R.L. Webb and M.A. Powell; London: T&T Clark, forthcoming).

54 Leon Morris, *The Gospel according to John*, NICNT (Grand Rapids, MI: Eerdmans, rev. edn, 1995), p. 172.

55 Perrin, *Jesus the Temple*, p. 102.

56 Perrin, *Jesus the Temple*, pp. 109–10.

57 Keener, *Gospel of John*, 1:615.

58 Keener, *Gospel of John*, 1:617–18.

59 Barrett, *St John*, p. 239.

60 Cf. Josephus, *Ant.* 18.85–87.

61 Cf. Painter (*Quest*, p. 405) who notes: 'For Jn the quest for the Messiah, the quest for God and the quest for life all find their fulfillment in the Jesus who is proclaimed and defended in the Gospel.'

62 Richard Bauckham, 'Monotheism and Christology in the Gospel of John', in *Contours of Christology in the New Testament* (ed. R.N. Longenecker; Grand Rapids, MI: Eerdmans, 2005), p. 159.

63 Cf. Wayne A. Meeks (*The Prophet-King: Moses Traditions and Johannine Christology* [Leiden: Brill, 1967], p. 25) who declares: 'the prophetic and royal elements in Johannine christology are not to be understood separately, but exactly in their combination and mutual interpretation'.

64 Craig R. Koester, *The Word of Life: A Theology of John's Gospel* (Grand Rapids, MI: Eerdmans, 2008), p. 93.

65 Michaels, *Gospel of John*, p. 450.

66 Michaels, *Gospel of John*, pp. 451–2.

67 Martyn, *History and Theology*, pp. 94–9.

68 John W. Pryor, *John: Evangelist of the Covenant People: The Narrative and Themes of the Fourth Gospel* (London: Darton, Longman & Todd, 1992), pp. 135–6; Keener, *Gospel of John*, 1:719; Bauckham, 'Messianism', p. 64.

69 Martyn, *History and Theology in the Fourth Gospel*, p. 113; Pryor, *John*, pp. 132–3; Carson, *Gospel according to John*, p. 319.

70 Carson, *Gospel according to John*, p. 329.

71 Köstenberger, *John*, p. 241.

72 Cf. too Justin, *Dial. Tryph.* 78, though on the lips of Justin.

73 Lincoln, *Saint John*, p. 258. Barrett (*St John*, p. 331) points out that the 'birth place of Jesus is a trivial matter in comparison with the question whether he is ἐκ τῶν ἄνω or ἐκ τῶν κάτω (8.23), whether he is or is not from God . . . It follows that all disputes about the birth place of the Messiah, the heavenly Man, are far wide of the point.'

[74] Cf. Edward Klink, 'Expulsion from the Synagogue? Rethinking a Johannine Anachronism', *TynBul* 59 (2008): pp. 99–118.

[75] On the link between messianism and the Son of Man in John 9, see Martyn, *History and Theology in the Fourth Gospel*, pp. 131–4.

[76] Lincoln, *Saint John*, pp. 286–7.

[77] Chae, *Jesus as the Eschatological Davidic Shepherd*, pp. 19–25 (esp. pp. 21–2).

[78] Cf. survey of the OT imagery for shepherds in Chae, *Jesus as the Eschatological Davidic Shepherd*, pp. 25–172.

[79] Painter, *Quest*, p. 411; cf. Koester, *Word of Life*, pp. 94–5.

[80] John A. Dennis, *Jesus' Death and the Gathering of True Israel*, WUNT 2.217 (Tübingen: Mohr Siebeck, 2006), pp. 270–71.

[81] Andrew C. Brunson, *Psalm 118 in the Gospel of John: An Intertextual Study of the New Exodus Pattern in the Theology of John*, WUNT 2.158 (Tübingen: Mohr Siebeck, 2003), pp. 233–8.

[82] James D.G. Dunn, 'Let John be John – a Gospel for Its Time', in *Das Evangelium und die Evangelien*, WUNT 28 (ed. P. Stuhlmacher; Tübingen: Mohr Siebeck, 1983), p. 328.

[83] Brunson, *Psalm 118 in the Gospel of John*, p. 233. Similar is Koester (*Word of Life*, p. 96): 'His crucifixion will be a victory in which Jesus wields divine love as a weapon against demonic hatred, divine truth against the world's falsehood, and the power of life against the forces of death.' Note also James McGrath (*John's Apologetic Christology: Legitimation and Development in Johannine Christology*, SNTSMS 111 (Cambridge: CUP, 2001], p. 213): 'John, we may suggest, found a way to appeal to Jewish tradition in order to present the death of the Son of Man on the cross as not only scriptural, but also a victory over the forces of evil, which is therefore not incompatible with the claim that he is the Messiah.'

[84] Cf. Lincoln, *Saint John*, p. 105.

[85] Ramsay, *Gospel of John*, pp. 922–3.

[86] Koester, *Word of Life*, p. 96.

[87] Cf. Metzger, *Textual Commentary*, pp. 219–20.

[88] Note the similar caution by G.R. Beasley-Murray, *John*, WBC (Waco, TX: Word, 1987), p. 387.

[89] Dodd, *Interpretation of the Fourth Gospel*, p. 9; Schnackenburg, *John*, 3:338; Carson, *Gospel according to John*, p. 662.

[90] Constantine R. Campbell, *Verbal Aspect and Non-Indicative Verbs* (New York: Peter Lang, 2008), p. 56.

91 Constantine R. Campbell, *Basics of Verbal Aspect in Biblical Greek* (Grand Rapids, MI: Zondervan, 2008), pp. 87–8.

92 Richard Bauckham, 'John for Readers of Mark', in *The Gospels for All Christians* (ed. R. Bauckham; Grand Rapids, MI: Eerdmans, 1998), pp. 147–71.

93 But note Ben Witherington's (*John's Wisdom: A Commentary on the Fourth Gospel* [Louisville, KY: Westminster John Knox, 1995], p. 226) remark: 'Despite all the polemics, there is no indication that the community had given up its witness or some hopes of its success even in the synagogue, despite rejection, ejection, and persecution. Jesus and his followers still longed for all sorts of people to be drawn to the Christ and so become children of light.'

94 F.F. Bruce (*The Gospel and Epistles of John* [Grand Rapids, MI: Eerdmans, 1983], p. 395) stated: 'Probably we are not shut up to two mutually exclusive alternatives, regardless of the reading adopted: John's record has the power to awaken new faith and to revive faith already awakened.' Carson (*Gospel according to John*, p. 663) comments: 'Even if John's purpose is primarily evangelistic, it must be admitted that throughout the history of the church this Gospel has served not only as a means for reaching unbelievers but as a means for instructing, edifying and comforting believers. Still, one must not confuse purpose with result. A modern evangelist aiming at the conversion of hearers may still find that Christians who attend his ministry are greatly edified. John's *purpose* in writing was to evangelize; the impact of his Gospel, *i.e.* the *result* of his writing, has far exceeded any hope he could have entertained.' For Painter (*Quest*, p. 104): 'Jn is a church book, written for those who believe, to enable faith to grow so that the Johannine community might, not only survive, but fulfil God's purpose for it in the world. Thus Jn is a missionary document in the sense that it gives expression to a theology of mission for the believing community. The Johannine community is commissioned to perpetuate the mission of Jesus to the world. In order to do this it was necessary to bind the believers to the revelation of God in Jesus and it was to fulfil this purpose that Jn was written.' R.E. Brown (*The Gospel according to John*, AB [2 vols; New York: Doubleday, 1966–70], 2:1060): 'In conclusion then, we admit that there may well be an apologetic motif in xx 31, as John seeks through the signs to prove that Jesus is the expected Jewish Messiah . . . Nevertheless, the major thrust of the statement in xx 31 reflects the evangelist's desire to deepen the faith of those who

were already Christians so that they would appreciate Jesus' unique relations to the Father.'

95 Cf. Edward M. Klink, 'The Gospel Community Debate: The State of the Question', *CBR* 3 (2004): pp. 60–85; idem, *The Sheep of the Fold: The Audience and Origin of the Gospel of John*, SNTSMS 141 (Cambridge: CUP, 2007); Michael F. Bird, 'Bauckham's *The Gospels for All Christians Revisited*', *EJT* 15 (2006): pp. 5–13.

96 Cf. Stanley E. Porter, *Idioms of the Greek New Testament* (Sheffield: Sheffield Academic Press, 2nd edn, 1999), pp. 109–10.

97 Cf. D.A. Carson, 'The Purpose of the Fourth Gospel: John 20:30–31 Reconsidered', *JBL* 108 (1987): pp. 639–51; idem, 'Syntactical and Text-Critical Observations on John 20:30–31: One More Round on the Purpose of the Fourth Gospel', *JBL* 124 (2005): pp. 693–714.

98 Carson, *John*, p. 662.

99 Carson, *John*, pp. 90, 662.

100 Daniel B. Wallace, *Greek Grammar beyond the Basics* (Grand Rapids, MI: Zondervan, 1996), pp. 46–7.

101 Dunn, *Unity and Diversity*, p. 47. Cf. William Loader (*The Christology of the Fourth Gospel: Structure and Issues* [Frankfurt am Main: Peter Lang, 1989], p. 80): 'The author employs confessional messianic state-ments that Jesus is the Christ and the Son of God, but integrates them primarily within his overall christology of Jesus as the Son of the Father whose coming was the event of revelation.' Pryor (*John*, p. 135): '"Messiah" needs more precise definition and is liable to misun-derstanding. In 11:27 and 20:30 it is further defined by "Son of God", and in this way Jesus' messiahship is seen to be of such a kind that he needs to be understood as the divine, pre-existent Son.' Hurtado (*Lord Jesus Christ*, p. 360): 'To be sure, GJohn affirms more about Jesus than his messianic status. Or perhaps we should say that GJohn defines the meaning of Jesus' messianic status with additional affir-mations of his significance (e.g., as divine "Son"). But the additional claims it makes for Jesus are never at the expense of insisting that he is also the Messiah of God, the true and proper fulfillment of biblical prophecy and hope, the one in whom Israel should find the climactic expression of God's faithfulness and redemptive purpose.'

102 Beasley-Murray, *John*, p. 338; Pryor, *John*, p. 135; Michaels, *Gospel of John*, p. 1023.

103 Brunson, *Psalm 118 in the Gospel of John*, p. 233 (italics original).

104 Pryor, *John*, p. 142.

[105] This essay also represents a rejection of the thesis of Marinus de Jonge ('Jewish Expectations about the "Messiah" according to the Fourth Gospel', *NTS* 19 (1973): pp. 246–70) who thinks that John criticizes both Jewish and Jewish Christian conceptions of messiahship. In response I contend: (1) Simply because the evangelist did not mention Elijah's relationship to Jesus does not mean that he repudiated the Jewish view taken up by Jewish Christians that Elijah's function was to reveal the Messiah. When the evangelist has the Baptist deny that he is Elijah (John 1:21,25) he seems to mean either a priestly figure or a miracle-worker rather than the forerunner to the Messiah who the Baptist clearly is by function (see John 10:21 about the Baptist not doing miracles); (2) Contra de Jonge, we do have good reason for linking John 7:27 with Trypho's notion of a hidden Messiah. For the evangelist, only the mode of his revelation differs from common expectations (*Dial. Tryph.* 8.4; 49.1); (3) The role of prophet and Messiah are not separated but blended, and the fluid tradition of Jewish exegesis could add miraculous deeds to the Messiah's CV. This is evident in 4Q521 which was not published when de Jonge wrote his original article. (4) Qualifying the title 'Messiah' with 'Son of God' is not a criticism of Jewish Christian views of messiahship since early synoptic tradition depicts Jesus as Son of God and Messiah as well (see Matt. 16:16; 26:23; Mark 15:32,39; Luke 4:41). (5) John 7:40–44 does not repudiate the view that Jesus was born in Bethlehem since the evangelist, who evidently knows synoptic or synoptic-like traditions (see Barrett, *St John*, p. 330; Brown, *John*, 1:330), believes that Jesus fulfils all of Scripture (as de Jonge acknowledges), but the point is irony in that Jesus' origins are unknown to his detractors, but readers know that he actually does meet the qualifications for being the Messiah. (6) The only real point of discontinuity between John and his Jewish contemporaries is the view given in 12:34 that the Messiah, as the Son of Man, must be lifted up.

[106] Köstenberger, *A Theology of John's Gospel and Letters*, p. 315.

[107] McGrath, *John's Apologetic Christology*, p. 194.

[108] Cf. Dodd, *Interpretation of the Fourth Gospel*, p. 87.

## Conclusion: Believing in the Messiah

[1] Cf. Markus Bockmuehl, 'A "Slain Messiah" in 4Q Serekh Milhûamah (4Q285)?' *TynBul* 43 (1992): p. 167.

[2] Longenecker, *Christology*, p. 82.

# General Index

Abraham 59–67, 110, 143, 146, 187

Apocalypse 10, 84, 108, 113, 127, 197

Augustus, Caesar 19, 52

Baptism 36, 39, 49–50, 66, 75, 77, 90, 106–7, 181, 187

Baptist, John the 6, 8, 36, 68, 70, 73, 83, 101–2, 104–13, 118, 121, 204

Biography, Graeco-Roman 1

Caiaphas 9, 39, 43, 48, 51, 133

*Christos*, as proper name 3, 13, 16, 21, 24, 59, 103, 137, 168, 174

Covenant 11, 37–38, 61–66, 84, 87, 99, 115, 169, 189

David, Son of 1, 5, 7, 10, 19, 27, 30, 45–47, 52–54, 58–60, 64–70, 72, 75, 77–78, 86–87, 141–143, 146, 184, 187

Dead Sea Scrolls 8, 34, 84, 139

Disciple, Beloved 3, 132

Disciples, twelve 8

Elijah 36, 50, 84–85, 105–6, 142, 197, 204

Entry, triumphal 8, 23, 36, 53–54, 68–69, 86, 101–2, 130–31, 184

Exaltation, of Jesus 2, 3, 11, 21, 23–25, 39, 43, 50, 53–54, 75–77, 87, 89, 91, 95, 111, 132, 172, 184

Exile, of Israel 2, 60–67, 69, 78, 113, 127

Genealogy, of Jesus 58–62, 66–67

God, Son of 2, 5, 12, 17–18, 24, 26, 30, 35–36, 38–39, 42, 45, 49–52, 54–56, 67, 72–77, 80, 82, 84, 98, 100, 102–4, 110–12, 122, 124–26, 129–30, 134– 40, 141–46, 179, 182–85, 191, 198, 203–4

Interpretation, messianic 22, 26, 30, 48, 52, 91

Israel,
    King of 1, 27, 39–41, 47, 76, 101, 103, 110–11, 119, 122, 125, 130– 31, 133, 138–40, 181
    Restoration of 8–9, 11, 14, 36, 60, 62–63, 69, 70, 82, 90, 95–96, 113, 127, 143

Kingdom of God 8, 9, 37, 39–40, 46, 54, 93–94, 185, 190

Logos 3, 99–100, 139

Man, Son of 5, 11, 22–24, 26, 28, 30, 36–37, 39, 45–49, 51, 54–56, 70, 74, 78, 85–88, 110–12, 125–26, 130–32, 138–43, 175, 182–84, 201

Melchizedek 53, 139

Messianism,
    Historical Jesus 6–10.
    Jewish 5–6, 20
    Pauline 15–22, 27, 33, 92–94, 98, 144
    Priestly 11, 28, 53–54, 103, 106–7, 119, 147, 167, 197, 204
    Royal 5, 8, 11–12, 17, 20, 27–28, 52–53, 69, 75, 80–83, 102, 105, 121, 127, 130, 142–43, 167, 172– 73, 181, 183, 190, 200

Miracles 24, 56, 75, 102, 104, 112, 118, 120–21, 125, 182, 204

Monotheism 53, 99, 117, 144

*Parousia*, of Jesus  12, 23–25, 30, 175,
    181
Peter, Apostle  7, 36–37, 46, 48, 71–74,
    76, 84, 90–91, 109, 129, 147
Pharisees  35–36, 57, 67, 73, 100, 120,
    121, 123, 126, 128–31
Pilate, Pontius  40–41, 52, 74, 76, 103,
    133–35
Pre–existence, of Messiah  82, 99–112,
    139–40, 196–97, 203
Procession, triumphal  41–42, 75
Prophet, the  5, 79, 85, 102, 103, 105–6,
    118, 121–22, 193
Resurrection, general  129
Resurrection, of Jesus  3, 6–7, 10–11,
    18, 20–26, 29–30, 37, 45, 54, 56, 77,
    79, 85, 87–91, 111, 114–15, 125, 132–
    33, 135, 139, 141–42, 173, 184
Revolt, Maccabean  130
Saying(s)
    "I am"  117
    "I have come"  8
    Material  173
    Ransom  37
Secret, messianic  7, 36, 53, 112
Servant, Suffering  11, 25, 37, 51, 75,
    78, 83, 108, 182
Solomon  8, 10, 50, 69, 120
Spirit, Holy  8, 11, 14, 17–18, 21,
    49–50, 52, 60, 64, 71, 77, 80, 82–83,
    87, 89–90, 95, 107–8, 116, 121–22,
    125, 135, 172, 187, 190
Temple, demonstration  51, 74, 87,
    114, 199
Titulus  9, 24, 32, 40
Trial, of Jesus  9–10, 23, 51–53, 74–76,
    115, 117, 130, 133
Worship, of Jesus  34, 38, 40–41,
    76–77, 178
Zealots  114